PLANET EARTH
2000 A.D.

Will Mankind Survive?

Hal Lindsey

Western Front, Ltd.
Palos Verdes, California

Library of Congress Cataloging-in-Publication Data

ISBN 0-9641058-0-2

Library of Congress Catalog Card Number:
96-60756

Scriptures quoted in this book are from the New American
Standard Bible (NASB) unless otherwise noted.

Western Front, Ltd.
416 Paseo Del Mar
Palos Verdes, CA 90274

Book design and production: Publication Services
Manufactured in the United States of America

Contents

A NOTE TO MY READERS

By Hal Lindsey

In the short time that has passed since I wrote *Planet Earth 2000 AD*, so much has happened. What used to take a decade to happen now takes a year. One of the most difficult parts of putting together a book on Bible prophecy in this generation is the fact that it is developing so rapidly.

When I wrote *The Late Great Planet Earth*, the signs of the times were all around us—but in embryonic form. Trends were developing that were gradually pushing in the direction Bible prophecy indicated, but slowly.

Today, almost before I finish explaining a developing trend—it's already an accomplished fact. When I wrote *Planet Earth 2000 AD*, the peace process in the Middle East was being hailed by the mainstream press as "the beginning of a new era of peace in the Middle East." As I indicated in my original manuscript, the Bible says this will be a period of false peace. As I finish this new, updated version, Israeli warplanes are shelling Hezbollah outposts in southern Lebanon. The press is screaming about an accidental Israeli strike against a United Nations base located near the Hezbollah position that killed 75 civilians and several UN soldiers. Peace looks remarkably like war. It seems the Bible is right, after all.

Things change—when I first wrote the manuscript for this book, there was speculation that Israel might discover oil. Since then, Reuters has reported an oil strike near the Dead Sea—the problem is figuring out how to extract it. But the oil is there.

When I first wrote the book, the enduring image of ethnic unrest and the media attacks on the justice system in the U.S. was Rodney King—but that was before O.J. Simpson. The World Trade Center gave way to the Oklahoma City Bombing, the killer heat waves of 1994 gave room to the killer blizzards of 1995 and 1996. The Northridge earthquake was dwarfed by the Kobe, Japan quake and the Yunan quake in China that claimed thousands of lives.

The original manuscript pointed out the dangers from new plagues—but that was before the Ebola virus outbreak, "Mad Cow" Disease, swine TB and other killers.

I detailed the inconsistencies of the "new" Russia following the collapse of the Soviet Union—but that was before the resurgence of Communism that has captured a quarter of the popular vote there.

The world is spinning out of control—or so it seems. But, as you will discover, everything is in order. God told us these things would happen—in advance—to give us assurance that He has things under His direction.

As we grow ever closer to the end of this century—and the beginning of a new millennium—the debate grows more pertinent. A new day is about to dawn, and the question remains; *Planet Earth 2000 AD, Will Mankind Survive?*

Introduction

COUNTDOWN TO THE THIRD MILLENNIUM

In 1970, *The Late Great Planet Earth* began introducing tens of millions all over the world to what was then a rather arcane subject—Bible prophecy. A subject too often neglected, ignored or misunderstood, even by the modern church, somehow came to life in those pages, providing the spark that led countless people who were not otherwise interested in the Bible to find a new faith in it.

It would be nearly impossible to catalog all the prophecy books that have been published since then. It was the beginning of new kind of broad-based interest in prophecy. Some of the new books have been enlightening, while others have served only to mislead people with unscriptural date-setting or confuse them with mysterious doctrinal debate.

Meanwhile, for 25 years I resisted the mammoth undertaking of writing a book that would go beyond where *The Late Great Planet Earth* left off, mostly because prophetically meaningful events were occurring so quickly. I wasn't sure how a book could do justice to the subject. Instead of focusing on writing prophecy books that might be out of date by the time they reached the stores, I devoted my attention to radio and television shows, video and audio tapes and a monthly news and prophecy journal. Only now, as mankind approaches the third millennium, do I feel like the Holy Spirit has provided me with the proper perspective—the Big Picture, so to speak—on the mind-blowing experiences of the modem world.

The Significance of 2000

Is there anything magical about the year 2000? I don't think so. Christians need to keep things in perspective. As the year 1000 approached, we know that apocalyptic fervor reached absurd levels. The Bible warns against date-setting. God clearly wants certain knowledge obscured from mankind. We should never try to outsmart our Heavenly Father. Even Jesus, when He walked on Earth, said He did not know the day or hour of His own return.

But, nevertheless, it would be equally foolhardy for any serious student of prophecy to ignore the approach of the next millennium—especially at a time when the entire prophetic scenario is being fulfilled literally before our eyes. Frankly, I don't know if the year 2000 will be meaningful in relation to Endtimes events. I do know this: The final countdown leading to the return of Jesus could occur even before the year 2000. It could literally begin today, tomorrow or next week.

No other period in human history has ever seen so many formidable perils to the survival of the human race. This is not just my opinion, by the way. This view is shared by many secular analysts and scientists.

That's why I felt the urgency to write about the flood of prophetically significant events that have happened in the last 25 years. There has been no time in the history of mankind in which the stage has been so well set for this main event. The geopolitical alliances have been forged. The climatic conditions are in evidence. The spiritual status of the world is just what we would expect. Examined together, these signs lead inevitably to one conclusion: The long-awaited Messiah of the Bible is coming soon.

Not Much Time Left

Jesus promised us that the generation that witnessed the restoration of the Jewish people to their homeland would not pass until "all these things"—including His return to Earth—would be done. The Jewish people declared the rebirth of their nation in 1948. They recaptured Jerusalem in 1967. A biblical generation is somewhere between 40 and 100 years, depending on whether you take the example from Abraham's day or from the discipline of Israel in the Wilderness of Sinai. In either case, you do the arithmetic, folks. No matter how you cut it, there's not much time left.

While most of *The Late Great Planet Earth* was, by necessity, spent looking backward, this book devotes more time to looking ahead. In the late 1960s and early 1970s, the world was blissfully unaware of biblical predictions about the fate of the human race. That's why I spent so much time in *Late Great* illustrating the fact that the prophets had a 100 percent accuracy rating and that Jesus really was who He said He was. While it is my sincere hope that this book, too, can serve as a wake-up call to the world at large, you will notice something dramatically different about this work.

This book doesn't dwell on the past, it looks to the future. Because we are so close to the final, climactic stages of world history, it is considerably easier today for the student of Bible prophecy to see with some accuracy what's coming next. No, I am not a prophet. But I have studied the prophets. And I am certain that all of what they predict for mankind up to and including the Second Advent will occur in the next few years—probably in your lifetime.

Twenty-five years ago, when I wrote *The Late Great Planet Earth*, I made a series of predictions based on my understanding of what the Bible tells us about the last days. Again, these weren't prognostications based on my own wisdom, nor were they soothsayings based on some mystical form of extra-sensory perception. They were simply the result of my own careful study of Scripture as to what conditions would prevail on Earth in the days just before Jesus returns.

What I Foresaw in *Late Great*

Not surprisingly, then, I'll confidently hold up my track record against that of any modern-day astrological charlatan or New Age clairvoyant. I will deal with many of these issues in more detail throughout this book, but here's what I warned *The Late Great Planet Earth* readers to look for in the years ahead way back in 1969 (I wrote the last sentence on November 1, 1969):

- Major denominations would be captured by those who reject the essential truth of the Bible and the deity of Jesus Christ.

- Denominations would merge and ecumenicism would become more prevalent as the historic truths of the Bible are discarded.

- Ministers, losing their power along with their link to the supernatural, would resort to "social action gimmicks."

- Followers, especially young people, would flee the main-line churches in droves.

- Bible-believing Christians would be openly persecuted for their beliefs—sometimes even by so-called ministers of the gospel.

- We would begin to see the first evidence of an underground Christian church being established.

- We would begin to see more movement toward a one-world religion.

- Jerusalem would become the focal point of world concern as the Muslims and Israelis would begin to fight in earnest over who owns it.

- We would see movement toward the rebuilding of the Temple in Jerusalem by the Jews.

- The Middle East would become a constant source of tension in the world.

- Israel would become more prosperous.

- The Muslim-Israeli conflict would become a constant world-threatening crisis.
- The U.S. would begin to lose its pre-eminent leadership position in the world.
- Europe would begin emerging as the most powerful economic force in the world.
- We would see Europe move toward unification.
- The Communist takeover of the world would be stopped abruptly.
- The political power and influence of the pope would increase.
- People all over the world would be looking and yearning for a leader to bring them together.
- The worst famines the world has ever known would break out.
- Moral and social chaos in America would tear apart the fabric of our society and begin to destroy our economy.
- Drug addiction and abuse would escalate as problems in America and throughout the Western world.
- Crime, riots, unemployment, poverty, illiteracy, mental illness, illegitimacy and other social problems would increase at an unprecedented rate.
- There would be more interest in and acceptance of Eastern religions, extra-sensory perception, astrology and witchcraft.

Did I miss any?

Now, you know how those supermarket tabloid psychics work. Every year they make a bunch of predictions and, thanks to the law of averages, occasionally they are right. But they never tell you about the dozens of forecasts they made that never materialize. Unlike those false prophets of a false religion, I will admit that one prediction I made has not yet occurred. I suggested 25 years ago that we could expect to see some limited use of nuclear weapons in the world that would so frighten people that they would gladly sacrifice their freedom for a little more security.

I'm not copping out, though. I still say something like this scenario—whether it's nuclear arms or chemical weaponry or biological warheads—is likely very soon. Something terrifying on a mass scale will be necessary to shock people into accepting—even welcoming—a global political and religious leader.

I also said that *"if"* a generation was 40 years and *"if"* the generation of the "fig tree" (Matthew 24:32-34) started with the foundation of the State of Israel, then Jesus *"might* come back by 1988."* But I put a lot of ifs and maybes in because I knew that no one could be absolutely certain.

But imagine if some New Age guru came along 25 years ago and made more than 20 fairly specific predictions of world events and trends that were borne out over time. Today, such a person would be sought out by all the major news networks. World leaders and Hollywood celebrities would be courting his or her attention. My forecasts are different, of course. They're not taken seriously by the secular world. Why? Because they are grounded in the Bible. And the Bible, today, is too often an object of scorn and ridicule. But, you know, even that fact is itself further evidence that we are in the last days.

"Behold, you scoffers, and marvel, and perish," we are told in Acts 13:41. "For I am accomplishing a work in your days, a work which you will never believe, though someone should describe it to you."

The Power of the Word

And that is all I seek to do with this book. I am attempting to describe to you what God is doing for us in these last days as they pass like sand through the hourglass. I seek only to make these sometimes difficult to understand biblical prophecies more accessible to the uninitiated reader.

You know, everywhere I have gone for the last 25 years I have run into people who say *The Late Great Planet Earth* was instrumental in bringing them to faith in Jesus as their Messiah and Savior. Imagine how thrilling and satisfying that is for me. I am thankful daily that whatever gifts I have been given can be used effectively to help others understand the prophetic scenario that is coming together before our very eyes. Even today *The Late Great Planet Earth* is still reaching people in ways I could never have imagined. How do you follow an act like that? But after analyzing the intervening world events over the last two and one-half decades, I felt compelled to write again and show how breathtakingly close we are to the climax of history. I hope you will agree after reading this book that it was worth the effort.

Chapter 1

THE PERILOUS CONDITION OF THE HUMAN RACE

But realize this, that in the last days difficult times will come. For men will be lovers of self, lovers of money, boastful, arrogant, revilers, disobedient to parents, ungrateful, unholy, unloving, irreconcilable, malicious gossips without self-control, brutal haters of good, treacherous, reckless, conceited, lovers of pleasure rather than lovers of God; holding to a form of godliness, although they have denied its power; and avoid such men as these.
—2 TIMOTHY 3:1-5

A friend of mine has recently been brushing up on her French linguistic abilities. One of the techniques she finds most useful—and stimulating—is to pick up and read popular French-language periodicals. This allows her to familiarize herself not only with the language, but also with the trends, issues and the social climate in France. In other words, she gets to understand the dialogue, not just the dialect. One day she purchased a copy of *L'Express*, roughly the French equivalent of Time magazine.

Now, I think most people familiar with France would agree with me that the French people are among the most skeptical on Earth. France has long been one of the least religious nations. It was, after all, the birthplace of the so-called "Age of Reason," a period second only to the 20th century in unbridled godlessness, barbarism and all manner of perversion.

Commentary on the End of the World

So, no one would make the mistake of confusing the modern-day French with fans of Bible prophecy. Right? Well, then, you can imagine my surprise when my friend pointed out the cover story of the Sept. 2, 1993, issue of *L'Express*— "Commentary Concerning the End of the World." And this title was no mere hyperbole. Inside the publication was one of the most sobering assessments of where we are as a people and as a planet.

We're threatened with overpopulation, pollution, deforestation, nuclear proliferation, ozone depletion, new and deadlier strains of diseases, famine, war, lawlessness and disorder. No matter where we turn today, we are confronted with the sad state of human race. There's no escaping it. It's no longer just a few religious zealots out there wearing sandwich boards proclaiming "The end is near!" More often than not, it's the cool, calculating scientist who is most likely to suggest that Earth and mankind are hurtling toward destruction.

And it doesn't take a priest, minister or rabbi to recognize the devastating effects mankind is experiencing due to the general breakdown of morality around the globe—but especially in the West, the historic heartbed of Judeo-Christian values.

What's Happening to Us?

Think about it. What in the world is happening to us? Preteen pregnancies...free condom distribution in the public schools...drive-by shootings...kiddie porn...abortion on demand...suicide machines...rampant child abuse....

Would somebody please explain to me how the Boy Scouts of America became a subversive organization? And when did church-going Christians become "intolerant religious fanatics"? How did America, a nation founded on a bedrock of godly principles, go so far astray?

It reminds me of the passage in Judges 17: "In those days there was no king in Israel; every man did what was right in his own eyes." That's what is happening today in America—the leader of the free world. Standards of right and wrong have been discarded. Try to suggest nowadays that there are eternal moral absolutes and you will likely be branded as an "intolerant bigot" or a "right-wing fundamentalist."

The Cultural Meltdown

I warned about this cultural breakdown in *The Late Great Planet Earth*, but just think about how conditions have deteriorated since then:

- Since 1960 there has been a 560 percent increase in violent crime.[1]

- In the last 30 years, illegitimate births have increased 419 percent.[2]

- Divorce rates have tripled.[3]
- The number of children living in single-parent homes has tripled.[4]
- The teen-age suicide rate has increased 200 percent.[5]
- Student Achievement Test scores have plummeted 80 points.[6]

"The West," explained Alexander Solzhenitsyn, "has been undergoing an erosion and obscuring of high moral and ethical ideals. The spiritual axis of life has grown dim."[7]

America today is caught in the cross-fire of a "culture war" that literally threatens to destroy the nation's political heritage. The Founding Fathers understood that democratic rule and the principles of justice and freedom depended on a population grounded in a God-given morality. That view is now under siege from those who contend the nation is not bound to any fixed truths.

The Late Great United States

Ultimately, this war of values could bring about the collapse of democracy and the rule of law. After all, if people are not accountable to God for their actions, there is no way to make them accountable to society except by coercion and terror. Government's job becomes much bigger in a nation whose inhabitants believe they answer only to themselves.

As difficult as it is for me to admit it, America is very much on the decline. And this is exactly what I have been expecting and predicting for this country since 1956.

"The United States will not hold its present position of leadership in the western world," I wrote in *The Late Great Planet Earth*. "Lack of moral principle by citizens and leaders will so weaken law and order that a state of anarchy will finally result. The military capability of the United States, though it is at present the most powerful in the world, has already been neutralized because no one has the courage to use it decisively. When the economy collapses, so will the military."[8]

Remember, folks, these words were written in 1969, not the 1990s! Today, more than ever, we understand their significance. I added: "The only chance of slowing up this decline in America is a widespread spiritual awakening."[9] That's still true, but our hope for the kind of major revival that would be required to shake America out of its spiritual doldrums is growing dimmer by the day.

Look what else I wrote about this subject in *Late Great*: "Look for the present sociological problems such as crime, riots, lack of employment, poverty, illiteracy, mental illness, illegitimacy, etc., to increase as the population explosion begins to multiply geometrically…Look for drug addiction to further permeate the U.S. and other free-world countries. Drug addicts will run for high political offices and win through support of young adults." [10]

Disrespect for Military

Does any of this sound familiar? All of the problems I listed have evolved into "crises." Now we have had a president of the United States who smoked marijuana but "didn't inhale." The American military is completely demoralized. Its mission has been radically altered from fighting force to "humanitarian" force. And as the defense budget is hacked away mercilessly, America's naive political leadership keeps finding more remote parts of the world in which to commit our confused young troops.

Some military affairs experts are predicting that this changing mission could actually someday undermine civilian control of American defense forces and ultimately even lead to a coup d'etat.

In 1992, Air Force Lt. Col. Charles E. Dunlap Jr. wrote an award-winning National War College student essay called "The Origins of the American Military Coup of 2012." In it he warns that a military takeover could be prompted by such trends as "the massive diversion of military forces to civilian uses."

He points out that the "Military Cooperation with Civilian Law Enforcement Act of 1981" was "specifically intended to force reluctant military commanders to actively collaborate in police work." This was a historic, if little noticed, change of policy, Dunlap explains. "Since the passage of the Posse Comitatus Act in 1878, the military had distanced itself from law enforcement activities.... By 1992 combating drug trafficking was formally declared a 'high national security mission.'" [11]

Our Thinking Has Changed

It's undeniable. Something's happening in America. The way people think about their country is changing. And it's not by accident, but by design. There is an agenda behind this "culture war."

My good friend, journalist Joseph Farah, explains it well: It all began, he says, in the early part of the 20th century, when an Italian Communist by the name of Antonio Gramsci theorized in his relatively obscure prison writings that it would take a "long march through the institutions"—meaning the media, the universities, public interest groups, etc.—before socialism and relativism would be victorious. By capturing those institutions and using their power, cultural values would be changed, morals broken down and the stage would be set for the political and economic power of the West to literally fall into the hands of the radical left.

Gramsci showed the left that the best way to change a society—permanently—was to change the way the whole society thinks about problems. Priority No. 1, he wrote, was subverting and undermining belief in God. If you could convince the masses that there is no real set of divinely inspired moral absolutes, you've already won half the battle. Everything more or less begins to fall into place for the socialist-relativist hordes.

Today, Farah explains, Gramsci's ideas have been adopted by the modern left—not only in the United States but worldwide. The obscure Italian Communist succeeded in defining a strategy for waging cultural warfare. And this new tactic has become the new great hope of the chronic America-bashers.

In other words, folks, there are other ways to power in a democratic, pluralistic society than getting someone elected to office. If you control the press, the arts, the universities, the schools and other key cultural institutions, the battle is basically over.

The Agenda of Moral Relativism

And that is the type of campaign that the moral relativists and secular humanists have waged over the last 25 years. Boy, have they been successful!

What exactly is their agenda? Dr. James Dobson of *Focus on the Family* may have summarized it best:

- "Convince the public that the training and development of children are far too important to be left to the whims and errors of parents.

- "Teach students that gay and lesbian lifestyles are no less moral than heterosexual relationships.

- "Remove all references to God from school literature."

- "Require churches, businesses and schools to hire gays, lesbians and others who contradict their faith.

- "Expand the power of government and its bureaucracies to control every vestige of private life.

- "Implement an aggressive sex-ed program, beginning in kindergarten, that is guided by no moral code.

- "Fight tooth and nail to retain the right to abortion.

- "Operate aggressive 'death education' classes in public schools to desensitize children to dying and to help them see life materialistically. [12]

You have to admit it. The humanists have done their job well. The Judeo-Christian ethic, the fundamental tenet of western civilization, has been broken down. Moral relativism rules the day. Its rules? There are no rules. Except those imposed capriciously by big government.

The Abortion Holocaust

So today, many women think nothing of destroying their unborn babies because a pregnancy might be "inconvenient." This is something that was practically unheard of at the time I wrote *Late Great*. In fact, no federal agency even kept statistics on the number of abortions taking place before 1972. Now, between 1.5 million and 2 million abortions take place every year in America—a hefty percentage of which are subsidized with your tax dollars.[13] Abortion in one generation has become the most common surgical procedure in America.

Why did abortion become so popular? Well, back in the early 1970s, abortion proponents told us that if we simply eliminated unwanted children from the planet the incidence of child abuse would plummet. Were they right? Of course not. In fact, just the opposite has occurred. As the value of life has been cheapened by abortion, child abuse has reached epidemic proportions.

Again, back in 1969, no one was even keeping tabs on the reported cases of child abuse. But since 1976 the number has increased from about 670,000 cases to nearly 3 million in the early '90s.[14] Some solution, huh? But don't expect the humanists to admit they failed. In fact, they are more driven than ever and their agenda grows more frightening every day.

The Brave New World?

Time magazine laid out the program for us titled "Beyond the Year 2000: What to Expect in the New Millennium." It provided a glimpse of what the brave new world of the humanists will soon look like:

- The traditional nuclear family will be dead. It turns out, the liberals who run *Time* magazine tell us, that the family was never anything more than an interesting cultural phenomenon. So, don't be overly sentimental about its demise.

* In place of the family, we'll have multiple marriages. Some marriage agreements will actually have "sunset clauses" to automatically terminate at a given age. Divorce will become far more commonplace—almost a matter of routine.

* Many women will live with other women. The "Golden Girls" television show might well be a model of such living arrangements.

* Children will live with many different relatives—and nonrelatives.

* The taboo against *incest* will be broken.

* There will be more older people and fewer children around as the value of life itself diminishes.

* Children will be victimized and abused even more routinely than they are today. It will not be unusual to see bands of boys and girls roaming the streets of urban America as they already do in Brazil.

* The study of God and the Bible will nearly disappear. Schoolchildren will have no knowledge of spiritual matters and—if the humanists have their way—no interest in such things.

* And here's a direct quote: "The triumph of feminist religion will cause many Christians and Jews to shun references to God in personal terms [no more Lord or Heavenly father]. This in turn [will] strengthen the groups that worship a mysterious nature-force to seek to deify the self."

* Forced abortion will become the rule of the land—just as it has in China.

End of the Family?

To sum it all up, *Time* tells us, "an even more radical approach may evolve. It is reasonable to ask whether there will be a family at all. Given the propensity for divorce, the growing number of adults who choose to remain single, the declining popularity of having children and the evaporation of the time families spend together, another way may eventually evolve. It may be quicker and more efficient to dispense with family-based reproduction. Society could then produce its future generations in institutions that might resemble state-sponsored baby hatcheries." [15]

Now, I don't suggest to you that all of these things will actually occur. In fact, I believe many of these ideas are mainly wishful thinking by the humanists. But it is nonetheless important to understand the agenda that is being promoted by powerful special interests. And it is also clear that if even half of this program is put into place, America and the free world will be considerably weakened as a result.[16]

The Vicious Cycle of Abuse

Unfortunately, we don't have that far to go. As children are more neglected and abused, they in turn become abusers themselves. Thus, the fastest growing segment of the criminal population is the children. Juvenile arrests are skyrocketing not only among the "disadvantaged minority youth in urban areas," but "all races, all social classes and lifestyles," says the FBI. And because the population group of 10-to-17-year-olds is going to increase significantly throughout the 1990s, authorities expect the level of violence to escalate dramatically. [17]

Defying the statisticians, however, is another trend. Criminologists have long theorized that juvenile crime rises along with the juvenile population—almost in direct correlation. However, new studies show that when the young male population actually started to decline in the early 1980s, their criminal activity and violent behavior increased rather than decreased as expected.[18]

Things are getting so bad that among the unsafest places to be in America today are in school or at work. Murder has jumped to No. 3 as a leading cause of death in the workplace— tripling in incidence during the 1980s.

"Some people are perceiving murder as one of their options when they're feeling frustrated," says Thomas Harpley, clinical director and founder of National Trauma Services in San Diego. [19]

Crime—The Worldwide Epidemic

Even though the United States leads the industrialized world in murders, sexual assaults and other violent crimes, most other nations are experiencing similar disturbing trends:

- South Africa is experiencing record numbers of murders and every category of crime is way up.

- In Germany, a record 6.1 million crimes were reported in 1992, up from the previous high of 5.3 million in 1991.

- In Israel, the prisons are bursting at the seams. The Police Ministry is running newspaper ads seeking to buy, lease or rent buildings to be turned into penitentiaries.

- In Russia, Boris Yeltsin is considering putting army troops into Moscow and other cities to serve as anti-crime patrols. [20]

Twisted Morality

And elsewhere around the world, misguided humanistic policies are resulting in tragic breakdowns of morality. In China, for instance, the government's strict population controls are resulting in a major surge in kidnappings. Thousands of young children are disappearing—from their beds, on their way to school, from their kindergarten classes, from open-air markets and from the paddy fields.[21] In addition, that same policy is resulting in thousands of baby girls being aborted. Knowing they can have only one child, parents are resorting to using ultrasound testing to determine the sex of unborn babies and aborting them if they are girls. Official figures show that for every 100 girls born in China, 113.8 boys are born.[22]

I'm afraid matters are only going to get worse on a global scale. God intends to use crime and violence as a judgment against man for his immorality and disobedience. The Scriptures give a prophetic report of the runaway crimes that will dominate society in the days immediately before Christ's return, and that man will even then not repent even after witnessing unprecedented supernatural catastrophic events ravage the planet:

> And the rest of mankind, who were not killed by these plagues, did not repent of the works of their hands, so as not to worship demons...and they did not repent of their murders nor of their sorceries [occult practices] nor of their immorality nor of their thefts" (Revelation 9:20-21).

But it's not just crime sweeping the landscape. It's a more general breakdown of values. Huge percentages of American students admit they cheat on tests and lie to their employers. According to a two-year study of nearly 9,000 high school and college students, lying, cheating and stealing comes fairly easily to kids these days.[23]

"In the short term, individuals can prosper from cheating," explained Ralph Wexler, executive vice president of the Josephson Institute for Ethics in Marina del Rey, California, who conducted the study. "But in the long term, society as a whole suffers. *The well-being, perhaps the survival of our civilization, involves a caring citizenry with sound moral character.*" [24] (emphasis added). Amen to that! But why do we need a study to tell us something we should all understand intuitively?

Drugs Make a Comeback

In the late 1960s, I could already see the devastating effects of drug abuse on an entire generation. But today, in the 1990s, drug abuse knows no generational boundaries. From the very young to the very old, drug use has reached epidemic proportions. I know businessmen who routinely test potential new employees for drugs who say they have trouble finding anyone not using marijuana, cocaine, psychedelics or the even more dangerous new synthetic narcotics.

With the "new morality" of the '60s came the "sexual revolution." Out went the old taboos about multiple sex partners, same-sex partners and promiscuity of all forms. With that, of course, came the judgment of AIDS and a whole host of other sexually transmitted diseases. The liberal social engineers told us that would be enough to discourage these "unsafe sex practices." But, despite all the publicity about AIDS, the latest statistics show people are more sexually active outside of marriage than ever.

"The enormous tensions and backlash generated by these devastating sexually transmitted diseases made the practitioners of casual sex pause," wrote the research team of Samuel and Cynthia Janus, who studied 8,000 people over a nine-year period. "In a sense, it was a time of national reassessment. Rather than lapsing into the sexual 'dark ages' however, Americans as a whole decided to move forward. This really marked the beginning of the 'Second Sexual Revolution,...an overall willingness to engage in a variety of sexual practices, some of which may once have been considered 'deviant' or at least 'unacceptable' by society."[25]

Well, so much for that kind of close-mindedness, right? On with the revolution. Forget the taboos. Who's to say what's right or wrong? If there are no absolutes (and without the Bible there are none), who's to say what is right or wrong? "If it feels good, do it" is the logical conclusion of a society that has pushed the true God out of their memory. The spirit of the '60s—which I'm convinced was inspired by demons—is still alive and well as we hurtle toward the third millennium.

The New Sexual Hedonism

Back in the late '60s, heterosexual promiscuity, open marriages and group sex were considered avante garde. Today, that stuff is considered child's play among the social crusaders. Even homosexuality and lesbianism are considered mainstream. On the cutting edge now are such bizarre practices as incest, sadomasochism, pedophilia and bestiality.

Anyone who opposes such behavior better watch out. In the name of "tolerance" and "diversity" even the Boy Scouts of

America will be shut out of funding, picketed, sued and boy-cotted in this new wacky, upside-down world of ours. I knew things were going to get strange, but even I am shocked by how far and how quickly depravity has progressed.

You know, I could cite statistics from now until Jesus comes and not make my point nearly as effectively as I can with a cou-ple of illustrations—modern-day parables, if you will.

A Sign of the Times

Two days before Christmas 1992, the Friedrick von Schiller Elementary School in a poor section of Chicago held a party for more than 325 students. It was to be a time of great joy and cele-bration. Each of the kids would receive a present provided by local businesses.

A group of parents offered to help the school inventory the gifts in the school auditorium before the children were allowed in. But while the adults were arranging the bags by grade and room number, some started unwrapping them and taking what they wanted. One parent described the hoarding as a wild animal fight.

"Some children went home crying," said Principal Marshall Taylor. "There was wrapping paper all over the floor—just as if somebody had said, 'Hey, help yourself!' When the kids came, they saw their parents hoarding the gifts."[26]

And we wonder why our kids are so troubled? We wonder why they have no standards? What ever happened to decency and civility? How barbaric can we get as a society?

I'm afraid the next illustration may provide a partial answer to that last rhetorical question. You've had your Christmas story, now here's a Halloween treat for you. This is no joke.

Obsession with Death

A new store opened up on fashionable Melrose Avenue in Los Angeles recently. It's called Necromance, and if you have a vivid imagination, you might be able to figure out what they

sell. Among the hip adornments available in this chic establishment are human fingers on a leather cord, necklaces of human
teeth, bone beads, human skulls and even a tiny fetal one. Mind
you, folks, this is not some secret bazaar in Bangladesh. This is
Melrose Avenue in supposedly civilized L.A. Worse yet, the *Los
Angeles Times* reports that business is booming for this shop of
horrors. [27]

Dr. Jack Kevorkian's acquittal in March, 1996, validated the
position of right to die advocates and increased public sympathy
for physician assisted suicides. As his trial in Michigan was on-
going, the California Ninth Circuit Court overturned a
Washington State law banning assisted suicide. In Europe,
Dutch legislators are debating the concept of involuntary
euthanasia for the mentally retarded, the terminally ill and the
criminally insane.

This is what we've come to, folks. This is the way our great
civilization has advanced. Truly, how much longer can we
expect it to last? You know, the Bible predicted there would be
days like this. Paul told Timothy there would be days like this.
Jesus warned us about days like this.

They would come in the "latter years," the "last days," the
"endtimes." They would be followed by a period of great tribulation and crisis in the world. They would precipitate mankind's
judgment. They would come just before the return of Jesus the
Messiah to planet Earth.

Do you have any doubts that we are living in that time? If
so, remember, this kind of trouble and foment—the kind so well
depicted in 2 Timothy 3:1-5—is just one of the many signs we
are told to look for in the closing of the age. Stay tuned for even
more compelling evidence.

References

[1] Federal Bureau of Investigation statistics
[2] National Center for Health Statistics
[3] Ibid.

[4] Census Bureau statistics

[5] National Center for Health Statistics

[6] The College Board

[7] The *Wall Street Journal*, March 15,1993

[8] *The Late Great Planet Earth*, 1970, chapter 14

[9] Ibid.

[10] Ibid.

[11] Charles J. Dunlap Jr., *The Origins of the American Military Coup of 2012,* National Defense University, National War College, 1992

[12] Dr. James Dobson, *Focus on the Family* magazine, July 1992

[13] The Alan Guttmacher Institute

[14] American Humane Association and the National Committee for the Prevention of Child Abuse.

[15] "Beyond the Year 2000: What to Expect in the New Millennium," *Time* magazine special edition, January 1993.

[16] A poll taken at the end of March, 1996, revealed that 71 percent of Americans polled denied there was any such thing as a moral absolute, or an absolute truth.

[17] Federal Bureau of Investigation, *Crime in the U.S. 1991: Juveniles and Violence 1965-1990.*

[18] *Sacramento Union*, October 15, 1992

[19] *San Francisco Chronicle*, November 8, 1992

[20] Edward Epstein, *San Francisco Chronicle*, February 4, 1993

[21] Deutsche Press Agentur, January 9, 1993

[22] Associated Press, June 22, 1993

[23] *San Francisco Chronicle*, November 13, 1992

[24] Ibid.

[25] *Los Angeles Times*, March 7, 1993

[26] Associated Press, December 24, 1992

[27] *Los Angeles Times*, March 12, 1993

Chapter 2

THE RISE OF
DECEIVING SPIRITS

Beloved, do not believe every spirit, but test the spirits to see whether they are from God; because many false prophets have gone out into the world.
—I JOHN 4:1

And many false prophets will arise, and will mislead many.
—MATTHEW 24:11

I've said it before and I will no doubt say it again: When the Rapture occurs, many churches will not have to find a new pastor. That's how badly infected the modern church is with deceiving spirits. Much of the flock has lost its way, but the so-called shepherds are even further off course in many cases.

This is tragic, but, once again, just what we should expect in the time just prior to our redemption.

Let me take you back to *The Late Great Planet Earth* once again, and what I said to look for regarding the future of the church based on my study of Bible prophecy. The very first thing I warned readers to watch for was the falling away of mainline churches from biblical teaching.

Whither the Church

"In the institutional church, composed of professing Christians who are in many cases not Christian, look for many things to happen," I wrote. "With increasing frequency the leadership of the denominations will be captured by those who completely reject the historic truths of the Bible and deny doctrines which according to Christ Himself are crucial to believe in order to be a Christian. In some of the largest Protestant denominations this has already taken place. The few remaining institutions which are not yet dominated by the disbelievers will go downhill in the same manner.

"There will be unprecedented mergers of denominations into 'religious conglomerates.' This will occur for two reasons. First, most denominations were formed because of deep convictions about certain spiritual truths. As more of these truths are discarded as irrelevant because of unbelief in biblical authority, there will be no reason to be divided. Unity is certainly important to have, but never, according to the teachings of Christ, at the expense of the crucial truths of Christianity.

"Second, as ministers depart from the truths of the Bible they lose the authority and power that it has to meet real human needs, and as many ministers are not truly born spiritually themselves and are consequently without the illumination of God's Spirit, they no longer will be able to hold their present congregations, much less attract others. So they resort to 'social action gimmicks,' super-organization and elaborate programs as a substitute." [1]

The Heresy Road

What I had in mind here were two converging and complementary trends: one toward apostasy and the other toward greater ecumenicism. What I did not see with as much clarity 25 years ago was the absolute explosion of the New Age movement and the greatly heightened interest in the occult, the supernatural and even the outright open worship of Satan.

But, first things first: Let's look at what's happening inside the church today.

Liberalism within the modern church has caused even some major denominations to move away from Scripture. It's not unusual today for some Christian groups to be more involved in politics—or the so-called "social-action gospel"—than in the Word of God. This is just as I predicted.

Several studies have shown that both U.S. Catholic and "mainline" Protestant church leaders lean far to the left of the American people.[2] Many of the leaders advocate an outright socialist agenda.

How Liberal Can You Get?

In surveys conducted by the Center for Media and Public Affairs, three of five Catholic leaders and four of five mainline

Protestant leaders categorized themselves as liberals, compared to only 13 percent of the fundamentalists questioned. In the survey by Robert Lerner, Stanley Rothman and S. Robert Lichter of the Center for Media and Public Affairs, 25 percent of mainline Protestant leaders and 31 percent of Roman Catholic leaders said they thought the U.S. should move toward a socialist economic system. Only 4 percent of fundamentalists agreed.

About one in five of the Catholics and mainline Protestants agreed that "big corporations should be taken out of private ownership and run in the public interest." Fifty-two percent of the Protestants and 64 percent of the Catholics said they thought capitalism is fair to workers. Among fundamentalists, the number was 91 percent.

Four of five mainline Protestant leaders and Roman Catholics said the government should do something to reduce the income gap between rich and poor. Even on the issue of abortion there was widespread disagreement. Two-thirds of liberal Protestants said women should have the right to abortion.[3]

The mainline churches, those that affiliated themselves eagerly with the National Council of Churches and the World Council of Churches, have long been attracted to this social gospel. During the past 25 years, many of the major denominations were deeply infiltrated by Communists and socialists who used the credibility the churches provided for them as cover for their nefarious and subversive activities. Remember "liberation theology"? There are doubtless still some practitioners out there, but most of them went into hiding after their sponsors and benefactors in the Soviet Union fell from power.

Rise of the Eco-Church

There are still plenty of liberals in the church who care more about redistribution of wealth than they do about eternal salvation. But now their tactics and strategy have changed. Have you heard a message like this in your church recently: "We trash the earth, yet it is every bit as sacred as any place within this church."

That's the familiar refrain of a new breed of church activist preaching environmental protection from America's pulpits. Just as the liberal, apostate church was active in the anti-nuclear movement of the 1960s and 1970s and the pro-abortion movement of the '70s and '80s, too many clergy are getting caught up in the save-the-earth gospel.

Don't get me wrong. No one can deny that the Earth is facing grave ecological crises. There is probably no one in the church who has done more than me in calling this fact to the attention of millions. We all have an obligation and responsibility to be good stewards with the natural bounty God has provided. But there is a sinister side to the "greening of the church" as well.

The New Name for Socialism?

I still remember when nuclear weapons were considered a great rallying issue. You could get people marching around the world on the idea of banning the bomb. That was a cause that young people and liberals would rally around. What happened with that movement was that the Communists snatched it and stealthily moved in and began to manipulate it for their own cause.

Organizing behind the scenes, the Communists managed to hijack and discredit much of the nuclear freeze movement. Now, with the hindsight only time can provide, we understand the degree to which the freeze movement was an active measure of the Soviet disinformation machine. The proof of the pudding is in this simple question: Where are the nuclear freezers today? Now that the Soviet Union has broken apart, why don't we see the long marches and the civil disobedience by freeze activists? There are just as many nuclear weapons in the world and they are just as dangerous. They are still aimed at the major population centers of the world. So where are the protests?

The answer, of course, is that they disappeared along with

their benefactors. But as they faded, a new movement caught the fancy of the liberal church—the green movement. While concern for the Earth is, as I have said, a legitimate cause, what concerns many conservative Christians is the fervor and the solutions the green movement proposes. In addition, there are so many familiar faces involved in it—many of the same ones who rallied around the nuclear cause are now rallying around the environmental issue and proposing totalitarian, one-world, socialistic, New Age-style solutions.

Politics Makes Strange Bedfellows

What's so strange about the church's excitement and fascination with this cause is the company it is keeping. Many of the New Agers who direct the environmentalist movement actually suggest that the church—indeed, the Judeo-Christian heritage in general—is arrogant toward the Earth and nature. Some are suggesting this is another reason such beliefs actually need to be eliminated before our problems can be resolved.

Let me tell you, folks. When church leaders work hand-in-hand with those who have vowed to destroy them and their core beliefs, they are indeed sowing the seeds of their own destruction. And they deserve what they get. Will turning away from biblical principles help avert ecological catastrophe? No way. In fact, turning away from those principles only ensures mankind's demise. It is the Bible itself that instructs mankind to be a good steward with his environment. Where do these environmentalist extremists think these ideas come from?

The Real Agenda

We all must do what we can to protect the earth's environment for ourselves and our children. But we must not allow such a political movement to be hijacked, as the antinuclear crusade was, by socialists and totalitarians.

Here's the bottom line: The Earth will not be saved from environmental destruction by the powers of big government. In fact, the worst polluters on the planet have been and continue to be socialist governments. Respect for private property and God's creation are essential elements to conservation. Those are elements missing in the environmental movement.

Unfortunately, the environmental movement has become little more than a tool of the radical socialist extremists. It is seen as the latest excuse to seize property, redistribute wealth and empower government. Without a doubt, the far left has made the environment its No. 1 issue for the foreseeable future. And too much of the church has become complicit in this extremist agenda.

The New Apostates

At the same time, there are other destructive forces working within the church. One of the most insidious is a group called the Jesus Seminar. Once a year, this arrogant, pompous group of self-proclaimed biblical scholars gets together to decide what Jesus really said or didn't say to His disciples and how the Bible has distorted that message. Talk about insolence! But, nevertheless, every year the proclamations of the Jesus Seminar receive national attention thanks to the cynicism and bias of the secular media, which are openly hostile to real Bible-based Christianity in the first place.

But even the scriptural revisionists of the Jesus Seminar can't compare in presumptuousness and blasphemy to Bishop John Shelby Spong of the Episcopal Church. Just in time for the holidays in 1992, Spong came out with a book claiming that Jesus was illegitimate, perhaps even the product of rape, and that most of the rest of the biblical Christmas story—from the Wise Men to the star to the angelic hosts—is sheer mythology.[4]

Spong is one of many liberal theologians who has been blinded to the truth of the Bible by their need and desire to be "politically correct." Suffice it to say that church leaders who forsake revealed truth about God and His plan for salvation in favor of reclaiming the powers of this world are apostates. There is no other way to say it. They are traitors to their faith and to God.

With such heresy being preached from the pulpits of Christian churches throughout the world is it any wonder so many people are becoming spiritually disenfranchised? Is it any wonder people are leaving the mainline denominations in droves? Is it any wonder young people especially are turning elsewhere for their spiritual needs?

The Church Loses Its Way

"If long-term trends continue, the once-dominant liberal and moderate denominations will soon become a minority in American Protestantism." Who wrote that? Not me—though it sounds strikingly similar to words I used in *The Late Great Planet Earth* nearly 20 years earlier. No, this statement was made by *Los Angeles Times* religion writer John Dart in a front-page news report.[5]

Dart pointed out that back in 1920, mainline Protestant churches like the Presbyterian, Episcopal, Methodist and Lutheran constituted 76 percent of the Protestant population in the U.S. But by the mid-1980s, that figure was down to about 50 percent.[6]

The Good News

And even though church membership overall was gaining in the 1990s, the liberal mainline denominations continued to experience steady annual declines in membership.[7] Where are all the people going? Well, just as I predicted in *The Late Great Planet Earth*, many, especially the young, are turning to more conservative evangelical churches that emphasize the fundamental eternal truths of the Bible. Note that the more conservative denominations—Presbyterian Church in America and Southern Baptist Convention continue to show increases in membership.[8] But the real story is told in the explosion of growth in small, unaffiliated, non-denominational churches that emphasize basic Bible teaching.

That's the good news. Many millions of people have come

to know Jesus Christ in a personal way. They have come to understand that salvation has nothing to do with the church you go to. It's an individual choice and a gift from God Almighty. Lots of people have been saved in the last 25 years. Again, that's just what I foresaw and just what you would expect in these days of grace before the final judgment begins.

The Lost Sheep

But there is also bad news on the horizon. While many of those turned off to the social gospel and hollowness of the mainline denominational message have been led to the truth, a great many others have been seduced by an even more insidious lie. This development is even more striking in prophetic significance than the apostate movements within the church. I refer to the Eastern religious mysticism sweeping the globe.

We call it the "New Age" movement. But there is very little "new" about it. Most of its tenets are inspired from ancient pagan religions. Yet, dressed up in their Yuppified, '90s garb, these beliefs and practices are considered chic, hip—even divinely revealed.

This is an accurate fulfillment of I Timothy 4:1, which says, "But the Spirit explicitly says that in later times some will fall away from the faith, paying attention to deceitful spirits and doctrines of demons."

The Rise of False Prophets

False prophets abounded in Old Testament days. In many cases, they were people motivated not by loyalty to God, but by a desire for popularity. While Jeremiah warned the nation of imminent disaster, the false prophets were assuring the people that peace was at hand and all was well.

After all, Israel was God's people and the holy Temple was in Jerusalem. The people generally preferred this soothing message. In Isaiah 30:10, they actually say: *"Prophesy not to us what is right; speak to us smooth things, prophesy illusions..."*

But Jeremiah (Jeremiah 4:1-9) warned the people of Israel not to be fooled into thinking the nation was immune from suffering.

The message of the false prophet continued because it was motivated by self-interest and given to please the people. In the New Testament, Jesus warned against those who disguise themselves as sheep but are in fact wolves ready for the kill.

Know Them by Their Track Record

Moses gave the test of a true prophet of God. Their prophecies had to come true with 100-percent accuracy. Near misses earned a prophet death by stoning (Deuteronomy 18:20-22). The prophet's message and life has to also check out with the Bible (Deuteronomy 13:1-5). In the last days, Jesus warned there would be an increase in the number of false prophets, and one in particular so convincing that even the elect would be fooled, if that were possible (Matthew 24:24).

Once again we have seen evidence of this prophecy being fulfilled, particularly in the 1990s as we near the next millennium. Cultists have attached great significance to the year 2000, and as we get closer, we will no doubt see an even greater rise in the number of false prophets and doctrines.

As the world approached the year 1000, false prophets were predicting events ranging from famines to flying dragons. Today, New Age cultists are predicting the dawn of the Age of Aquarius. The hysteria is only likely to get worse as we edge nearer the year 2000.

Doctrines of Demons?

Doctrines of demons are accepted phenomena today. You can't watch a talk show or a sitcom or read a newspaper without hearing about them. But we don't call it necromancy, or calling up demons, in our culture. We call it "channeling" or following your "spirit guide." It's become a parlor game over in Malibu and other places where the cultural elite congregate. But, you know what? It's no game. They are making contact with very real and powerful spirit beings whose ability to deceive covers their deadly evil intent. Without the Bible, no human being has a clue as to how much danger they are in with these demon spirits. Literally, their eternal destiny is at stake.

The New Age is big business. It sponsors magazines that claim circulations in the millions. Books by Shirley MacLaine and other authors are best sellers. While it is considered bad taste or at least "unhip" to produce TV shows or movies that put Christianity in a positive light, countless productions do just that for New Age philosophies.

Religion á la Carte

Another name for the New Age might well be "Religion á la Carte." Take one doctrine from column A and another from column B. Who's to say what's right and wrong? Isn't it up to each individual to discover the truth within himself? That's the core of the New Age philosophy. There is no fixed set of beliefs. New Age tends to mean any belief system other than strict monotheism. But the New Agers tend to be most hostile to Christianity. Some liberal churches—ever concerned about being "pluralistic" and "open-minded"—have embraced some of the teachings of Buddhism, yoga and other New Age spiritualities with open arms.

How many new cults are there? Depending on whom you believe, anywhere from 700 to 5,000.[9] The New Age is even making inroads into our political establishment. In the 1980s, we found out that one of the most powerful men in the Senate, Claiborne Pell of Rhode Island, who headed the Foreign Relations Committee, had steeped himself in all facets of New Age belief. He dabbled in ESP, near-death studies, psychic powers, unconventional healing techniques and UFOs.

Hollywood Joins in the Fun

New Age "solutions" to problems—from interpersonal to international—have been widely trumpeted by the media for the last 15 years. In fact, Hollywood seems to be particularly under its spell. For instance, the latest "Star Trek" TV series, "Deep Space Nine," routinely promotes many Eastern religious ideas.

"There are simply too many Eastern religious concepts in that one show to deal with at one time," says Vishal Mangalwadi, a Christian theologian at the Himalayan L'Abri Resource Center. "It seems like the gurus are making the films."[10]

In studying the series and other "Star Trek" films, Mangalwadi found they consistently promote an Eastern worldview with themes like these:

- We are the Creator: In one movie, Capt. James T. Kirk and crew go looking for God and find a projection of themselves.

- The cosmos is merely a creation of human consciousness. Over and over, "Star Trek" episodes seem to suggest that perception may be reality and that life is merely the product of consciousness rather than the creation of a transcendent God.

- Time is cyclical. In Eastern religions, you are always repeating your life over and over.

- Karma, the energy generated by a person's actions, is a recurrent theme in the series and films. [11]

The New Age Establishment

But it's not just the media. Our government, our schools, indeed, most of our major cultural institutions are promoting New Age ideas. When you hear about efforts to improve the public's self-esteem or ability to resolve conflict, know that you are likely in the presence of a New Age evangelist. And these ideas are quickly seeping into the curricula of our public schools and being legislated into our lives through government action at the local, state and federal levels.

Much of the New Age agenda sounds harmless. But it is part of a different Gospel—a different world view than the Bible-centered Judeo-Christian perspective. And there is a more overtly dark side, a more blatantly evil side to the New Age.

The Slide to the Dark Side

Hardly a day can go by now that we don't hear about ritualistic child abuse, animal sacrifice, Satan worshippers, etc. It is a continuing and horrifying story that even the secular media cannot ignore any longer.

These occurrences are becoming increasingly commonplace in our society as the traditional Judeo-Christian beliefs, mores and values take a back seat to secularism, relativism, humanism and, most of all, the open-door philosophies of the New Age. Because, while the New Age movement rejects orthodox tenets of Christianity and Judaism, it can find no wrong in ancient occultic beliefs and practices, including even the once unthinkable worship of Satan.

The fact of the matter is that today's brand of Satanism can be traced directly to the rise of the New Age counterculture in the 1960s. In 1966, the high priest of modern Satanism, Anton LaVey, declared the dawn of the Satanic age. He proclaimed that God was dead. Within a few months, the Sexual Freedom League came into prominence, and the free sex culture developed.

While the bizarre, hateful, murderous practices of Satanism may seem almost a perfect contradiction to the peaceful, harmonic themes of the New Age movement born of the '60s and '70s, one of the common denominators is rebellion. Both share a vehement hostility to traditional, orthodox religious belief. Rather than opposites, the differences between the superficially benign occultism of the New Age and the openly violent and depraved practices of Satanism are really only a matter of degree. What does the stereotypical New Ager talk about? Love, peace, unity, pacifism, non-violence, the brotherhood of man and so forth. Right? But there is a less-understood, seldom-discussed side to the equation that is—like Satanism—darker, diabolical and completely intolerant of Christianity.

The Corruption of the Church

Nevertheless, many in the church are led to associate with these ideas and beliefs. It is a major corrupting influence. And it is leading many away from grace and salvation and toward death and damnation. It is also leading to the day—in the not-too-distant future—when all the world sings one hymn. But it won't be "Rock of Ages," folks. It's going to be a song sweet only to the ears of Satan.

That's right. The occultic beliefs of the New Age and Satanism spring from the same well. I'll prove it to you. The spiritual godmother of the New Age movement is Helena Petrovna Blavatsky. In 1875, she founded the Theosophical Society in New York. Theosophy's teachings varied very little from today's brand of New Age mumbo-jumbo. You'd recognize the universalist pronouncements about how we're all part of the "brotherhood of man" and how we all need to unite behind one belief system, etc.

But, from its very earliest roots, New Agers always made it clear that all were welcome to partake of this communion but those who believe in one God—and particularly Christians. Here, for instance, is an excerpt from an early Theosophical Society statement: "To oppose...every form of dogmatic theology, especially the Christian, which the Chiefs of the Society regard as particularly pernicious...to counteract, as far as possible, the effects of missionaries to delude the so-called 'Heathen' and 'Pagans' as to the real dogmas of Christianity and the practical effects of the latter upon public and private character in so-called Christian countries." [12]

Know Them by Their Enemies

Blavatsky detested God, Jesus and Christianity. She went so far as to suggest Satan was an innocent victim of God's capricious and intemperate wrath: "The appellation Sa'tan, in Hebrew Satan, and Adversary...belongs by right to the first and cruelest "Adversary" of all other Gods—Jehovah; not to the serpent which spoke only words of sympathy and wisdom." [13]

So enamored of Satan were Blavatsky's followers and successors that in the 1890s they launched the Lucifer Publishing Company, which, among other things, published their periodical *Lucifer*. Realizing later that for public relations purposes a less-explosive name might be preferable, they changed the name to Lucis Publishing Company. The Lucis Trust, established by Blavatsky disciple Alice Bailey in 1922, remains to this day a prominent foundation supporting New Age and one-world causes and organizations. [14]

Where It's All Leading

The increasing acceptance of New Age beliefs by the world in general and the apostate church in particular is leading the world irrevocably toward the one-world religious system the Bible tells us will exist on Earth just before the return of Jesus. Have any doubts? How's this for a preview:

> Buddhist monks draped in saffron robes joined black-turbaned Sikh priests in gold and white. Roman Catholic Cardinal Joseph Bernardin mixed with Jain nuns with mouth coverings that prevented them from harming even an insect. During the opening processional of the 1993 Parliament of the World's Religions, Jewish and American Islamic leaders marched side-by-side down three aisles in a packed ballroom. [15]

Is it really such a stretch to consider that shortly one man will be able to unite all of these disparate seekers into one planetary religion that worships a New Age god? In fact, can't you already hear the throngs cheering this new unity—this new "brotherhood of man"? After all, this new world religion will allow so much diversity under its wide umbrella. You will be able to worship any God, practice any belief and attend any church you want—as long as it's not the God of the Bible, the belief in Jesus Christ and a church that preaches personal salvation and relationship with the true God.

The Religion of the U.N.

We're very, very close, my friends. Let me tell you how close. Let me show you how even the hallowed halls of the United Nations—the world's leading promoter of globalism and world government—have become a hotbed of idol-worship and the kind of militant paganism that the prophets warned us would arise and spread in these last days.

The United Nations today works hand in glove with the Lucis Trust. Remember how that organization got its name? According to the foundation, it is "represented at regular briefing sessions at the United Nations in New York and Geneva." The group's weekly broadcasts are beamed to a worldwide audience from the U.N. University for Peace in Costa Rica. Donald Keys, who is a disciple of Lucis Trust founder Alice Bailey, serves as president of Planetary Citizens. Listen to what he says goes on at the U.N. today:

"We have meditations at the United Nations a couple of times a week. The meditation leader is Sri Chinmoy, and this is what he said about this situation: 'The United Nations is the chosen instrument of God; to be a chosen instrument means to be a divine messenger carrying the banner of God's inner vision and outer manifestation. One day, the world will...treasure and cherish the soul of the United Nations as its very own with enormous pride, for this soul is all-loving, all nourishing and all-fulfilling.'"[16]

Could the U.N. really provide the basis for not only a one-world government but also a global religion? Let's just say that many New Agers are promoting just that.

One Big Happy Family

"A worldwide citizens' movement is born around the U.N. system and will be in the years ahead a central focal point for the New World Order which Alice Bailey wrote about many decades ago and which is going to be politically free, socially fair, economically efficient and environmentally sustainable," declared the Union for Natural Environment Protection following the 1992 Rio de Janeiro Earth Summit. [17]

Notice the interconnection between the Lucifer-loving Blavatsky disciple Alice Bailey, the environmentalist extremists, the New Age spiritualists and the globalists at the U.N. About one thing all these folks are right: We are truly on the cusp of a major planetary transition. Hold onto your seats, folks. The future is now.

References

[1] Hal Lindsey, *The Late Great Planet Earth*, Zondervan, 1970

[2] Allan C. Brownfeld, *Human Events*, June 6, 1987, page 11

[3] Center for Media and Public Affairs

[4] *The Sacramento Bee*, January 2, 1993

[5] John Dart, *Los Angeles Times*, April 6, 1985

[6] Ibid.

[7] *Christianity Today*, November 11, 1991

[8] Ibid.

[9] *Newsweek*, March 15, 1993

[10] *Washington Times*, February 27, 1993

[11] Ibid.

[12] Theosophical Society brochure, quoted by Constance Cumby, *The Hidden Dangers of the Rainbow: The New Age Movement and Our Coming Age of Barbarism*, Huntington House, Shreveport, Louisiana, 1983, page 43

[13] Tal Brooke, *When the World Will Be As One*, Harvest House Publishers, Eugene, Oregon, 1989, pages 175-176

[14] William Jasper, *Global Tyranny...Step By Step*, Western Islands, Appleton, Wisconsin, 1992, page 215

[15] *San Francisco Examiner*, September 5, 1993

[16] Jasper, Ibid., page 212

[17] Ibid., page 221

Chapter 3

THE NEW WORLD DISORDER

And they said, "Come, let us build for ourselves a city, and a tower whose top will reach into heaven, let us make for ourselves a name; lest we be scattered abroad over the face of the whole earth."
—GENESIS 11:4

And it was given to him to make war with the saints and to overcome them; and authority over every tribe and people and tongue and nation was given to him.
—REVELATION 13:7

As American was celebrating Independence Day 1990, a chilling confirmation of the one-world environmentalist agenda was revealed over an international computer bulletin board and news service for the far-left globalists. Little noticed anywhere beyond my own monthly news journal *Countdown*, the "Declaration of Interdependence," a political manifesto for socialists parading as environmentalists, was set forth on July 4 that year.

"When in the course of human events, it becomes necessary to acknowledge the ecological bands which have connected them with each other, and to assume among the powers of the Earth the united and equal station to which the laws of nature and nature's God entitle them, a decent respect for the opinions of humankind requires that they declare the causes which impel them to the Union," the statement beamed out over a computer database called "Socialism On-Line."[1]

Despite the overwhelming evidence of destruction to the environment by central planning in Eastern Europe, the Soviet Union and other socialist governments, the environmental extremist movement continues to direct most of its hostility toward the West. This Declaration of Interdependence was in reality a re-packaged version of the same old Marxist declaration of war against governments which permit free enterprise, respect private property ownership and provide for a national defense.

What They Will Believe In

But the Declaration of Interdependence is more a religious document than a political one. For it sets out a spiritual basis—

fraudulent though it may be—for what is shaping up to be a one-world government, or, as some call it, the New World Order.

"To establish a new world order of compassion, peace, justice and security, it is essential that mankind free itself from the limitations of national prejudice, and acknowledge that the forces that unite it are incomparably deeper than those that divide it—that all people are part of one global community, dependent on one body of resources, bound together by the ties of a common humanity and associated in a common adventure on the planet Earth," the document reads.

The Trend Toward Centralization

Unfortunately, there is a force at work throughout the world that aims to unite people, nations, communities and other groups into larger units. Centralization, you might call it. While it may seem logical to people that bigger countries, bigger groups, bigger governments are by definition better, we have seen an overwhelming body of evidence which contradicts that truism. That's why the Soviet Union disintegrated.

Bigger is not better. It is usually worse. That's why talk of a New World Order and a global government is frightening. The Bible warns of a time coming very soon when the world will be divided into a few spheres of influence and when, in fact, there will be a giant world federation that controls virtually all human activity and commerce. To achieve that goal, people are being convinced—brainwashed really—into believing there are no significant differences between cultural and religious traditions. This movement is commonly called "multi-culturalism," and it is at the root of the trend in our universities that sees Western Civilization being phased out as the bedrock of academic pursuit.

The Role of Multiculturalism

The current drive to include multicultural and non-Western books in the core curriculum of American universities is justified in its goals, but misguided in its approach, explains Dinesh D'Souza, author of the best-seller *Illiberal Education*. Mr. D'Souza says that studying other cultures and their traditions is a worthy pursuit if the goal is to learn about their achievements and failings. Unfortunately, he adds, many of the most prestigious institutions of higher learning in the West now require students to take non-Western or ethnic studies but do not require them to study the basic ingredients of Western history, politics or literature.

Mr. D'Souza, a true student of other cultures, took the time to prepare a list of great non-Western books worthy of study:

- *The Upanishads*—Written in Sanskrit between 800 and 400 B.C., they are at the heart of Hinduism. "They have contributed to a widespread conviction, across the Indian subcontinent, that it is a waste of time to combat social injustice, as true liberation comes from the inner soul's receptivity to the divine calling," he writes.

- Confucius' *Analects*—They are the foundation of Chinese thought. "Western students who study Confucius confront a worldview that takes a fatalistic approach to reforming social institutions, emphasizes unqualified obedience within the family, and embraces rigid class structures and emperor worship."

- *The Koran*—It has much in common with the Judeo-Christian tradition from which it sprang, says D'Souza. "At the same time, its teachings regarding male superiority and authority over women, polygamy and criminal deterrence... will be difficult for many Westerners to embrace. The Koran does not distinguish between religious and political activity: It calls for Muslim domination and limited rights for others, and it urges a jihad, or holy war, against non-Islamic states to bring them under the rule of Allah," says D'Souza.[2]

What's wrong with this picture?

There are many other great books cited by Mr. D'Souza, but the point is that all of them are fatally flawed from a Western, Judeo-Christian worldview—the tradition that gave us the U.S. Constitution and unparalleled freedom and opportunity. So don't be fooled by the talk of "interdependence," "Multiculturalism," and a "New World Order." They are nice sounding words. But all of them together spell tyranny, oppression and death.

There are other nice sounding words being spoken by well-respected men. But it's time to look beneath the veneer. Take, for example, everyone's friend, good old Jacques Cousteau. Here's a guy that the whole world loves. He seems harmless enough when you see him on TV swimming around in the coral with the dolphins. But, again, he deserves a closer look. In recent years, he has become a champion not only of radical environmentalism—but of one-world socialism, as well.

The New Bill of Rights

Not unlike the backers of the Declaration of Inter-dependence, the Jacques Cousteau Society has developed a "Bill of Rights for Future Generations" that it is circulating and seeking support in the United States and elsewhere. The idea is to collect 10 million signatures in support of the plan and present them to the U.N. General Assembly in hopes that the world body will adopt the new rights plan.

Cousteau says the U.S. Bill of Rights is outdated and "no longer suffices." He adds: "Free enterprise is leading to scandalous inequalities." Cousteau is openly calling for the nations of the world to abdicate their sovereignty, "because there is no other solution but to define global laws." He also wants the U.N. to create an environmental police force of "green helmets."[3] I'm not making this up, folks; you can find this proposed new bill of rights that Cousteau is advocating being promoted all over as if it were the least controversial plan ever devised. I found it being hyped in a California supermarket.

What's the main difference between the old Bill of Rights and the new? Well, the old plan basically served to limit the powers of government. "Congress shall make no law…is a frequent device used to restrict government meddling. Cousteau's plan places no limits on government. Instead, it is a plan to curtail freedom—to shackle people and industry and to empower a world government.

Most Powerful Man in the World?

Who is the most powerful man in the world today? No, it's not the president of the United States. It's not even Jacques Cousteau. Instead, by sheer will and a vision for a New World Order, United Nations Secretary General Boutros Boutros-Ghali has become arguably the most influential individual on the face of the planet.

The Egyptian diplomat has at his disposal virtually limitless military and financial resources (thanks to the pliancy of the United States) with almost no accountability or the kinds of checks and balances on power that confine elected leaders in civilized nations.

Boutros-Ghali, with the full complicity of an inexperienced U.S. chief executive, is using this clout and seizing the opportunity created by the end of the Cold War to place his globalist designs on the fast track. And what are his plans?

What He Wants

In a candid article in a publication of the Council on Foreign Relations, Boutros-Ghali revealed his ambitious plans: "The machinery of the United Nations, which had often been rendered inoperative by the dynamics of the Cold War, is suddenly at the center of international efforts to deal with unresolved problems of the past decades as well as an emerging array of present and future issues."[4]

Like the socialists who direct many nations of the world, Boutros-Ghali dreams of being able to micro-manage international affairs, resolving every dispute and, most importantly, maintaining stability and preserving the world order. Also like the socialists and liberals of the West, Boutros-Ghali plays upon the good nature and compassion of the liberal democracies in his crusade for centralized world authority.

The Age of Manipulation

How do you motivate Americans to send their sons and daughters to die in Somalia chasing around warlords who pose no possible threat to their nation's vital interests? Easy. Just show pictures of starving children on television and call it a "humanitarian mission." How do you get Americans to agree to place their kids in the crossfire of an ancient ethnic war in Bosnia? Easy. Just show pictures of starving adults and injured children on television. How do you get Americans to blockade Haiti and intervene in a pointless civil war? Easy. Just ask Bill Clinton.

Call it manipulation by compassion. Using such tactics, Boutros-Ghali has managed to deploy record numbers of U.N. "peacekeeping" troops around the globe. Between 1948 and 1978, U.N. troops were called out to respond to 13 different operations. But in the last three years alone, more than twice that number of U.N. deployments have occurred.

The U.N. Mission

"Together, the international community and the U.N. Secretariat need to seize this extraordinary opportunity to expand, adapt and reinvigorate the work of the United Nations so that the lofty goals as originally envisioned by the charter can begin to be realized," Boutros-Ghali writes.[5]

And what are those goals? Where is the U.N. taking us all? The U.N. Charter has four objectives:

- "To practice tolerance and live together in peace with one another as good neighbors;

- "To unite our strength to maintain international peace and security;

- "To ensure, by the acceptance of principles and the institution of methods, that the armed forces shall not be used, save in the common interest;

- "To employ international machinery for the promotion of the economic and social advancement of all peoples."[6]

The New World Cops

Do you see anything in there about maintaining an army? Even Boutros-Ghali admits that the peacekeeping forces flung far and wide around the planet today are an invention of the U.N.

"It was not specifically defined in the charter but evolved as a non-coercive instrument of conflict and control at a time when Cold War restraints prevented the Security Council from taking the more forceful actions permitted by the charter," he explains.[7]

Like the utopian dreams of socialists everywhere, successful results are not the standard by which peacekeeping ventures are measured. It is a matter of faith that more troops means more peace. Therefore, Boutros-Ghali is selling the world on the need for a permanent, standing U.N. army.

"One of the lessons learned during the recent headlong expansion of U.N. peacekeeping is the need to accelerate the deployment of new operations," he writes. "Under current procedures three or four months can elapse between the Security Council's authorization of a mission and its becoming operational in the field. Action is required on three fronts: finance, personnel and equipment."[8]

Guess Who Pays for It?

Therefore, Boutros-Ghali is organizing an effort to create military hardware and munitions depots around the world for use by U.N. forces. He is pushing hard for more commitments of money and troops by the West—particularly the United States.

Before it's too late, Americans need to ask the following questions: What does the U.S. Constitution say about compromising our national sovereignty to foreign powers or international bodies? How are U.N. missions serving our national interests? Do we really want our children serving in foreign wars under foreign command? Did our founding fathers ever envision us becoming the world's mercenaries?

But America doesn't seem to be asking the right questions. In fact, in the 1990s, the United States has broken with its traditional military policies and the principle of U.S. sovereignty and expanded its role in United Nations peacekeeping operations that will on a routine basis allow U.S. soldiers to serve under foreign commanders.

U.S. Troops Under Foreign Command

A presidential policy directive, which apparently does not need to be approved by Congress, was signed in 1993. How much of a departure is this decision from past practice? Since the end of World War II, the United States has been scrupulous about detailing only individual officers as monitors in U.N. peacekeeping missions or providing air and sea transport for operations.

In fact, before the recent U.N. operation in Somalia, the United States had only once placed an American military unit under direct United Nations command—and that was a small air transport unit in Western New Guinea during the Kennedy administration. American troops fought in United Nations sanctioned missions in Korea and the Gulf War, but, in both cases, the commanders were U.S. officers.

The move by President Clinton represented a bold and dangerous step toward the New World Order that international socialists have been dreaming about for years. It is also a step toward the kind of one-world government the Bible predicts will exist on earth just before the return of the real Messiah of the Bible, Jesus Christ.

This directive goes well beyond anything envisioned even by former President Bush, who seemed to work tirelessly and enthusiastically toward the goal of a new world order that diminished the commitment to national sovereignty. It was the Bush administration that first pushed openly for what it called "a multilateral approach" to regional conflicts. But even Bush never proposed placing the lives of American soldiers in the hands of foreign commanders.

.

And then there is the case of former Army Specialist Michael New. He was ordered to join a unit under the command of the United Nations. He refused to wear the UN insignia on his uniform just before being shipped out from Germany to be part of the UN monitoring mission in Macedonia, a small country between Greece and war-torn Bosnia. He was tried, convicted and given a bad conduct discharge from the military. New's attorney, retired Army Colonel Ron Ray said, "I feel that the only reason they convicted him at all was because they had to do what was good for the whole Army, which was to convict Michael New. Military court isn't like civilian court, where the rights of the defendant are first and foremost. To acquit him of any wrongdoing would, in essence, convict the Army and the president and acknowledge that America's participation in these U.N. peacekeeping missions is illegal." [9]

U.S. Loses Its Bearings

I have been warning for years that, because of the last-days geopolitical alignment portrayed in the Bible, it is not likely that the U.S. will remain the pre-eminent world power very long. There are many ways America could quickly slide down the road toward second-rate power:
• moral collapse
• financial disaster
• war
• natural disaster
No one can be sure how it will happen or when it will happen. But I'll tell you I think the most likely scenario for America's decline is that the United States will simply compromise its own national sovereignty in the way we see it happening right now.

Not only is America placing its troops under foreign command, it is also sacrificing its sovereignty in international treaties, some of which don't permit the United States to change its own laws without the consent of other nations.

Who's Pulling the Strings?

Why is this happening? I hate to sound like some kind of conspiracy nut, but the evidence is becoming overwhelming that there is a plan, perhaps one being orchestrated by an international elite.

If you ever had any doubts that key leaders are conspiring together to bring about a one-world government, a prestigious French publication has offered proof. The smoking gun was published by *Lecturers Francaises*, which managed to sneak a representative inside 1991's meeting of the highly secretive Bilderberg Group.

As always when this coterie of elite one-worlders meets, there were many media insiders in attendance at a recent conference in Sand, Germany. But, as usual, the representatives of the big media did not let their readers in on the agenda of the meetings.

Thanks for the Cover-Up

"We are grateful to the *Washington Post*, the *New York Times*, *Time* magazine and other great publications whose directors have attended our meetings and respected their promises of discretion for almost 40 years," the French periodical quoted David Rockefeller as telling the group. "It would have been impossible for us to develop our plan for the world if we had been subject to the bright lights of publicity during these years. But the world is now more sophisticated and prepared to march towards a world government which will never again know war but only peace and prosperity for the whole of humanity. The supranational sovereignty of an intellectual elite and world bankers is surely preferable to the national autodetermination practiced in the past centuries. It is also our duty to inform the press of our convictions as to the historic future of the century.'[10]

Could it be any more obvious what he's saying? Rockefeller was thanking the media for keeping their plans for one-world government quiet. So maybe the conspiracy folks are onto something, after all.

Regional Alliances

It's still theory and conjecture, but, in my opinion, here's how the grand plan will begin to unfold: The insiders who meet under the auspices of the Trilateral Commission, Council on Foreign Affairs, the Bilderberg Group, etc., intend to use the United Nations and the European Community as the models for other regional groups of nations. Already the Islamic nations of the world have formed a coalition. Latin American nations have grouped together through an "integration association." The nations of Southeast Asia have their own association. West African states have their own economic community. And, of course, the U.S., Canada and Mexico formed the North America Free Trade Area in 1989, which resulted in a treaty ratified by the U.S. Congress in October, 1993.

But these international groupings are merely an interim step toward total world unification. And in the 1990s, the world seems to be on a fast track toward global government. It's never been so clear before.

A Vision of Global Peace

"'What is emerging is a more complex global structure of international relations, an awareness of the need for some kind of global government—one in which all members of the world community would take part—is gaining ground," explains Mikhail Gorbachev. [11]

Those who support it say it is a "vision of global peace," that it would represent an effort in "collective security." It has also been called "a new partnership of nations moving toward a historic period of cooperation." And some have described it as "a new era, free from the threat of terror, strong in the pursuit of justice, more secure in the quest for peace."

To a world tired of war, rumors of war and sometimes unspeakable brutality and incivility, the New World Order can sound pretty appealing.

But when you get beyond the lofty rhetoric and analyze just

what is meant by global government, the reality can be even more frightening than the instability of a hostile world governed by the aggressive use of force.

End of American Sovereignty

The most important thing to remember about the global vision, the New World Order or the "new paradigm," as Mikhail Gorbachev sometimes calls it, is that it would mean an end to national sovereignty. Now, in many nations, that might not be such a bad thing. When the world imposed sanctions on Iraq, for instance, who could complain? But are Americans ready for a United Nations-style authority to tell us that our beloved Constitution is declared null and void? Are Americans prepared for an outside force telling them that they must adopt new laws protecting sexual deviancy? Can you imagine America being governed by anyone other than Americans?

And, of course, along with world government would come a world police force, world courts and a world bank and a universal currency. To top it all off, there would be a world elite— probably made up of the kind of internationalists who have run the Trilateral Commission and the European Community in recent years—to control it all.

Just imagine what that world would be like. America could no longer decide to do what is in its best interest. American taxpayers would not only be forced to carry the heavy tax burden they carry now—on top of that they would have to support international welfare. America would be placed on an equal footing with nations like Libya, Iran and China. Because the U.S. has only 5 percent of the world's population, we would be limited to a 5 percent level of geo-political influence. Your First and Second Amendment rights would mean little under the new setup—the U.S. Constitution would have to take a backseat to the higher authority.

And if freedom-loving Americans ever got too far out of line, why you could just call in the blue helmets of the United Nations to quell any disturbances. Whereas U.S. military troops might be reluctant to fire on fellow Americans, do you think those from Turkey or Pakistan would have second thoughts?

The United States has entered into treaty law with the World Trade Organization. By ratifying the United Nations Convention on Civil and Political Rights, it has, by treaty, placed itself under the jurisdiction of the United Nations. The UNCPR contains provisions that authorizes the UN to take military or economic action against the United States for a wide range of reasons. Under the provisions of the UNCPR, the UN grants rights, rather than the Constitutional recognition that certain "inalienable rights are granted by the Creator." What the UN can grant, it can rescind. Article 29, paragraph 2 says the following:

> 2. In the exercise of his rights and freedoms, everyone shall be subject only to such limitations as are determined by law solely for the purpose of securing due recognition and respect for the rights and freedoms of others and of meeting the just requirements of morality, public order and the general welfare in a democratic society.

What it doesn't say is whose law, what limitations, and who defines the "rights and freedoms" of others. Could pedophilia become a protected freedom? Why not? Homosexuality is. What about freedom of worship? Could cults be declared illegal? Undoubtedly. Could evangelical Christianity be described as a cult? Well, that would depend on who was making the distinction, wouldn't it?

There are those who dismiss fears of a UN "thought police" brigade by pointing out the fact that the Constitution guarantees freedom of worship. Article VI of the Constitution says; "This Constitution, and the laws of the United States which shall be made in pursuance thereof; and all treaties made, or which shall be made, under the authority of the United States, shall be the supreme law of the land."

There are two interpretations of this statement. One view holds that the Constitution is supreme, the other contends the clause makes treaty law supreme. The correct interpretation depends on which side of the fence you are on.

The Draining of America

One thing is almost certain to occur in such a scenario: The world government would decide to drain the wealth of America and redistribute it around the globe in a more "equitable" fashion. In his excellent book *The New World Order*, Pat Robertson says the master plan calls for "the prevailing economic disparities in the world to be abolished." We're talking about massive transfers of wealth from the United States to the developing nations—and you won't have a thing to say about it.

Robertson describes today's United Nations as "corrupt, inept and ineffective." It is an agency, he says, that hates free enterprise and favors planned economies and socialism. He also fears that if it ever has real authority over the world, it would be biased against freedom of the press and would mandate a cowardly peace-at-any-price policy.

The Global Plan for Your Family

Better than anyone else who has written on the subject before, Robertson explains how the American liberal establishment's anti-family policies of the last 20 years are contributing to the move toward a one-world government. The plan, he says, requires young Americans to become indoctrinated as "citizens of the world." Today they are being conditioned to believe that the traditional American way of doing things and the Judeo-Christian heritage of the nation are simply anachronistic, oppressive, racist, sexist and imperialistic.[12]

The liberal establishment in this country has, he points out, forced us to bus our children, mandated that businesses hire by quota rather than by merit, made sure banks lend money to people who won't repay, and required landlords to rent to undesirables.

"What could we expect if population control is held by foreigners with no background in self-government?" he asks.[13]

To answer that question, one needs only to look at the practices and policies of today's World Bank—a precursor to a one-world monetary system.

The Eugenics Crowd

"Operating under the deceptive slogan of 'safe mother-hood,' a gaggle of world population control policymakers recently gathered in Washington to hatch their latest plot against children and families in less-developed nations," says Father Paul Marx, founder and president of Human Life International. "World Bank President Lewis T. Preston has promised to pump $2.5 billion into abortion, contraception, sterilization and other 'women's health' programs by 1995—double the amount the World Bank has been spending. Clearly, the World Bank and its anti-life, anti-family sister organizations in the so-called Safe Motherhood Initiative have put a bounty on the lives of unborn children."[14]

Just imagine what would happen if the World Bank had absolute authority. Would the sterilizations be mandatory? Would families be forced into the abortion option? Big Brother knows no limits.

Furthermore, world government, according to advocates like Mikhail Gorbachev, would mandate international intervention in the affairs of any nation-state whenever and wherever "human rights violations" occurred. And what does that mean? It means restraints and shackles being placed on the United States, seen by many jealous nations in the world as "public enemy No. 1." Imagine, also, what bad news that would be for the state of Israel, which has been persecuted by the world community for the last 20 years.

How Close Are We?

How close are we to the establishment of the New World Order? Well, would you believe that Mikhail Gorbachev has set up shop at the Presidio, one of America's most hallowed military posts which has stood guard over the San Francisco Bay area for two centuries? It's true. The former dictator of the Soviet Union has opened an office for his Gorbachev Foundation USA, billed as a pro-democracy organization.

The Gorbachev Foundation was invited to take over part of the Presidio as part of the post's conversion from the home of the 6th U.S. Army to a national park. The base occupies a stunning piece of real estate and is just one of dozens set to close as the U.S. military downsizes. The Army is leaving the Presidio and the National Park Service is reviewing proposals for how the park might be used. One of the most commonly mentioned plans is for the establishment of a center for global environmental studies.

The Gorbachev Foundation's stated goals are working toward global peace and strengthening democracy in the former Soviet Union. Former Sen. Alan Cranston, a longtime globalist and one-world dreamer, chairs the board of directors for the foundation and helps it raise money. Cranston also maintains an office at the Presidio.

In accepting his new office from a U.S. military officer, Gorbachev commented: "This is the symbol of our irreversible transition from an era of confrontation and militaristic insanity to a New World Order, one that promises dividends for all."[15]

Peace and Security?

But where is this New World Order leading us? And what role will a sovereign United States play in it? Are military threats to the United States a thing of the past? Are we really entering into an era of world peace and harmony?

Don't bet on it. Though we are entering an era in which the world is proclaiming "peace and safety," there is trouble brewing on many fronts around the world.

Arms expert Ian Anthony of the Stockholm International Peace Institute points out that the developing nations of the world are shelling out on average nearly $70 million a day for weapons, ammunition and military hardware. Two areas of the world, in particular, are responsible for this new arms buildup—Asia and the Middle East. Since the United States packed up and pulled out of its two big bases in the Philippines, regional powers have stepped up their arms acquisitions and positioned themselves for strategic advantage.

Indonesia has purchased 39 ships of the old East German navy and two submarines. Malaysia, according to reports, is purchasing front-line fighters and naval frigates. Thailand is buying a helicopter carrier. Taiwan is ordering U.S. and French warplanes and China has boosted its military spending by 15 percent.

The International Arms Bazaar

But even more troubling, with the knowledge of what the Bible predicts for the region in the last days, is what is going on in the Middle East. Anti-submarine weapons are the hottest new item on the arms bazaar, as Iran recently bought three used Russian conventional subs for $1 billion. The United Arab Emirates has purchased more than $4 billion worth of French battle tanks. Saudi Arabia is buying large orders of American F15 fighters. Kuwait is purchasing hundreds of M-1A2 Abrams battle tanks.

Don't be fooled by the wishful thinking of the one-world crowd. Planet Earth is more unstable today than it has been at any time in human history. We must never put our faith in false prophets preaching about a false peace.

Gorbachev, the one-time ruler of the most brutal military machine on the face of the earth, doesn't have the credentials or the credibility of a peacemaker. His friend Cranston has done his best over the years to chip away at the U.S. Constitution's guaranty of a sovereign America. Now these two are joining hands with socialists masquerading as environmentalists in an effort to create a new global order created in their own image.

God has frustrated attempts in the past to overthrow His divine will, and He will do the same in the future. God forever rejected man's attempt to establish a one-world government at the tower of Babel. The fact that we all speak different languages on this planet should be a constant reminder of this. God knew that there could never be a benevolent dictator or one world leader as long as man has an old sin nature. In God's wisdom, the best chance for world order was to keep national governments so that Satan couldn't so easily take over one man or one group of elite and wipe out faith in Him. Every historic case of multi-national government has resulted in tyranny, suffering and departure from the truth of God.

References

[1] Primary intelligence sources

[2] Dinesh D'Souza, *Illiberal Education.*

[3] Jacques Cousteau Society

[4] *Foreign Affairs*, Winter 1993

[5] Ibid.

[6] U.N. Charter

[7] *Foreign Affairs*, Ibid.

[8] Ibid.

[9] Boulder, Colorado *Weekly News* article: "UN or US, Who Will We Die For?" — Wayne Laugesen

[10] *Lectures Francaise*

[11] Mikhail Gorbachev in a speech at Westminster College in Missouri in May 1992.

[12] Pat Robertson, *The New World Order.*

[13] Ibid.

[14] Father Paul Marx, *The Wanderer.*

[15] *Los Angeles Times*, April 17, 1993

Chapter 4

THE COMING GREAT DECEPTION

And there will be terrors and great signs from heaven.
—LUKE 21:11

. . . I saw a star from heaven which had fallen to the earth; and the key to the bottomless pit was given to him.
—REVELATION 9:1

It's been the source of countless science fiction plots—from Arthur C. Clarke's "Childhood's End" to the popular movie "The Day the Earth Stood Still." Usually the basic scenario goes something like this: A flying saucer—obviously of extraterrestrial origin—parks itself conspicuously in the sky above the Earth. The mere sight of this craft sends the population of the planet into hysteria.

"What do they want?" the people wonder. "Who are these beings? Are they human? Are they gods? What will become of us?"

The plot usually thickened when we got our first glimpse of the aliens. There were two possibilities: They were beautiful, noble-looking humanoids or, conversely, they were strange, menacing-looking—perhaps even a little terrifying—creatures who sent more shivers down the spines of the populace.

A New World Order

Almost invariably, the aliens came for a specific purpose: They intended to straighten out the Earth and teach its inhabitants a new way of life. In "Childhood's End," this close encounter of the third kind was a nightmare from the beginning. When the aliens disembark from the crafts, they appear as stereotypical demons, complete with horns and leathery wings.

Now, I believe if such a thing happens in the future, they will look more like the ETs in the movie *The Day the Earth Stood Still*. These visitors are attractive and polite. Nevertheless, in both scenarios the creatures leave no room for doubt about who's in charge. In both movies a new world order was started—and earthlings served only in supporting roles from that day forward.

Imagine the impact of a visitation like that. Is there anything you can think of—short of the visible return of Jesus Christ — that would more abruptly and dramatically turn the world upside-down?

Signs from Outer Space

Jesus told us to expect *"terrors and great signs from heaven* [or outer space]" in the last days. The Greek word for "sign" literally means a supernatural phenomenon intended to point its observer to a profound truth. In Greek, "heaven" can mean several things: the atmosphere around the Earth, outer space, or the place where God dwells.

I believe in the case of Luke 21:11, Jesus is referring to the physical skies above the earth. Later, in that same chapter, Jesus adds: "There will be signs in the sun, moon and stars. On the Earth, nations will be in anguish and perplexity at the roaring and tossing of the sea. Men will faint from terror, apprehensive of what is coming on the world, for the heavenly bodies will be shaken."

Jesus is telling us to watch for unprecedented and frightening events among the planets and stars, events which will, apparently, affect our atmosphere and weather.

The Comet Hyakutake made its appearance in January 1996. It provided riveting celestial theater until May. Coming on the heels of the comet bombardment of Jupiter in 1994, it also re-awakened the debate concerning our vulnerability to celestial objects. The government now has a committee whose sole responsibility is to formulate defenses against potential meterorite strikes against the earth. Millions of tax dollars are now being spent to discuss ways to protect us from falling space rocks. It is very possible that this is the sort of phenomenon Jesus foresaw, "And there will be signs in sun and moon and stars, and upon the earth dismay among nations, in perplexity at the roaring of the sea and the waves, men fainting from fear and the expectation of the things which are coming upon the world; for the powers of the heavens [outer space and earths's atmosphere] will be shaken" (Luke 21:25-26). Large meteorites would tend to further change global weather patterns as well. We're already seeing some of those manifestations, in my opinion. And one of those is the phenomenon of unidentified flying objects—or UFOs.

The Meaning of UFOs

Since the publication of *The Late Great Planet Earth*, I have become thoroughly convinced that UFOs are real. They are not all swamp gas. They are not all hallucinations. They are not all weather balloons. Some of these sightings, I believe, are of real spacecraft. And I believe they are operated by alien beings of great intelligence and power.

Where I differ with most "ufologists" is in the question of origin. I believe these beings are not only extraterrestrial but supernatural in origin. To be blunt, I think they are demons. The Bible tells us that demons are spiritual beings at war with God. We are told that demons will be allowed to use their tremendous powers of deception in a grand way in the last days. Call it the Great Deception—it is described by Paul in II Thessalonians 2:8-12:

> And then that lawless one will be revealed whom the Lord will slay with the breath of His mouth and bring to an end by the appearance of His coming; that is, the one whose coming is in accord with the activity of Satan, with all power and signs and false wonders, and with all the deception of wickedness for those who perish, because they did not receive the love of the truth so as to be saved. And for this reason God will send upon them a deluding influence so that they might believe what is false."

The Great Deception

In other words, there is going to come a time in our age when God is going to permit all those on Earth who are unsaved to be deceived by some great wonder. This deception will close their minds and hearts to the truth of God's Word.

We're already seeing many people deceived today by all manner of false doctrines. But I believe this passage refers to something even more dramatic. I think it might be pointing to something along the lines of the scenarios in "Childhood's End" or "The Day the Earth Stood Still."

I could be wrong, but I think it is very possible for demons to stage a spacecraft landing on Earth, probably claiming they are from an advanced civilization from another part of the universe. This is about the only thing colossal enough to cause Hindus, Moslems, Bhuddists, false Christians, et al., to forget old differences and get together into a one-world religion.

What They Might Say

Judging from some of the wild, counterfeit creation theories being spread today, they may even claim to have been the race that "planted" human life on this planet. They may tell us they are here to check up on our progress and steer us on a better course—prepare us for some great "quantum leap" forward.

Take, for example, this wacky and woolly scenario dreamed up by Edward O. Wilson, not some crackpot but a respected professor of science at Harvard University: "Imagine that on an icy moon of Jupiter—say, Gannymede—the space station of an alien civilization is concealed. For millions of years its scientists have closely watched the Earth. Because their law prevents settlement on a living planet, they have tracked the surface by means of satellites equipped with sophisticated sensors, mapping the spread of large assemblages of organisms, from forests, grasslands and tundras to coral reefs and the vast planktonic meadows of the sea. They have recorded millennial cycles in the climate, interrupted by the advance and retreat of glaciers and scattershot volcanic eruptions.

Awaiting "The Moment"

"The watchers have been waiting for what might be called The Moment. When it comes, occupying only a few centuries and thus a mere tick in geological time, the forests shrink back to less than half their original cover. Atmospheric carbon dioxide rises to the highest level in 100,000 years. The ozone layer of the stratosphere thins, and holes open at the poles. Plumes of nitrous oxide and other toxins rise from fires in South America and Africa, settle in the upper troposphere and drift eastward across the oceans. At night the land surface brightens with millions of pinpoints of light, which coalesce into blazing swaths across Europe, Japan and eastern North America. A semicircle of fire spreads from gas flares around the Persian Gulf.

"It was all but inevitable, the watchers might tell us if we met them, that from the great diversity of large animals, one species or another would eventually gain intelligent control of earth. That role has fallen to Homo Sapiens, a primate risen in Africa from a lineage that split away from the chimpanzee line five to eight million years ago. Unlike any creature that lived before, we have become a geophysical force, swiftly changing the atmosphere and climate as well as the composition of the world's fauna and flora. Now in the midst of a population explosion, the human species has doubled to 5.5 billion during the past 50 years. It is scheduled to double again in the next 50 years. No other single species in evolutionary history has even remotely approached the sheer mass of protoplasm generated by humanity."

Is Man Suicidal?

Wilson's doomsday message can be summed up by saying that man is basically suicidal. And without the objectivity and wisdom of a more advanced race, there is little that humanity can do to save itself. Is this a science fiction novel? A treatment for some movie of the week? No, this is an excerpt of an article by an eminent scientist published in the *New York Times Magazine*! [1]

Many scientists are putting forth theories like this. And it has been the sub-plot for plenty of motion pictures, novels, pseudoscientific books as well as New Age beliefs. If demons did pull off such a deception, it would certainly lead the world into total error regarding God and His revelation. It certainly is a possible meaning of what II Thessalonians 2:8-12 is predicting will usher in the world's acceptance of the Antichrist. It could also be the catalyst the New Age, Tribulation religion requires to assume power.

UFOs in the Bible

Strange and fearful sights in the heavens are not new. Ezekiel, for instance, saw four angelic creatures riding in "wheels within wheels."[2] The Bible describes some kind of heavenly chariots that violated all the known physical laws of the universe.[3]

But while this kind of unexplained activity has always been with us, the last two and half decades have been a time of increased UFO sightings and, more importantly, a period in which the world was readied for a real close encounter with the alien beings that inhabit them.

- Hollywood more than any other medium laid the groundwork for the acceptance of super-humans from outer space. "Close Encounters," "E.T.," "Star Man" and other science fiction movies often put the best possible face on such creatures.

- One of the best-selling books of the 1980s was Whitley Streiber's *Communion*, the story of a man who claims to have been abducted by these beings.

- Russian cosmonauts returning from a visit to their space station told a story that caused much concern. They reportedly videotaped seven gigantic angels—the size of 747s, according to official reports—who smiled at them "like they knew something we didn't know."

- Surveys show tens of thousands of Americans believe they have not only experienced close encounters with alien creatures, but have been abducted and subjected to experimentation and study by extraterrestrials.

Are We Conditioned Yet?

Never before has planet Earth been so prepared for an encounter with space beings. Throughout the last two and half decades, but particularly toward the end of it, unidentified flying objects were prominent in news reports, TV specials and the hot topic on many talk shows.

In Russia, a rash of UFO sightings coincided with a tremendous upsurge in all kinds of religious activity—from Bible-based evangelism to the most far-out cult worship. One Western diplomat observed: "Russians are by nature deeply religious people and are now desperately looking for something to believe in."

More and more people are becoming convinced that UFOs are real and that they are visitors from other planets. One Christian leader even suggested that we attempt to witness and preach the Gospel to these beings who obviously possess a higher intelligence.

I definitely believe there have been accurate sightings of UFOs. There may even have been actual encounters with intelligent beings on these crafts. But, let me reiterate: These creatures are not space aliens. They are demons. And I believe the UFO phenomenon is all part of a Satanic plot to set up a great deception.

When It Might Happen

Such a deception will likely take place around the same time as the Rapture—in which every living believer on the face of the Earth will be snatched up to be with the Lord. After all, some very dramatic changes will have to occur in the last days to change people's perceptions of truth, to distort the reality of developments and to motivate people to work within the end-times New World Order.

The discovery of extraterrestrial life, said NASA administrator James C. Fletcher, "would eclipse all previous discoveries of mankind." Robert Pinotti, a sociologist from Florence, Italy, had this to say: "The news of the existence of extraterrestrial intelligence could be devastating. It will affect every field of human activity. Contact with superior beings would be shattering." Why would it be so devastating? Because it would mean humans would suddenly find themselves inferior to other beings.[4]

"If there is a single consensus among those involved in the search (for extraterrestrials), it is that success would change the world forever, and the first few days would be sheer madness," said a report on the subject in the *Los Angeles Times*.[5] Just the kind of scenario it would take to set the stage for a new world order—politically, religiously and economically.

Aliens from Where?

The idea that aliens operating spacecraft might be other than extraterrestrials is being supported by some researchers. Jacques Vallee, an astrophysicist and computer scientist, is one of the world's most credible UFO researchers. In his book, *Dimensions: A Casebook of Alien Contact*, he writes: "Some witnesses have thought that they had seen demons because the creature had the unpredictability and mischievousness associated with popular conceptions of the devil. If you wanted to bypass the intelligentsia and the church, remain undetectable to the military system, leave undisturbed the political and administrative levels of society, and at the same time implant deep within that society far-reaching doubts concerning its basic philosophical tenets, this is exactly how you would act. At the same time, of course, such a process would have to provide its own explanation to make ultimate detection impossible. In other words, it would have to project an image just beyond the belief structure of the target society. It would have to disturb and reassure at the same time, exploiting both the gullibility of the zealots and the narrow-mindedness of the debunkers. This is exactly what the UFO phenomenon does."[6]

But I think the most compelling case for demonic control of UFOs was made, inadvertently, by Whitley Streiber, author of

Communion and *Transformation*. Read what he says in *Communion* regarding his own encounter with an alien creature: "Increasingly I felt as if I were entering a struggle for my soul, my essence, or whatever part of me might have reference to the eternal," he wrote in his latest book. "There are worse things than death, I suspected. And I was beginning to get the distinct impression that one of them had taken an interest in me. So far the word demon had never been spoken among the scientists and doctors who were working with me. And why should it have been? We were beyond such things. We were a group of atheists and agnostics, far too sophisticated to be concerned with such archaic ideas as demons and angels."[7]

Just Listen to the Experts

Streiber continues: "I felt an absolutely indescribable sense of menace. It was hell on Earth to be there, and yet I couldn't move, couldn't cry out and couldn't get away. I lay as still as death, suffering inner agonies. Whatever was there seemed so monstrously ugly, so filthy and dark and sinister. Of course they were demons. They had to be. And they were here and I couldn't get away. I couldn't save my poor family. I still remember that thing crouching there, so terribly ugly, its arms and legs like the limbs of a great insect, its eyes glaring at me."[8]

It is interesting to note that UFO vocabulary has come to include the term "contactees". These are individuals in communication with, usually telepathically, "alien entities." Satan, the prince of demons and father of the occult, has many religions. His most subtle and insidious is the New Age Movement. Another term for a "contactee," linking UFOs with the New Age, is "channeler." By the same token a synonym for channeler is a "medium," revealing an unmistakable connection with the occult.

UFOs and the Occult

It's undeniable that many or even most of those who have experienced so-called "close encounters" of this kind already had occult ties. This is a clear tip-off as to why they were picked. What they are seeing is real. But it is not what they think. Those Russian cosmonauts, for example, saw seven gigantic angels. Atheistic Russian leaders didn't know what to make of it, so their official explanation was that they were intelligent beings from another galaxy.

I say more likely they were from Galaxy H—heaven. But I don't think that's the origin of many other extraterrestrial visitors. For several years now, Russia and the former Soviet Union have been experiencing a dramatic increase in encounters with unidentified flying objects. In 1989 there were a number of well-publicized reports of bizarre UFO sightings and close encounters with giant aliens in the Russian city of Voronezh. Later, in Pensacola, Fla., the Mutual UFO Network, the world's largest research organization in the field, heard a report by Antonio Huneeus called "Red Skies: The Great 1989 UFO Wave in the USSR."

Strange Signs in Russia

Perhaps the most compelling case occurred in the city of Borisoz in Byelorussia. It began with the scrambling of two Soviet jets. "The crews of two Soviet aircraft reported seeing a large flying disk in their vicinity with five beams of lights emanating from it: three beams were directed toward the ground and two were projected upward when the object was first sighted," the report said. "The ground controller instructed one of the planes to alter its course and approach the object, at which point the disk flew to the same level and aimed one of its beams at the approaching Soviet plane, illuminating the cockpit."[9]

The pilot's log stated: "At this time, the co-pilot was at the controls. He observed the maneuver that the object had just carried out and was able to raise his hand to shield himself from the unbearable light. The aircraft commander was resting in the adjoining seat, and a bright ray of light, projecting a spot with a diameter of 20 centimeters, passed across his body. Both pilots felt heat."

Both of the crewman later became quite ill, according to the report.

"The co-pilot was forced to leave his job due to a sudden deterioration in his health, including the onset of sudden prolonged periods of 'loss of consciousness.' The aircraft commander died within a few months. The cause of death was listed in the official medical record as 'cancer' and 'injury to the organism as a result of radiation from an unidentified flying object.'"[10]

Later, Igor Maltsev, General of Aviation, discussed a radar-visual and jet scramble incident in the Pereslavl-Zalesskiy region, east of Moscow on the night of March 21.

"I am not a specialist on UFOs and therefore I can only correlate the data and express my own supposition," said Gen. Maltsev. "According to the evidence of these eyewitnesses, the UFO is a disk with a diameter from 100 to 200 meters. Two pulsating lights were positioned on its sides. When the object flew in a horizontal plane the line of the lights was parallel to the horizon. During vertical movement it rotated and was perpendicular to the ground. Moreover, the object rotated around its axis and performed an 'S-turn' flight both in the horizontal and vertical planes. Next, the UFO hovered over the ground and then flew with a speed exceeding that of the modern jet fighter by two to three times. All of the observers noticed that the flight speed was directly related to the flashing of the side lights: the more often they flashed, the higher the speed."[11]

The general's report continued: "The objects flew at altitudes ranging from 1,000 to 7,000 meters. The movement of the UFOs was not accompanied by sound of any kind and was distinguished by its startling maneuverability. It seemed the UFOs were completely devoid of inertia. In other words, they had somehow 'come to terms' with gravity. At the present time, terrestrial machines could hardly have such capabilities. The object was observed as a 'pip' from a radar target on the screens of aircraft radar sights and on the screens of several electronic surveillance sub-units. One station did not establish an observation."[12]

Searching for Answers

The detailed military reports on this incident contrast with the sometimes wild reports in the popular Russian press of sightings in the city of Voronezh. Many suggested those incidents had more to do with a deep spiritual hunger in the country and escapism than real extraterrestrial visitors.

"I believe the spaceship was a message from Jesus," concluded Alexander Mosolov, a member of the local team investigating the incidents in Voronozh. "He was telling us we have to be as innocent as children, which is why only the young saw the spaceship land." [13]

UFO sightings have been a matter of record for thousands of years—from ancient "celestial chariots" and "flying shields" to 18th century "phantom airships" and modern "flying saucers." And they have been associated with Jesus, who warned of signs in the heavens accompanying the destruction of Jerusalem (Luke 21:11, 20), just before the Jewish war with the Romans in AD 66. And indeed, the Jewish historian Josephus recorded that people in Jerusalem witnessed such signs. [14]

Of course, as I've mentioned, Jesus also said there would be signs in the heavens just before His return to Earth (Luke 21:25-33). Is it plausible that spiritual beings might be causing these signs? Frankly, it seems likely, based on what Scripture tells us about the second advent.

The War in the Heavens

Revelation 12:7-9 tells us that Satan and his angels will be expelled from heaven just before Jesus' return. This might be part of what the Earth is witnessing with this increase in UFO activity. There's a war raging in the heavens. It's a spiritual war, but there are physical manifestations to it, the Bible says. That's what I believe the world could be witnessing today as we approach the end of the second millennium and the imminent return of Jesus Christ.

And why? Because something truly dramatic, sensational

and spectacular will be necessary in these endtimes to ensure that a skeptical world buys into the new world religion the Bible predicts will be in place before the second advent. Something remarkable must occur to deceive the entire population of the world and line them up eagerly—behind a god-man political and spiritual leader.

Speculation? Yes. But the evidence is growing more persuasive every day.

If you are reading this book with tongue in cheek, do remember I said something like this may happen, especially if you hear that millions of those "born again Christians" have mysteriously disappeared.

References

[1] Edward O. Wilson, *New York Times Magazine*, May 30, 1993, page 24.

[2] Ezekiel 1:4-28

[3] Ezekiel 1:12

[4] News media reports

[5] Ibid.

[6] Jacques Vallee, *Dimensions: A Casebook of Alien Contact.*

[7] Whitley Streiber, *Communion*, Beech Tree Books, William Morrow, New York, 1987.

[8] Ibid.

[9] Soviet newspaper *Socialist Industry*, Sept. 30, 1989

[10] Ibid.

[11] "UFOs on Air Defense Radars," April 19, 1990, *Rabochaya Tribuna.*

[12] Ibid.

[13] News media reports

[14] Josephus, *War*, VI, v. 3

Chapter 5

EARTHQUAKES AND BERSERK WEATHER

And there will be signs in sun and moon and stars, and upon the earth dismay among nations, in perplexity at the roaring sea and the waves, men fainting from fear and the expectation of the things which are coming upon the world; for the powers of the heavens will be shaken.
—LUKE 21:25, 26

And there will be great earthquakes...
—LUKE 21:11

One of the major birthpangs Jesus predicted would increase in frequency and intensity shortly before His return is earthquakes. Those of us who live in California are only too aware of the increase in earthquake activity in recent years.

But California is not the only place where earthquake activity has increased. There has been a destructive series of quakes in Armenia, Australia, Japan, China, India as well as California. The whole world has become conscious of the phenomenon. Are there really more great quakes today than there were 100 years ago? Or are we just more aware of them because of better communications and tracking systems?

I think that it is important to point out that every culture from the earliest times has left records of earthquakes. They are such fearful, uncontrollable and unpredictable catastrophes that all peoples have remembered and recorded them from the earliest recorded history. So keeping track of quakes is not a recent phenomenon.

The Great Quake Wave

Let me give you some startling statistics:

- From 1890 to 1899, there was only one "killer" quake—6.0 or greater— recorded anywhere in the world.
- From 1900 to 1910, there were 3.
- From 1910 to 1920, there were 2.
- From 1920 to 1930, there were 2.
- From 1930 to 1940, there were 5.
- From 1940 to 1950, there were 4.
- From 1950 to 1960, there were 9.
- From 1960 to 1970, there were 13.
- From 1970 to 1979, there were 51.

- From 1980 to 1989, there were 86.
- And in the first four years of the 1990s there were *more than 100*.

These are not my figures, folks. They are from statistics kept by groups like the U.S. Geological Survey in Boulder, Colorado.[1]

You see, it is not just our imaginations. The track record is now documentable. There has been a rapid increase in major California quakes in the last 15 years. Since 1980, the state has experienced 18 quakes worse than 5.0. That's the same number of 5.0-plus quakes the state experienced in the entire century before 1980. And this is not counting the four greater than 5.0 aftershocks of the January 17, 1994 earthquake that hit catastrophe-wracked California.

According to data from the state Seismic Safety Commission, from 1990 through January 1994, the state sustained six 5.0-plus quakes—an average of 1.5 a year. That's up from the record-setting pace of the 1980s average of 0.9 per year, which, in turn, was 50 percent greater than the 1970s rate of 0.6 per year.

"Following the earthquake in 1911 (an aftershock of the San Francisco quake of 1906), we went through a long time before there was a significant earthquake along the line of the 1906 San Andreas rupture," explains William Bakun of the U. S. Geological Survey in Menlo Park. "Then we went for several more years, with not much going on.

"Then, starting in the late 1970s, we started seeing a pickup in the rate of magnitude 6 earthquakes."

The experts say this rapid increase in seismic activity suggests that the state of California is headed toward a cataclysm that, according to one news report, would make L.A.'s devastating quake "look like a picnic."

Los Angeles' Third Catastrophe in Two Years

The great Northridge quake of January 17, 1994 has turned out to be the most costly natural disaster in U. S. history. It will cost more than $30 billion to repair the damage to Los Angeles' freeways, schools, office buildings, homes, apartments and utility pipes and lines. Sixty-one people were killed. The city traffic was almost paralyzed. And this was only a 6.8 earthquake. The great damage was done because of the type of fault that caused it and the location of the epicenter under a heavily populated area. The cause was an heretofore unknown thrust fault lying eleven miles beneath the earth. The two sides of the fault slipped past each other at a steep upward angle. This caused the release of shocks that exploded upward, raising the ground as much as 12 feet in some places.

Is there any doubt that earthquakes have increased in frequency and intensity in recent years? Everywhere that fault lines exist there has been a great increase in seismic activity.

The Coming "Big One"

Even after the massive 7.1 Bay Area quake in October 1989, earthquake authorities are still predicting a major killer quake of the same magnitude of the San Francisco quake of 1906 to strike California—within the next 10 years. That quake was estimated at an almost incomprehensible 8.3 on the Richter scale. The coming predicted quake of 8.0 plus, according to *Time* magazine, will be more than 85 times stronger than the 6.8 Northridge quake. But don't tell the residents of Los Angeles who experienced that quake! It would be hard for them to imagine something more destructive.

A friend of mine said that his family in the eastern U. S. challenged him that he was foolish to continue living in Los Angeles. They said "You don't even have four seasons." He replied, "Yes we do have four seasons: riots, fires, floods and earthquakes."

The fact that earthquakes are on the rise is obvious to even the most casual of observers. (With the exception of the Dominionist Theologians, who seem to be willing to go to any length to discredit contemporary prophetic fulfillment.) In fact, so many people have contacted the US Geological Study inquiring about the topic, that the USGS has apparently decided to bury the evidence. I visited the USGS website as part of my research into the subject, and found the following (newly posted) section entitled, *Are Earthquakes Really on the Increase?*; it offers the following explanation: *"We continue to hear from many people throughout the world that earthquakes are on the increase. Although it may **seem** that we are having more earthquakes, earthquakes of **magnitude 7.0 or greater** have remained fairly constant throughout this century and, according to our records, have actually seemed to decrease in recent years"* (emphasis mine).

Note the portion I have emphasized. They say we "seem" to be having more earthquakes. The USGS traditionally defined a major earthquake as being "6.5 magnitude or greater, and causing significant death or damage." That is still the category heading used when they compile their own statistics. By the simple expedient of raising the minimum magnitude level for the basic criteria, earthquake statistics can be manipulated to support their contention of no noticable increase in major earthquakes.

But let's take a look of just one single month—February, 1996. (Still using the standard USGS criteria—6.5 or greater or causing significant death or damage—taken directly from the USGS official report.) [2]

- Feb. 1996 Yunnan, China — Mag 6.5 (251 dead, 4027 injured, 1 million homeless)
- Feb. 1996 Kuril Islands — Mag 7.1
- Feb. 1996 Honshu, Japan — Mag 6.7
- Feb. 1996 Irian Jaya Region — Mag 7.9 (including a tsunami that reached 22 ft)
- Feb. 1996 Irian Jaya Region — Mag 6.7
- Feb. 1996 Irian Jaya Region — Mag 6.6
- Feb. 1996 Irian Jaya Region — Mag 6.6
- Feb. 1996 Irian Jaya Region — Mag 6.5

- Feb. 1996 Ascension Island — Mag 6.5
- Feb. 1996 Northern Peru — Mag 7.3
- Feb. 1996 Oaxaca, Mexico — Mag 7.1

That is ten major, killer earthquakes in a single month! Now turn back to the beginning of the chapter and review the frequency of earthquakes from the beginning of this century to the present.

By selectively manipulating the criteria used to determine a "major quake," the USGS can effectively argue against any increase in seismic activity. But why would they do such a thing? It would seem fairly obvious. Acknowledging a discernible increase in earthquake activity could induce a panic. Since there is no explanation—apart from the Bible—any scientist who would allow scientific data to support such a conclusion would find himself unable to honestly accept other "scientific" evidence to support "theories" like evolution, the Big Bang or other humanist views. Without these views, geology as a science would have to start from scratch. Much of what is called scientific fact would be put at risk because the whole edifice would be exposed as based on unprovable assumptions.

The Effect of Weather on Civilizations

Have you ever heard of the Akkadians? They were a people who lived in the southern Mesopotamia region, nestled in the lush valleys of the Tigris and Euphrates rivers in what is now called Syria and Iraq.

The Akkadians ruled over and dominated the entire Middle East for 100 years before disappearing about 2200 BC. Do you know why they disappeared and why you likely never have heard of these people even though theirs was considered to be the very first human empire?

Well, we now know why their civilization collapsed. It was due to an abrupt climatic change. New soil evidence indicates that the rich farmlands of northern Mesopotamia were hit with a sudden drought that rendered the region uninhabitable for 300 years.

The Lesson of the Akkadians

Driven off their lands by starvation, the farmers flocked to southern cities, overwhelming the rich resources of the urban society. Things got so bad that the written records show that city leaders had to erect walls to keep the waves of immigrants out. Urban riots helped lead to the fall of the empire.

"For the first time, we've identified abrupt climate change directly linked to the collapse of a thriving civilization," explains archeologist Harvey Weiss of Yale University. [3]

And the same researchers who have unraveled this 4,000-year-old mystery story are now suggesting that the demise of the Akkadian empire serves as a parable for what could happen to modern society in terms of environmental upheaval.

Is the natural environment really capable of making things that inhospitable for us? Isn't man smart enough now to adapt to global climate changes? Is nature really that powerful a force in our lives?

The Power of Nature

Well, let me answer those rhetorical questions with a few more. Did you know that a thunderstorm can cover as much as 180 square miles at one time? Did you know that thunderstorms have bursts of power that are equal to a billion volts of electricity? Did you know that the power in just one thunderstorm is equivalent to 200 Hiroshima-size atomic bombs? Did you know that one thunderstorm can dump as much as 18 million tons of water on the Earth each hour?[4]

Now, we've all seen thunderstorms. They are, of course, common occurrences in almost every part of the world. But there is incredible and awesome destructive power in even the most common thunderstorm. And the interesting thing, from a prophetic viewpoint, is that these storms are now generating weather that is unparalleled in ferocity in all recorded history.

Changing Global Weather Patterns

The storms that hit the United States in the early 1990s have been rated among the worst natural disasters. It all started off with Hurricane Andrew, which devastated Florida and other parts of the East Coast. That was followed by what meteorologists called the greatest ice and snow storm in the history of the country and "one of the worst coastal storms ever,"[5] wreaking havoc and destruction in its wake. Then came one of the most expensive catastrophes in history—the floods of the Mississippi Valley. The natural disasters of 1992 alone cost insurers more than $20 billion.[6] All of that devastation coincided in one 12-month period—and all in just the United States!

Let me tell you, folks, the Western world is not alone. A *Life* magazine cover story in 1993, titled "The Year of the Killer Weather: Why Has Nature Gone Mad?" made just that point. In a sudden rash of violent storms, what were once freakish deadly occurrences became the norm for planet Earth in the early 1990s:

- The worst deluge in 60 years left thousands dead in Nepal and millions homeless in India and Bangladesh.

- It rained hard enough in the Philippines in the summer of 1993 to set off an explosion of Mount Pinatubo, when rainwater seeped under lava flows and became super-heated.

- Similar flooding has hit hard in places like Russia, China, Japan, Korea, Mexico and the United Kingdom.[7]

Floods, droughts, heatwaves and freak snowstorms underscore the less sensational weather events like the endless winter of 1996 in the Northeast. Wild temperature fluctuations set records across the nation. In January, winter-weary residents of Buffalo, New York sighed with relief when the mercury climbed to a record-breaking 64°F. Another record was shattered—this one for an all time low, when the temperature plummeted to -5 ° F the very same day! San Antonio, Texas, also shattered both the high and low temperature records in a single day that same winter. Globally, the weather situation gets crazier and crazier.

- Azerbaijan—October 1995: Heavy rains flood the country, leaving 5 dead and 3,000 homeless

- Benin—October 1995: Torrential rains and flooding affected 86,000 people

- China—August, 1995: Flooding there affected 11.1 million people, 2 million marooned, 3.04 million evacuated

- Korea—July 1995: Flooding resulted in 70 dead or missing, 500,000 homeless

- Morocco—August 1995: Flash flooding kills 230 with 500 missing

- Myanmar—September 1995: Floods kill 50, 15 missing

- Philippines—September 1995: Floods kill 48, injure 7, 382 missing

Add to that 20,000 affected by flooding in Sri Lanka in October, 4.2 million affected by November flooding in Thailand, 62 dead, 60 injured and 16 missing in floods in Turkey and similar statistics from Costa Rica, El Salvador, Ghana, Guatemala, India, Somalia and Vietnam, and bizarre weather patterns are undeniable. [8]

Looking for an Ark

Everywhere—even in radically secular New York City—these strange events got people thinking about the forces behind them.

"I feel like I'm caught in something biblical, you know, one of the great plagues," said one Manhattan shopper caught in the violent winter storm of 1992. "I'm expecting to see Noah's ark come floating up Third Avenue." [9]

Time magazine is calling it the "the weird weather phenomenon. And many are wondering what all this is about.

"What's going on?" asks *Time*. "Scientists have a standard reply to the question. It's the nature of the weather, they say, for wild fluctuations to occur. Their proof? There's a record broken every day somewhere in the world. But after last week's weather, which showed every sign of being this week's weather as well, the standard reply starts to wear a little thin. Why are so many records being set in so many places right now? Could it have anything to do with the holes we've drilled in the ozone layer? The forests we've leveled? The greenhouse gases we've pumped into the atmosphere?" [10]

The Role of El Niño

The changing weather patterns of the 1990s are usually attributed by scientists to El Niño, a condition caused by warming waters in the western Pacific. But El Niño conditions normally last only from 12 to 18 months. And the one that brought hurricanes to Hawaii, drowned the Midwestern United States and disrupted lives throughout the world during the late 1980s continued for more than four years.

This fact has scientists re-evaluating what it is that they are examining.

"It's unlike anything we've seen among the El Niño," said Donald Hansen, a University of Miami oceanographer. "Maybe it's not just an El Niño, but is really signaling that two or three years ago we had a relatively persistent change in climate." [11]

Gerald Bell, a meteorologist with the National Oceanic and Atmospheric Administration, confirmed that this El Niño condition was by far the longest ever recorded.

"No one is sure just what the world is experiencing," says Henry Diaz, a National Oceanic and Atmospheric Administration forecaster in Boulder, Colorado. [12]

El Niño, by the way, is Spanish for "The Christ Child", and is so named because it often coincides in South America with the Christmas season. I find it interesting that changing weather patterns, precisely like those caused by such conditions, were predicted in the Bible as heralding the Second Coming of Jesus Christ—this time not as a child but as a ruling Messiah.

The Role of Volcanoes

But there are other forces besides El Niño involved in the changing weather patterns that are causing record-breaking extremes worldwide. A big part of the responsibility lies with the violent volcanic eruption of Mount Pinatubo in the Philippines in June 1991.

This was the most powerful tropical eruption the planet had witnessed since Krakatoa near Java in 1883. Following that eruption, the world experienced five years of major storms and disturbances.

"For more than 10 years, I have predicted the same effect if a similar eruption occurred," says Dr. Paul Handler, a private crop and climate consultant and editor of *Atlas Forecasts*. [13]

The Power of a Volcano

How powerful was the Mount Pinatubo eruption? Well, it spewed sulfur dioxide gas 10 to 15 miles into the stratosphere. At that point, the gas condensed into sulfuric acid and formed a haze that reflects earth-bound sunlight back into outer space. During the two years following the eruption, the world lost between 1 percent and 3 percent of the sun's radiation.

"That doesn't sound like much," says Dr. Handler. "Few understand how sensitive our global climate is. A small change in radiation can cause drastic consequences." [14]

Let me give you an idea of the explosive power of Mount Pinatubo, and volcanic activity in general, which, we know, will increase dramatically in the last days. The eruption lasted 24 hours with a force equivalent to the detonation of an atom bomb per second...or launching 1 million space shuttles.

"The volcanic aerosol was distributed around the globe," explains Dr. Handler. "The consequence has been global oscillation of climate. Variability has gone up, so we are seeing more extremes of weather. After Mount Pinatubo's eruption, South Africa had the worst drought in 100 years...the Mideast had its coldest winter in 50 years...rains and flooding devastated Bangladesh, northern India, Japan, Korea and Nepal." [15]

Wacky Weather Not Going Away

Dr. Handler says the extremes in worldwide weather will last at least through 1996. In the United States, he predicts this will mean rising waters in Lake Michigan and the Great Salt Lake, an increase in more powerful tropical storms and hurricanes, more snow, colder winters and drier summers. [16]

The physical tribulations of the Earth and its environment has been one of the most significant developments—prophetically speaking—since I authored *The Late Great Planet Earth* 25 years ago. You can scarcely read a newspaper or watch a television program without being bombarded with information about the crisis of the environment.

Of principal concern to most environmentalists today is the so-called "greenhouse effect" or global warming trend, which, by the way, is directly related to the wacky weather and climatic changes throughout the world. Here are some of the major developments in global warming that have been well documented in scientific journals in the last 10 years:

Multiple Mega-killer Storms Begin in 1995

One of the world's leading experts on hurricanes links the new wave of mega-storms to the the global warming phenomenon. "A wave of killer hurricanes is long overdue, says the world's formost hurricane expert," the September, 1995 issue of *Popular Science* magazine declared. The article went on to further quote Dr. William Gray, "Gray predicts that three major hurricanes, five minor hurricanes, and twelve smaller tropical storms will form. (Indeed, one of these minor hurricanes, Allison, smacked into the Florida panhandle on June 5.) The overall hurricane intensity, a measure that takes into account sea surge as well as winds, should exceed by a large margin that of the 1992 season, when Andrew hit." These predictions were made before the hurricane season.

Gray warned, "Inevitably, long stretches of destruction will return. When this happens, Florida and the East Coast will see hurricane devastation such as they have never experienced before."

True to Dr. Gray's forecast, there were more hurricanes in 1995 than at any time in the recorded history of the Atlantic, Caribbean and Gulf of Mexico region. "Storms are going to get much worse because of the effect of global warming over the equatorial ocean area where these storms are spawned," Gray said gloomily.

This same phenomenon was recorded in the Pacific and Indian Oceans—where they are called typhoons. More killer typhoons of record ferocity were recorded in this region in 1995 than during any other year in recorded history. And remember, these types of disasters, like earthquakes, were recorded diligently in ancient history—even in primitive cultures. The ancients often saw disasters as direct acts of their gods, so they were even more awestruck and diligent to record them.

Hollywood Goes Weather Conscious

The movie industry seems to always perceive what is most on the minds of people, and keys their plots to capture each new wave of interest.

It is not insignificant that several recent movies reflect an almost prophetic view of the new weather changes taking place. "Water World" with Kevin Costner warned that the current global warming will melt the ice caps and send the world into another universal flood. (It is comforting to know that God promised He would never destroy the world again by a flood.)

Even Steven Speilberg has made a movie (for release in the spring of 1996) called "Twisters" , which he heralds as "the ultimate disaster movie on weather gone berserk."

The fact that all these disasters—earthquakes, plagues, berserk global weather changes, global warming, unprecedented killer storms, famines, weapons of mass destruction, ethnic conflicts and continuous wars, etc.—are occuring in the same time frame, and are increasing in frequency and intensity in concert, makes this a unique time in history. There has never been a more important time to understand that all of these history-making phenomena are fitting precisely into an exact scenario predicted long ago by the Prophets of the Bible. Jesus Himself predicted that these things would all happen within the generation that witnesses His Second Coming.

How Climate Is Changing

- There has been a sharp increase in methane gas in the atmosphere since 1978, which, most scientists agree, will probably make the Earth warmer and may worsen seasonal losses of protective ozone over Antarctica.

- The number of icebergs breaking away from Antarctica is increasing, possibly a symptom of a rise in the Earth's temperature.

- Climate changes, some scientists say, are already causing a "greenhouse effect"—with hotter deserts and more severe tropical storms—that could soon threaten cities with floods from rising seas.

Time magazine reported that the situation is far more precarious than the average citizen is aware of. "Sea levels could rise up to 3 ft., mostly because of melting glaciers and the expansion of water as it warms up. That could submerge vast areas of low-lying coastal land, including major river deltas, most of the beaches on the U.S. Atlantic Coast, parts of China and the island nations of the Maldives, the Seychelles and the Cook and Marshall islands. More than 100 million people would be displaced...Hurricanes, which draw their energy from warm oceans, could become even stronger as those oceans heat up. Temperature and rainfall patterns would shift in unpredictable ways...Natural ecosystems that have to adapt on their own, however, could be devastated."[17]

There is essentially no longer much debate in scientific circles about whether a buildup of carbon dioxide is warming the Earth. The only debate still taking place is over what—if anything—can be still done about it.

Understanding the Greenhouse Effect

What is the "greenhouse effect"? It is basically a threat to the Earth caused by the production of carbon dioxide. Man did not begin heavy use of the so-called "fossil fuels" that have created this abundance of carbon dioxide until this century. Then, as the world became industrialized, the use of oil, gasoline, coal, natural gas and so forth, became widespread. The use of those fuels has greatly increased every year since the beginning of the century. The result is the collection of an enormous amount of carbon dioxide in the atmosphere.

The gas has created a kind of shield that prevents solar heat from dissipating and leaving the atmosphere. Just like the glass ceilings of a greenhouse, the carbon dioxide traps the heat inside the atmosphere, causing a rise in temperature.

The worst part of this scenario is that it is a continuum. It gets worse and worse as the Earth's inhabitants continue to burn these fuels. At the current rate of use of these fuels, if we could freeze it at today's level—which we cannot—the experts predict the earth's temperature would rise an average of about 8 degrees. What that means in some parts of the world is absolutely horrible. It could mean an increase of 20 degrees in certain places.

And these are only projections based on computer models. The situation could deteriorate even faster.

Of one thing there is no doubt. The level of carbon dioxide in the atmosphere is rising rapidly. Ice cores from both polar caps, for example, show that the amount of carbon dioxide in the air has more than doubled from what it was thousands of years before the Industrial Revolution.

Deforestation of the Planet

Complicating and worsening the "greenhouse effect" is the deforestation of the planet. All plants, through photosynthesis, convert carbon in the air into biomass. The tropical rain forests convert carbon into plant material faster than it is released into the atmosphere through decay. But in recent years, a quarter of the net carbon releases into the atmosphere can be attributed to forest clearance, according to some authorities.

And just so you don't think I've turned into some kind of environmentalist wacko bent on destroying the free-enterprise system, I want to quickly point out that it is in the socialist world that the most environmental degradation and pollution is occurring. Take Cambodia, for instance. United Nations aerial photos of the western part of the country show that in Khmer Rouge-held areas the deforestation is "almost indescribable." [18]

It's a fact that the resources in private hands are always the most protected. After all, would you cut down all the trees on land you owned? What would be gained by such folly? Private landowners are, by far, the best stewards. Think about it in terms of so-called "endangered species." Have you ever heard any concern that pigs or cows or sheep might become endangered? Of course not. The reason is, there is a profit to be made in maintaining herds of these animals. People own them and preserve them. But bald eagles belong only to the public and are protected only by the government. That's why they are endangered.

So, please don't mistake anything I write here to suggest I am siding with those who use environmental scare tactics to incite strong-arm tactics by big government.

Changes Are Inter-related

It's interesting to me how so many of these conditions— deforestation, global warming, volcanoes, ozone depletion—are scientifically inter-related. And they all, of course, fit so exactly into the prophetic scenario for the endtimes.

The rise in global temperatures has come, the scientists point out, while several factors have actually worked toward lowering global heat. The sun has been radiating less energy during this time and an increase in volcanoes—also predicted in the Bible—has caused a reduction in temperatures because the dust tends to filter out some sunlight.

What does this buildup of heat mean? Later, I will address how these climatic conditions are helping lead us into an age of famines—also predicted for the last days before Jesus' return to Earth. Even a 1-degree rise of temperature in the farm belts can have a devastating effect on productivity. Some experts on global warming are suggesting that most of the world's wheat might have to be grown in the northern regions of Siberia and Canada before this century is out.

The Population Bomb

And, of course, there will be lots more mouths to feed in this brave new world. I believe overpopulation of the planet is apocalyptic peril No. 1 as we approach the new millennium. It's a problem completely out of control. Think about this: At the time Jesus walked the Earth 2,000 years ago, there were some 250 million people in the world. By the Renaissance, there were 450 million. In 1850, we first reached 1 billion. By 1900 there were 1.5 billion. In 1950, there were 2.5 billion. Today, as I put the finishing touches on this manuscript, we are approaching the 6 billion figure.

The experts tell us that in about 50 years there will be 10 billion. They also add that for the population of the world to enjoy the standard of living of modern-day Paris, the world's population would have to be reduced to 700 million. The earth can only sustain, at minimal survival levels, some 20 billion and that would mean the whole world's living standard would equal Bangladesh's present standard. [19]

The first pinch will be felt at the water faucet. Already, more and more politicians are discovering that our greatest global crisis may soon be a water shortage. Each country, to supply its population, needs about 725 gallons a day of replenishable water supply per person, according to the water experts. The Earth holds about 10 times this amount. But usage of water is up three times since the 1950s—primarily because of new agricultural techniques and wastefulness.

The Coming Worldwide Drought

"Water scarcity will affect everything from prospects in the Middle East to global food scarcity, the growth of cities and the location of industries," suggests Sandra Postel, author of *Last Oasis: Facing Water Scarcity.* "By the end of the '90s, water problems in the Middle East will lead either to an unprecedented degree of cooperation or a combustible level of conflict." [20]

See how all these problems—not just the environmental, but the political as well—seem to interconnect?

Just as frightening as the water crisis and the greenhouse effect is what is happening to the ozone layer. Do you know how thick the ozone layer is that protects all life on this planet? If brought down to sea level, it would be only three millimeters thick. That's a little more than an eighth of an inch. That's all that stands between us and an uninhabitable planet.

The Precariousness of the Ozone Layer

That delicate little shield that God put there in the upper atmosphere shields out ultra-violet rays. Already more than 3 percent of the ozone layer has been destroyed. Scientists estimate that if 15 percent of it is destroyed it will mean millions of hideous deaths by skin cancer.

Using satellites, aircraft and ground instruments, scientists have documented large holes in the ozone layer over both the north and south poles. Industrialization may be a contributing factor, but increased volcanic activity is by far the biggest culprit. When the radical elements in CFCs—either naturally or synthetically produced—drift up into the stratosphere, they are changed by the effect of the ultra-violet rays and become a form of chlorine. Then one atom of that chlorine destroys 100,000 molecules of ozone. The chlorine atoms each molecule of CFC contains can break apart thousands of ozone molecules in the stratosphere, which protect the Earth from ultraviolet radiation. CFCs are also thought to be a contributing factor in the "greenhouse effect."

Already the thinning ozone layer is being blamed for severe sunburns in the southern end of Chile. Rodolfo Mansilla says he was still badly burned after spending 30 minutes gardening outside his Puntas Arenas home. He says half his 1,200 cattle were so blinded by conjunctivitis that they have been crashing into each other like bumper cars. Trees are dying. Animals are starving because they can't find their food from blindness. Some are beginning to suggest that southern Chile, so near the Antarctic ozone hole, may be showing us what life might be like for all of us soon.[21]

"What's happening here is something totally new in the world," says Jaime Abarca, a local dermatologist. "It's as unusual as Martians landing." [22]

Bedrich Magas, a professor of electrical engineering from the University of Maganelles, is even more ominous in his assessment: "What's happening here is like AIDS from the sky."[23]

On the ozone front, things seem to be getting worse all the time. In late 1993, the hole over Antarctica grew larger than Europe-an area about 9 million square miles, according to the World Meteorological Organization.[24]

"We didn't think it was possible to get levels this low," said Rumen Bojkov, the United Nations' ozone expert. "Lower than this seems practically impossible."[25]

Once It's Gone, It's Gone

What's so scary about this is that there isn't anything we can do to repair a damaged ozone layer-yet it threatens to contribute to global warming, increased skin cancer risk and disruption of the world food supply. And even if man were able to stop producing CFCs used for industry, an increase in volcanic activity seems certain to aggravate the existing depletion.

The Blast Heard Round the World

Everyone is aware of the danger of earthquakes—especially in California. But few are aware of the dangers posed by volcanic activity in the Golden State. It is well-known to Californians that Mammoth Lakes, a major skiing, hiking and camping resort, is situated on top of a major volcano that has tremendous potential for damage. Just how much damage it could do was illustrated in this article.

"Mammoth is more than a vacation spot," one recent report said. "It's the epicenter of what may become the greatest natural catastrophe in historic times. Mammoth is located southeast of San Francisco, near Yosemite National Park.... It seems that there is a magma intrusion about 10 kilometers in width underlying the area at a depth of about seven kilometers, and this pre-volcanic body is rising at the phenomenal rate of two inches per year. That may not seem like much, but in geological terms, it's like a Saturn V launch. The situation has been closely monitored for years, using all kinds of advanced techniques, by various learned bodies, prominently including the U.S. Geological Survey, and there's agreement that something most unusual is going on." [26]

Sometime within the next 20 years, a genuinely catastrophic eruption could take place there.

"This anticipated catastrophe will trivialize Mount St. Helens, and be an order of magnitude bigger than Krakatoa, " the report said. "There was an eruption at this location 700,000 years ago that produced about 140 cubic miles of ash, which blanketed the western half of the continent; by comparison, the 1980 Mount St. Helens episode ejected only a quarter of a cubic mile of ash. To put that on a human scale, it means Fresno, and everything else within 75 miles of the epicenter, would be buried with at least a meter of ash, and likely with pyroclastic flows as well." [27]

Supposedly, when the volcano erupts, the noise will be loud enough to break people's eardrums in New York, and the shock waves will break glass there. Hot ash will bury Los Angeles and San Francisco like a heavy snowfall. The sun would darken for about a year and temperatures would plummet because of the decreased sunlight.

"Why isn't the looming end of civilization as we know it a better known story?" asks the report. "One man volunteered that although there were any number of serious geological trouble spots around the world, scientists generally aren't accustomed to promoting' their disaster potential in newsworthy terms simply because they're scientists, not *National Enquirer* reporters."[28]

What Can We Do?

In addition, it's worth pointing out, there's not much any of us can do about the matter. It's in God's hands. But the scale of such a disaster-which could come at Mammoth Lakes, Calif., or many other places around the world-should humble us before God and His awesome power.

I have written and talked a lot about the dramatic increase in seismic activity that has occurred in recent years. This, of course, fits in perfectly with prophetic warnings of an increase in earthquake and volcano activity in the last days.

Much of the concern about quakes in the United States has centered on the state of California, which has a long history of earthquake activity including some very recent jolts.

But it's not a potential quake in California that so concerned a group of experts recently. When a group of seismologists and structural engineers got together in New York they warned that the real catastrophic earthquake could well occur in the highly industrialized, densely populated and poorly prepared East Coast.

The reason that an earthquake in the East will devastate an area 100 times greater than one in the West is because of the presence of a great many faults in the West, which actually has the effect of thinning out shock waves.

Calamities and God

Calamities like earthquakes often tend to bring people closer to their spiritual roots and closer to God. And well they should, because the Bible has much to say about earthquakes and volcanoes, which are very much on the increase today. Both are mentioned as "signs of the times" that will confirm that our planet is entering the last days before the return of Jesus Christ.

But the greatest quake of all time is still yet to occur. It won't strike Los Angeles or even California, but will occur in an area not noted for its faults—the Middle East. Revelation 16:18-20 refers to a quake so severe it will destroy many cities, Jerusalem will shudder and whole islands and mountains will disappear.

This is the kind of disaster our planet is heading toward. But there is great hope for all who have come to accept God's gift of pardon in Jesus. Outside of this there is no hope according to the Bible prophets, who have always been 100% accurate. But stay tuned for a fuller explanation of that later.

No one is immune to natural disasters, especially as we proceed further into the last days—when the Bible warns that there will be an increase in these "birth pangs" and "signs of the times."

What the Scientists Say

Scientists tell us they are grim about the future of the planet. For more than 20 years, their primary concern was nuclear war. But today it's ozone depletion, global warming, soil erosion, overpopulation and other environmental crises.

"Human beings and the natural world are on a collision course, warned a report by 1,580 top scientists from 69 countries. "Human activities inflict harsh and often irreversible damage on the environment and on critical resources." [29]

There is no hope in mankind changing his destructive behavior. But there is sure hope for those who are intellectually honest with God's offer of forgiveness and accept it.

References

[1] *Los Angeles Herald Examiner*, May 22, 1984.

[2] Report heading from USGS Source document, March 1, 1996: *Significant Earthquakes of the World, 1996—Earthquakes of mag-*

nitude 6.5 or greater, or ones that caused fatalities, injuries or substantial damage.

[3] *Los Angeles Times*, August 20, 1993.

[4] Stephen Petranek, *Life Magazine*, September 1993, "The Year of the Killer Weather."

[5] *Los Angeles Times*, December 12, 1992.

[6] Reuters report, *San Francisco Chronicle*, Dec. 20, 1992.

[7] John Liscio, *The Sacramento Bee*, August 29, 1993 (reprinted from *Barron's*).

[8] *Global Disasters Report*, Vol 1: #1 WADEM, Safar Center, University of Pittsburg, 3434 Fifth Ave., Suite 243, Pittsburg, PA 15260

[9] *Los Angeles Times*, Ibid.

[10] *Time*, July 19,1993.

[11] Associated Press report, *San Francisco Chronicle*, October 22, 1993.

[12] Ibid.

[13] Dr. Paul Handler, *Bottom Line*, Oct. 30, 1993.

[14] Ibid.

[15] Ibid.

[16] Ibid.

[17] *Time*, Oct 2, 1995: "Heading for the Apocalypse" pg 42.

[18] *San Francisco Examiner*, January 10, 1993

[19] *L'Express*, September 2, 1993

[20] Associated Press report, *Sacramento Union*, November 15, 1992.

[21] *Wall Street Journal*, January 13,1993.

[22] Ibid.

[23] Ibid.

[24] Reuters report, *San Francisco Chronicle*, October 16, 1993.

[25] Ibid.

[26] U.S. Geological Survey, Boulder, Colorado

[27] *Los Angeles Herald Examiner*, Ibid.

[28] Ibid.

[29] Union of Concerned Scientists 1993 report, "World Scientists Warning to Humanity."

Chapter 6

IS "AIDS" JUST THE BEGINNING?

And there will be...in various places plagues...
—LUKE 21:11

And the fourth angel poured out his bowl upon the sun; and it was given to it to scorch men with fire. And men were scorched with fierce heat; and they blasphemed the name of God who has the power over these plagues....
—REVELATION 16:8, 9

Twenty-five years ago, I was debating proponents of "free love" on college campuses all across America. There was a "sexual revolution" taking place in the 1960s, and its pioneers were in academia.

Typically, I would be called in as a Christian speaker, working for Campus Crusade for Christ at the time, to present "the other side of the story" on the New Morality. It was the dawn of the "Age of Aquarius," and many young people had abandoned God and the values of the Bible in favor of a philosophy that could only have been inspired by Satan himself.

"If it feels good, do it," was the catch phrase of the day. A generation was convinced that you could experience total freedom without any sense of responsibility or consequence. I'm very sorry to say that the results were predictable.

Look What Happened

As discussed earlier, America—and the western world in general—experienced epidemics of teen-age pregnancies, abortions, sexually transmitted diseases, and the institution of the family eroded dramatically in less than a generation. We found out that there was indeed a price for "free love"—a heavy price that we are still paying today.

In fact, it was that perversion of morality that occurred in the '60s and early '70s that led to what will most assuredly be the worst plague in the history of mankind. Though, even in the height of the wild '60s, few could have imagined the power and influence exerted today by the homosexual political activists, this was the climate that created the "gay liberation movement."

After all, if there's nothing wrong with promiscuous heterosexual sex, what could be wrong with promiscuous homosexual sex? If the Bible's injunctions against adultery are not valid, who's to say that homosexuality is wrong? And, if there's nothing wrong with homosexuality, surely there can be nothing wrong with sado-masochism, pedophilia, bestiality and incest. This is the road we're on right now.

Sodom and Gomorrah are only the most notable of many cultures that went down this same road with catastrophic results.

The Rise of AIDS

It was this "anything goes" climate that created the AIDS epidemic. It was spread by promiscuous homosexual sex—just as certainly as other sexually transmitted diseases, from syphilis to gonorrhea to herpes, were spread so rapidly as casual heterosexual sex became widespread.

Yet, though the evidence could not be more clear, many are still confused and living in denial about this obvious link—this cause-and-effect relationship between sex and sexual epidemics. Though millions have gotten the message that God's laws are supreme, there are still others—including those who control the media, many government institutions and the health establishment—who believe it's all just some kind of crazy aberration. All we have to do is use condoms and have "safe sex" and everything will be all right, they insist.

Worse yet, many government agencies reacted in the 1980s to the AIDS crisis in a way that only made the situation worse. They turned AIDS into the first politically protected disease. Whereas less-serious ailments like syphilis required notification of sexual partners, victims of AIDS—a 100% fatal disease— were not asked to provide such information. It was as if the government was more concerned about protecting the diseased person than the public. The HIV positive person deserves compassion and humane treatment, but within the bounds of safety for the population at large.

Has Anyone Ever Heard of Sin?

The problem, of course, is promiscuous sex. The prevailing attitudes condoning casual sex come right out of the age of "free love." The "free love" generation more than made its point with the political and cultural establishment. In fact, a large part of the establishment bought into the "free love" ethic. And since the 1960s, most of our sex-education courses—even in elementary schools—teach about sex without any mention of morality. Morality is considered a personal issue (maybe even, God forbid, religious), separate and apart from the mechanics of sex.

The American Health Association reports that 2.5 million teen-agers contract a sexually transmitted disease every year. This is happening right now as the schools are devoting more time than ever before to sex education. A study by Jacqueline Kasun of California's Humboldt State University concluded that before sex education programs began in the 1960s, adolescent pregnancy rates were actually declining. After the programs were established, the rates went through the roof.

A Disease with Political Protection

In addition to the pleas for more sex education by groups like Planned Parenthood, throughout the 1980s we saw many communities and states passing laws which can only help spread the dreaded AIDS virus. Today, a majority of states have adopted policies prohibiting discrimination against people with AIDS. This means you don't know if the man preparing your salad in the restaurant is an AIDS victim. He could very well be. The restaurant owner could not dismiss him or even give him new responsibilities because of his disease.

And while this kind of lunacy continues, the media have been there to make sure it's all covered—covered up, that is.

"There has been no serious attempt at investigative journalism into the wealth of scientific scandals surrounding AIDS," said Dr. John Seale, a leading British expert on the disease who advises Margaret Thatcher. "[Journalists] have often given way to the tremendous pressure put upon them by scientists and homosexuals to understate the seriousness of the epidemic and...have capitulated to demands that AIDS is portrayed as an ordinary venereal disease."[1]

Biological Equivalent of Nuclear War

Dr. Seale has accurately called AIDS "the molecular biological equivalent of nuclear war." And he is shocked at how public health authorities have failed to take appropriate actions to curb the disease and how the media has spread so much disinformation about it.[2]

Today, in our major cities, AIDS has become one of the leading causes of death. And there is no cure in sight. What makes AIDS more horrible than any previous plague is its attack on the immune system, which leaves its victims helpless to defend themselves against every kind of sickness—from the common cold to tuberculosis to meningitis.

And though AIDS is certainly more horrifying in its destruction of the human body, mind and soul than any other such disease, it is not the only sexually transmitted virus that is seeing a dramatic increase. All of the so-called STDs are seeing record increases. And even scarier is the long list of new sexually transmitted diseases that are being discovered almost monthly.

AIDS—Tip of the Iceberg?

The Centers for Disease Control, for instance, found that a cancer thought to be a direct result of AIDS virus infections may actually be an independent sexually transmitted disease. For years AIDS researchers have wondered whether the cancer, Kaposi's sarcoma, occurred when the immune system was destroyed by the AIDS virus, as was widely assumed, or whether it was caused by some other process or organism.

The researchers at the federal centers in Atlanta said that accumulating data had led them to conclude that "Kaposi's sarcoma in persons with AIDS may be caused by an as yet unidentified infectious agent transmitted mainly by sexual contact."[3]

So, the fact of the matter is, the scientific and medical community just doesn't know the full story yet about AIDS, Kaposi's sarcoma and the health effects of homosexual practices and other promiscuous sexual activity. In the case of AIDS, Kaposi's sarcoma and many other STDs, an overwhelming number of victims are homosexual men. Even the non-homosexual cases can usually be traced back to a homosexual who donated blood or infected a drug user's needle. AIDS has been spread largely through homosexual practices. The No. 1 cause of AIDs transmission remains to this day anal sex. The gay activists have been completely unrepentant about this practice—urging their followers only to end so-called "unsafe sex" until a medical breakthrough is achieved.

How It Started, Spread

I can't document what I am about to say, but I can tell you it is information that comes from reliable sources. The medical establishment knows and understands this but is reluctant to admit it because of political fallout. Homosexual activists have tried for years to make the case that AIDS is not a "gay disease." They have pointed to Haiti and western Africa, for example, as places where AIDs is spread primarily through heterosexual contact. Let me tell you something about that. My sources say that AIDS got its start in Haiti and western Africa because both those places were considered hip and exotic vacation spots for homosexuals in the 1970s and early 1980s.

It was not unusual for well-to-do westerners to visit those places and pay young boys to be their sexual companions for a week or two at a time. That's how the disease got its start. Now, why does it spread so rapidly among heterosexuals there and not in the West? That has more to do with the sad state of nutrition, medical care and immunity in Haiti and western Africa than anything else.

The Nightmare in Bombay

Now, how scary is this disease for the rest of us? Well, very scary. If you want to see where the world is headed in terms of the AIDS nightmare, just look at what's going on in Bombay, India. It's a hellish scene. And if you have a weak stomach or are prone to bad dreams, skip over the next few paragraphs.

On Falkland Road in one of India's most notorious red-light districts, thousands of women are held captive in cages. Some have been kidnapped from their homes and villages, while others have been sold into bondage as rape or incest victims. Others are *devadasi*, devotees of a Hindu goddess forced into prostitution by unscrupulous priests. Then there are the young, often castrated, male prostitutes or *hijras*.[4]

"Crammed in dark tenements, in the stench of raw sewage, most prostitutes serve four men a night," said a report in the *Los Angeles Times*. "The lucky ones make $15 a month; others, including 9-year-old girls, are paid only in clothes, food and makeup. Waving and hissing from every doorway, dressed in bright saris, blood-red lipstick and jangling bracelets, the sad-eyed sex workers of these muddy lanes and dingy brothels draw hundreds of thousands of men every night from across India.

"Millions may die as a result. At least 35 percent of Bombay's prostitutes now carry the virus that causes AIDS, according to the World Health Organization. That's up from only 3 percent in 1988. By early next century, experts say, Bombay will be the epicenter of a catastrophe: India, the world's second-most-populous country, could outpace sub-Saharan Africa as the chief killing ground of the deadly disease."[5]

No One Is Safe Anymore

See how this time bomb works? It may be too late to defuse it. Certainly it cannot be set back by handing out condoms. Clearly this disease began and continues to be spread by people victimizing one another. Many so-called partners are actually unwilling victims. This is a disease from the pit of hell that affects not only the body, but clouds the mind and judgment of those afflicted with it. And it's spreading to all parts of the world; no one is safe any more.

The very reliable *Intelligence Digest* reports that AIDS "could change all assumptions about Africa." In 1994 that publication reported: "One aspect of South Africa's future that the liberal newspapers have been extremely cautious of reporting is AIDS. It is not a problem they can ignore for much longer. Last week the U.S.-based Population Research Institute, quoting Johannesburg physician and public health administrator, Dr. Claude Newbury, said that by the end of 1995 there could be as many as 12.8 million South Africans infected with the AIDS virus. This could mean a heavily depopulated South Africa by the end of the century."[6]

Even more shocking, though, is this assessment: The CIA

calculates that approximately 75 percent of Africa's population south of the Sahara could be infected by AIDS by the mid-1990s. Think of it! Seventy-five percent! The problems of famine in Africa will pale in comparison to the staggering crisis of AIDS if these estimates are even close to reality. This surely will be the worst epidemic the world has ever witnessed.

"Today's generation of African children will be largely consigned to lives of poor health and arrested growth," reports UNICEF. "The hopes of the continent will be frustrated well into the next century. Unless urgent action is taken...the human foundation for Africa's progress in the 21st century will not exist."[7]

The Pandemic Rages

The world has not even begun to grasp the magnitude of the AIDS pandemic. Even the conservative International AIDS Center at Harvard now predicts that as many as 110 million people worldwide will have contracted HIV by the year 2000. This is almost triple what the World Health Organization estimated just one year earlier.[8] Where we will actually be in a few years is anyone's guess.

"The world's vulnerability to the spread of AIDS is increasing, not decreasing," says Johnathan Mann, director of the International AIDS Center. "The pandemic is spreading to new areas and new communities. The disease has not peaked in any country and will reach every country by the end of the century because governments and international organizations lack effective means to control it." [9]

What We Don't Know Can Hurt Us

One of the reasons AIDs is so hard to control is because it is still such a mysterious ailment. There is much about the disease which remains unknown. In 1992, the first cases were discovered of people contracting AIDS who had tested negative for HIV-1 and HIV-2.[10] There is a growing fear that AIDS may be just the tip of the iceberg—the first sign of a wave of diseases in an age of plagues.

"We are also seeing other viruses like the AIDS virus—viruses that aren't even talked about in the press," says Dr. William Grace, the former chief of oncology at St. Vincent's Hospital in New York.[11]

Medical journals have begun discussing outbreaks of deadly mutant strains of AIDS. There was one horrendous wave of AIDS cases in the West African nation of Ghana in which most of those afflicted tested negative for HIV.

Deadly Mutant Viruses

"Our attention is now focused on the considerably large number of the seronegative group who were clinically diagnosed as having AIDS," said a report in the British medical journal Lancet in October 1992. "In relation to the AIDS cases in the U.S.A. without evidence of known retroviral infection, our African cases are especially intriguing. The existence of other agents causing AIDS-like syndromes might be possible among these so-called HIV-seronegative cases."[12]

But, remember folks, AIDS is not just some exotic, tropical plague. The epidemic is growing very quickly in the United States and most other industrialized western nations. In 1993, for instance, the number of Americans with AIDS jumped at a surprising rate—some 35,000 new cases.[13]

"That is higher than we expected," admitted Dr. John Ward, chief of AIDS surveillance for the Centers for Disease Control and Prevention in Atlanta. "Some of the 21 percent [increase] is a sign that the AIDS epidemic is continuing to grow."[14]

Let's Play Pretend

Yet, despite the alarming statistics and the heartbreaking reality of AIDS, the media and the liberal cultural establishment are still acting like ostriches with their heads in the sand. They are still perpetuating deadly myths on the public—especially young people. Who, for instance, becomes America's No. 1 spokesman on avoiding AIDS? Magic Johnson—a multi-millionaire sports star who tragically chose to live a promiscuous sex life in the age of AIDS. And his message? Not one of abstinence—the only hope for America's young people—but one of "safe sex." I like Magic and feel real compassion for him (as I do for all who are suffering this dread disease), but I do wish he would warn the young that the only safe sex is within a wisely chosen marriage.

In any case, people are now beginning to see that we are reaping the harvest of the sexual revolution of the '60s, of lowered standards of morality, of pandering to the whims of homosexual activists. That's good, but it may be too late.

Optimistically, we might see more individual homosexuals re-evaluating their lifestyles and turning away from that sinfulness. There's a myth perpetuated by the gay rights movement that no one ever leaves the lifestyle. But it's amazing what a relationship with Jesus will accomplish.

What It Would Take to Change

It's difficult to imagine we'll soon see America turning back to reaffirm our traditional beliefs in the moral principles of the Bible and Christian teaching about love, marriage, sex, family and faithfulness. But that's really what it would take to turn things around. And, even then, we would risk losing an entire generation to this horrible plague.

How, you might ask, does the AIDS disaster fit into the prophetic scenario? The Bible tells us there will be several great signals to alert us that the end of the age and the beginning of a new world is near. War, revolution, earthquakes, religious deception, strange occurrences in space, famines and plagues are all mentioned.

Only in the late 1980s did we begin to realize that we were in the midst of a plague as real and as dreadful as any the human race had ever experienced. The severity of AIDS, however, should not have surprised anyone.

The Biblical Precedent

The Bible is very clear about homosexuality and its consequences. In Leviticus 18:22, it says:

"You shall not lie with a male as one lies with a female; it is an abomination." The prescribed penalty? Death.

In the New Testament, let's look at Romans 1:24-28:

"Therefore God gave them over in the lusts of their hearts to impurity, that their bodies might be dishonored among them. For they exchanged the truth of God for a lie, and worshipped and served the creature rather than the Creator, who is blessed forever. Amen. For this reason God gave them over to degrading passions; for their women exchanged the natural function for that which is unnatural, and in the same way also the men abandoned the natural function of the woman and burned in their desire toward one another, men with men committing indecent acts and receiving in their own persons the due penalty of their error. And just as they did not see fit to acknowledge God any longer, God gave them over to a depraved mind, to do those things which are not proper."

Now, could that be any clearer? It leaves little room for misinterpretation.

The Due Penalty of Their Error

The most striking verse is Romans 1:27, which shows there is a natural consequence for sexual immorality. It says that homosexuals will receive in their own bodies *"the due penalty of their error."* In other words, there is a physical price to be paid for living this "lifestyle."

Though AIDS is a very recent discovery, there have been other deadly plagues that resulted from widespread sexual sin. The Bible recounts a time when the Israelites were faced with a plague in the Plains of Moab after they consorted with prostitutes. Moses contained the disease by killing every potential carrier on direct orders from God. Nevertheless, the Book of Numbers (Chapter 25:1-9) says that 24,000 died from the plague.

Historically, whenever rampant sexual promiscuity broke out in a society, a virulent plague would follow. Yet with all the evidence, some of our greatest medical, scientific and political minds fail to see the connection.

Other Plagues

But there is more to the plague story in the last days than AIDS and other sexually transmitted diseases. In part due to the spread of AIDS and its effect on the immune systems of millions of people, old diseases like tuberculosis are making a comeback —big time.

Los Angeles, San Francisco and New York are facing bonafide TB epidemics. The rate of infection is up 85 percent in Los Angeles. County health officials are suggesting that if millions are not spent on prevention and treatment right now, the public health menace may quickly escape their grasp.[15]

"Right now, under the current circumstances, it looks pretty bleak," says Graydon Shepherd, a senior public health adviser for the CDC in Los Angeles. [16]

What this means is that 90 years of tuberculosis control and treatment advances could soon be wiped out. A disease considered virtually extinct is generating terror in a new generation.

"It's perfectly clear that tuberculosis and HIV-AIDS walk hand in hand," explains Dr. David Rogers of Cornell Medical College. [17]

Whatever Happened to Malaria?

Another disease thought behind us is malaria. In 1955, the World Health Organization actually announced that the disease would soon be completely eradicated. It once killed more people around the world than any other disease. Well, it may again. Malarial parasites now infect an estimated 270 million people every year, killing up to 2 million (far more than AIDS right now) and causing at least 10 million cases of acute illness. [18]

People are flooding into malarial clinics in unprecedented numbers and Dr. Louis Miller, head of malarial research at the National Institutes of health in Maryland admits: "We're worse off than we were in 1950." [19]

Cholera's Comeback

Scientists are also concerned that the world is facing a new cholera epidemic—possibly the biggest this century. A strain resistant to all known vaccines has appeared in Asia and is already claiming thousands of lives. By the mid-'90s it is expected to spread into Africa, the Middle East and the Mediterranean. The number of cholera deaths is expected to increase tenfold by that time.[20]

In 1993 an epidemic of a mysterious flu-like disease broke out in the southwestern United States. But it was no surprise to virologists, who have been predicting for years that humanity's encroachment on nature will eventually unleash on America and other developed nations exotic diseases previously confined to the poverty-ridden Third World.

Strange New Viruses

The hantavirus—or "Four Corners" disease—is actually not so mysterious at all, but rather a common wildlife virus. The outbreak, say scientists, is a classic case of what can happen "when you keep fussing around with the environment."[21] Part of the problem in the southwestern U.S. is a population explosion by rats. Rodents are carrying strains related to the bubonic plague, which nearly destroyed Europe. Actually, that plague is carried not by the rodents but by their fleas.

And how's this for a biblical sounding plague? Pakistan and the east coast of Africa are now experiencing the worst plagues of locusts in recorded history. This is what you can expect when you have large disruptions and migrations of the population. No spraying is done by farmers when the population is on the move.

The World Health Organization identifies tuberculosis as the number one killer virus on earth today. It will infect fifteen million people this year. Three million will die. The recent film "Outbreak!" brought to life the risk of Ebola infection. The Ebola virus is one strain of a killer called 'haemorrhagic fever'. This disease literally liquefies internal organs, melting the victim internally. And the number of outbreaks continue to expand. A World Health Organization press release in early 1996 identified Ebola outbreaks in Gabon and Zaire. The fatality rate in Zaire was 77 percent!

A yellow fever epidemic was reported in Liberia. In Nicaragua in 1995, more than 1,000 people contracted a new and unidentifiable disease.[22] That prompted the World Health Organization to create a new entity: The Division of Emerging Viral and Bacterial Disease Surveillance and Control.

In Brisbane, Australia, a killer virus that ordinarily affects only horses made the jump to two humans, killing them both. The virus, equine morbillivirus, could infect others, according to reports. [23]

CNN reported in April 1996 that epidemics spreading across a northern Nigerian state have killed 15,000 people—mostly children.

Outbreaks of meningitis, cholera, measles and diarrhea ravaged Kano, which has a population of 5.8 million—the nation's second most populated state.

An outbreak of 'mad cow' disease in the spring of 1996 added another killer to the growing list—but this one is really terrifying. "Mad cow" disease, or bovine spongiform encephalopathy (BSE) showed up in humans as Creutzfeld-Jakob Disease (CJD). It is believed to be transmitted through infected beef. The virus is so hardy that, after burying a specimen for three years, a researcher dug it up and injected it into lab animals. They developed the disease.

CJD infects humans, but can remain dormant for years. When it becomes active, it literally eats the brain of the victim. [24] There is no treatment, and no cure. What is interesting is its origin. Investigators believe a protein supplement in cattle feed is the cause.

As early as the 1960s, British researchers at Bedford College in London proposed that a disease common in sheep, called scrapie, was caused by a transmissible protein that could somehow replicate itself in healthy brains. At the same time, researchers at the National Health Institute in Britain found that the disease known as kuru was passed from person to person among cannibals in New Guinea when they ate human brains!

Hang on to your stomachs for this next part, friends! In

Britain, a protein feed composed of offal (parts) from sheep—including sheep that died from scrapie—and from cattle was a regular dietary supplement for beef cattle. That made most British feed cattle cannibals. Scientists are still exploring that possible link. Among the cattle and sheep parts used in the protein feed was brain matter. Infected brain matter is the principal suspect in the British outbreak. The British banned the use of the protein supplement in 1993, but a report issued in the UK in September, 1995 showed that half the slaughterhouses in Britain were in violation of the regulations! [25]

The ten victims may be just the first ones. John Pattison, the microbiologist who headed the government commission [in Britain] said that since CJD has an incubation period as long as 15 years, "there could be thousands of more cases." Asked whether Britain might face an AIDS-like epidemic, he answered, "I cannot deny that is a possibility." [26]

Although the U.S. banned British beef in 1989, we have little to be relieved about. The US used the identical protein feed here until after the British epidemic began. It's use wasn't banned here until the late spring of 1996.

American cattle are subject to a milder form of the disease called 'downer.' 'Downer' cattle exhibit similar symptoms, falling, or remaining unable to stand for 24 hours or more at a time. Those cattle, when slaughtered, are rendered into protein feed for healthy cattle. Given the nature of the disease, and length of the incubation period, it's a ticking time bomb!

You know, so many of the endtimes prophecies overlap one another, with one sign pointing to another sign. Such is the case with plagues. For instance, famine is one of the birth pangs Jesus spoke of as being increasing in frequency and intensity before His return. Plagues, like those that have afflicted regions in Africa, devastating crops and the food supply, are one of the factors increasing hunger throughout the world.

Role of the Environment

In the same way, the environmental problems—such as the ozone hole—may be a contributing factor to the increase in plagues in the last days.

Revelation 16:9 talks about how the sun will somehow grow more intense in the endtimes:

> And men were scorched with fierce heat; and they blasphemed the name of God who has the power over these plagues; and they did not repent, so as to give Him glory.

With growing concern by scientists about holes in the earth's ozone layer coupled with the "greenhouse effect," is it any wonder that in the very near future such conditions will exist?

Two verses later in that same chapter of Revelation, the Scripture refers to future events that sound strikingly similar to a plague of skin cancer that erupts among the population of the world....And they blasphemed the God of heaven because of their pains and their sores," it says.

Of course, we are already beginning to see a measured rise in the number of skin cancer cases around the world. And the situation is expected to get much worse if the ozone layer continues to be depleted at current rates.

Total Ecosystem Breakdown

What the Bible is describing for these endtimes is not only a series of terrible armed conflicts, political struggles and a worldwide religious deception, but a total breakdown of the earth's ecosystem. How else can one explain the verse in Matthew in which Jesus says, "And unless those days had been cut short, no life would have been saved; but for the sake of the elect those days shall be cut short."

Only a supernatural event—the return of Jesus—is able to restore the planet to health again, to allow it to support human life again, to tame the hostile environment and to stop the resultant plagues.

References

[1] Radio interview with Dr. John Seale, "Week in Review with Hal Lindsey"

[2] Ibid.

[3] Centers for Disease Control and Prevention, Atlanta, Georgia

[4] *Los Angeles Times*, November 26, 1992

[5] Ibid.

[6] *Intelligence Digest*, November 8, 1991

[7] *Financial Times* report in *San Francisco Examiner*, December 27, 1992

[8] *International Health Watch Report*, May-June 1992

[9] Ibid.

[10] *International Healthwatch Report*, July-August 1992

[11] *International Healthwatch Report*, December 1992

[12] Ibid.

[13] Associated Press report in *The Sacramento Bee*, April 30, 1993

[14] Ibid.

[15] *Los Angeles Times Magazine*, October 24, 1993

[16] Ibid.

[17] *International Healthwatch Report*, October-November 1992

[18] *Newsweek*, January 11, 1993

[19] Ibid.

[20] *London Independent* report in *San Francisco Examiner and Chronicle*, May 30, 1993

[21] Scripps Howard News Service report in *San Francisco Examiner and Chronicle*, June 13, 1993

[22] WHO Press release: #WHO79 3 Nov, 1995

[23] CNN, October 26, 1995

[24] CNN, March 29, 1996

[25] *New York Times*, March 30, 1996

[26] *Time*, April 1, 1996

Chapter 7

THE AGE OF FAMINE

In various places there will be famines…
—MATTHEW 24:7

And I looked, and behold, an ashen horse; and he
who sat on it and had the name "Death"; and Hades
was following with him. And authority was given
to them over a fourth of the earth, to kill with sword
and with famine and with pestilence and
by the wild beasts of the earth.
—REVELATION 6:8

Homo Sapiens have to be the most suicidal creatures on Earth. We make lemmings look like self-preservation freaks. And today, as we approach the next millennium, we're in danger of committing what I call "cosmocide." What's cosmocide? Well, if suicide is the destruction of one's own life, cosmocide is the destruction of the human race.

I hate to sound like an alarmist, folks, but we're getting very close to that now. As I have mentioned earlier, overpopulation is completely out of control. I have called this Apocalyptic Peril No. 1 for the 1990s. It's clear that the Earth cannot continue to sustain the growing population without redistributing the wealth and resources of the planet. That's not something I want to see happen, though there are plenty of people around who would welcome such a scenario.

Man, however, is the kind of creature who doesn't like having things taken from him and redistributed. So the more the population increases, the more man is pushed to ensure he keeps what he's got or to get what his neighbor has. It is this trend that is pushing the world toward three trials prominently discussed in Revelation—the birth pangs Jesus said would precede His coming.

Three Trials of Revelation

They are: No. 1, plagues, which I have already addressed; No. 2, war, which I will discuss later; and No. 3, famine—our topic for this chapter. As the population increases, the push for food becomes more desperate. And, ironically, the greatest population increases are occurring in those parts of the world least able to provide for their inhabitants.

That's where we are today—marching on the inevitable, irrevocable path toward an age of famine. Now, it's easy to become numb to all this. I've been reading these prophetic signs for more than 38 years. I've been a student of Bible prophecy almost from the day that I became a Christian. It's easy to become numb. It's easy to get absorbed in the doom and gloom of it all. But, let me tell you, don't get numb!

All of these signs are happening right before our eyes, and they have enormous prophetic significance because they are all happening simultaneously—just as the Bible predicted they would before the return of Jesus. In other words, folks, we ought to thank God that we're alive at a time like this and can see His Word fulfilled in the pages of our daily newspapers. That's the way I look at it. We as believers need to be grateful for the gifts of grace and faith God has given us. And we need to use the time we have left to evangelize and fulfill the Great Commission. That's what this message is all about.

Spaceship Earth

Let me give you an analogy of where the world is today. Suppose you were on a spaceship. You know there are filters and machines responsible for circulating and purifying the air and water on a daily basis. You also have some reckless people on the ship who are hacking away at the life-support system. Food supplies are desperately short and there is no ability to replenish those supplies because the air and water supplies are compromised. That's about what's happening on planet Earth.

It's a bigger spaceship, but it's still a closed environment that is gravely threatened. The rain forests, the lungs of the planet, are disappearing at an astonishing rate. About 80,000 square miles vanish every year. That's a land mass the size of Austria. At that rate, the rain forests will be gone by the middle of next century. When the rain forests are gone, so is the air we breathe. Likewise, plant and animal species are disappearing at a rate of 100 a year. Between 5 and 30 million have already vanished, never to come back. [1]

Now, I hope I don't sound like a member of Earth First! Because my real concern is not for plants and animals and trees, but for people. But the destruction of the environment has awesome consequences for man.

The Human Toll

Already, drought, plagues, starvation and famines have become commonplace throughout Africa and Asia. We've all heard about Somalia, of course. But there is much more to the famine story than that East Africa nation.

"Somalia is a drop in the bucket," says Marc Cohen, one of the authors of *Hunger 1993*, a publication of the Bread for the World Institute.[2]

Here are some of the staggering statistics: Some 786 million people—nearly one in every six on the globe—are suffering from acute or chronic hunger. More than a billion more face serious malnutrition. About 2 billion of the world's 5.5 billion are malnourished in some way. Here are the three categories of the underfed as established by the United Nations Food and Agriculture Organization:[3]

Who are these people?

- Chronic hunger: This is a group of people whose daily food intake is inadequate for health, growth and minimum energy needs with the potential to endanger life. About 750 million of people in this category live in South Asia and sub-Saharan Africa.[4]

- Acute hunger: These are folks threatened with imminent death because of an absolute shortage of food. More than 35 million people fit this classification—mostly in the southern states of Africa.[5]

- Hidden hunger: These are people unable to meet requirements for an adequate diet on a prolonged basis with the potential of shortening their life span. Virtually every country in the world—including the United States—has pockets of this kind of malnutrition.[6]

Don't be fooled into thinking that hunger is a problem isolated to Africa and Asia. Surely that's where the worst of the problem is today—the real famines. But recently we've begun to see hunger becoming an increasing concern in Eastern Europe. The conflict, for instance, in the former Yugoslavia has been heightened in part because of drastic food shortages and distribution problems complicated by war.

The Problem Spreads

Hunger in Albania is, by some reports, as desperate as the levels in sub-Saharan Africa. Albania now relies on foreign aid for 75 percent of its food. There are also desperate situations in parts of Russia, Bulgaria and Rumania. In Bulgaria, 60 percent of the average household's expenditures go for food. Food prices in Czechoslovakia increased 70 percent between 1989 and 1991.

"People are getting poorer, and the rate of development growth, food production and wealth are not keeping up with the population," says Bronek Szynalski, director of emergency relief for the U.N. World Food Program in Rome.[7]

The gap between rich and poor nations grew significantly in the last decade. In 1981, the gross national product per capita in the developed world was $8,600, compared with $700 in poor countries. By 1990, per capita income in the developed world had more than doubled to $17,900, while in poor countries income rose by only $110, according to the Population Crisis Committee.[8]

I Warned about This

In the late 1960s, there were a number of projections being made by scientists of coming famines that would plague various parts of the world. I saw that those scientific predictions fit into the prophetic scenario of starvation and pestilences set forth in Scripture.

"Look for the beginning of the widest spread famines in the history of the world." That was one of my warnings in my book, *The Late Great Planet Earth*—that we would likely be entering an age of famines. That is exactly where we are today.

The situation has become so severe that it is not even newsworthy anymore. Did you ever notice that's how the media works? When something new happens, you'll see it on the news constantly. But when something becomes commonplace, they don't report about it anymore. Famines have become so horrible and widespread today, that you don't see a great deal reported about them by the press.

Man-made Famines

However, some of the worst famines in the history of the world took place in the last 10 years. They took tens of millions of lives. Some of them were man-made debacles—like the Marxist-created crisis in Ethiopia and the warlord-exacerbated problems in Somalia—while others were caused naturally by drought and plague.

According to the World Bank, nearly one-fourth of Africa's population—more than 100 million people—do not get enough to eat. Food consumption per person has been declining since 1980. Per capita income has been declining in Africa for several decades, falling by 25 percent since 1980, says Edward Jaycox, World Bank vice president for Africa.

Currently there are famines and threats of famines throughout much of the African continent. Never before has a condition like this existed. One of the facts that always staggers me is that more than half the people who have ever lived on this planet are alive today. That's how fast the population is exploding.

What's Causing the Hunger?

How will we feed these people? Obviously, we won't. Recently, I gave a sermon in my church in California and I told the congregation that before I had finished the message, some 80,000 people on the planet would perish from starvation. That sort of illustration somehow brings the point home more dramatically than citing figures of millions dying.

There are other causes besides inept and criminal government policies and overpopulation for the increase in famines. Industrial pollution of the air, water and soil is threatening the quantity and the quality of our food. In other words, even the food that is produced has less nutritional value today than it did a generation ago.

There is grave doubt being expressed today about how much chemical fertilizer some soils can take without deterioration. At some point, we know, heavy fertilization becomes counterproductive. Some experts believe we are reaching that point in some industrialized countries—the very nations that provide the most food to the most people.

Ignoring Biblical Concepts

Soil erosion and exhaustion are other problems. You know, the Israelites were commanded to give the soil a rest every seven years. This was to allow the land to recover its nutrients. (The Israelites didn't do this and were taken to Babylon in discipline because of it.) Modern industrialized farming makes no such allowances. And once soil fertility is depleted, crops will not produce without increasing levels of chemical fertilizers.

Modern agricultural techniques are also putting a strain on our water resources. Water tables are depleting at alarming rates in many parts of the world—including the United States. Irrigation is also leaving millions of acres of once-productive farmland desolate from salinization and erosion. These are problems that, in the past, have destroyed civilizations.

People from Los Angeles to Beijing to Riyadh, Saudi Arabia, are having to look farther and farther away for fresh water, and a new report says water scarcity is a spreading global problem. The report said expense is the big problem with the kind of water projects that would be necessary to keep pace with growing populations.[9]

One Big Thirsty World

"The bottom line of this is simply that the rate of population growth in countries experiencing water scarcity is vastly outpacing population growth of the world as a whole," said Bob Engleman, co-author of the report by Population Action International. "Expense keeps getting in the way."[10]

Erosion of topsoil is a worldwide crisis. Once the topsoil is gone in marginally arable parts of the world, it's gone for good. Increasingly there is more land, once capable of producing crops, now sitting idle.

According to the Worldwatch Institute, food production reached maximum levels in the early 1980s. We got to the point where technological improvements, including better fertilizers and irrigation techniques, could no longer improve yields. Everyone, the experts say, will have less to eat in coming years as worldwide food production fails to keep pace with burgeoning population growth. [11]

Food Production Slipping

Worldwatch predicts a bleak future, with farms, livestock ranches and ocean fisheries unable to boost their production of food for a hungry world. As an example of current trends, world per capita grain output, which climbed 40 percent between 1950 and 1984, has fallen 8 percent over the past eight years.[12]

Meat production, which rose 78 percent from 1950 and 1990 to bring yearly per capita meat production to 70 pounds from 39 pounds, fell 1 percent between 1990 and 1992. The threat of BSE in feed cattle could reduce production even more. And there are other threats. *The London Observer* reported that half the pigs in the United Kingdom are inected with a form of swine tuberculosis. *The Observer* quoted from a Mea Hygiene Service memorandum written in January, 1996—well before the BSE scare. The memorandum referred to swine TB as "evidence of a new problem."[13] Oceanic fisheries have also reached their limits, with annual catch topping at 10 million tons in 1989 and per capita output falling 7 percent since then. [14]

To compound those problems, the number of refugees in the world climbed to an all-time high of 18 million in the early 1990s.[15]

The Weather Factor

And, of course, most farmers around the world are still dependent to a large extent on the weather. We have already discussed the changing global weather patterns and what that portends for the future. Imagine what a sustained worldwide drought—lasting several years—would mean to the planet in its current state. Or, what would an increase in world temperatures of a degree or two mean? Or what about the kind of flooding witnessed in 1993 in the Midwest United States?

Acid rains and the greenhouse effect are already wreaking havoc for farmers from California's San Joaquin Valley to the wheat fields of Canada. And changing weather patterns may soon displace the United States as the world's breadbasket.

Uncle Sam Can't Help

You may think that the United States, because of our history of prosperity, is somehow insulated from such problems as hunger and overpopulation. If that's what you think, you might want to ponder a few little-known facts:

- Right now, the United States continues to welcome more legal immigrants annually than all the other nations of the world combined. Keeping in mind the tremendous problem of illegal immigration, you can quickly see how the character of our nation could change very rapidly.

- Second, George Borgstrom, in his book *Hungry Planet*, cautioned that no part of the world is more than one year away from critical starvation in the event of serious crop failure—except the United States. But we are only two years away! And when you consider the impending radical changes in weather patterns, you begin to see that we are vulnerable.

Still, with our grocery stores fully stocked, it's hard to take the idea of hunger very seriously in the West. But just think of the devastation wrought by the drought of 1988 and the floods of 1993. Do you know what this kind of calamity, two years in a row, could do even to prosperous North America? We are not invulnerable. We need to remember that. God does not appreciate arrogance. We take so much for granted in America and the other industrialized nations.

The situation concerning overpopulation, changing weather patterns and the hunger problem is quite grim. Famines, unfortunately, are only the beginning of the woes that Jesus predicted would afflict the planet just before He returns.

Like Birth Pangs

I am not going to pretend that I know exactly why it's going to occur, but I do know famines are going to be a reality for the world in this generation. Like the other "signs of the times," they will increase in frequency and intensity as we get closer to the time when Jesus returns.

How do I know this? Because the Bible tells me so. When asked by His disciples how the world would know the general time of His return to earth, Jesus said: "See to it that no one misleads you. For many will come in My name, saying, 'I am the Christ,' and will mislead many. And you will be hearing of wars and rumors of wars; see that you are not frightened, for those things must take place, but that is not yet the end. For nation will rise against nation, and kingdom against kingdom, and in various places there will be famines and earthquakes. But all these things are merely the beginning of birth pangs."

Birth pangs. Any of you who have children know what those are like. They start out mild and infrequent and they grow increasingly more intense and frequent. That's what these signs will be like, Jesus is saying in Matthew 24. And that's exactly what we're seeing today all around the world.

Sure, there have always been earthquakes and wars and famines and pestilences and fearful conditions. But there has never been a time like this in the world where all of these conditions are occurring simultaneously and in greater magnitude than ever before. That's why it is so significant that we are experiencing this age of famine at precisely the moment that all these other conditions are occurring—not just quakes and wars and famines, but also religious deception and the rebirth of Israel and the other geo-political alignments I'll be addressing in this book.

Jesus also tells us in that chapter that all of these things would happen at a time when it was actually possible for the entire human race to extinguish itself: "And unless those days had been cut short, no life would have been saved; but for the sake of the elect those days shall be cut short." Now let me ask you: Was it possible for man to annihilate himself through war and environmental degradation 2,000 years ago? No. Was it possible 1,000 years ago? No. But it is possible today, isn't it? In this age of nuclear weapons, chemical and biological warfare and environmental crisis, it is more than possible, isn't it?

Jesus also told us that once this chain of events got started, that generation would see all of the endtimes events fulfilled: "Truly I say to you, this generation will not pass away until all these things take place."

And this section of the Gospel of Matthew is not the only place in Scripture that describes this sequence of events. Jesus revealed to John (Revelation 6:5) prophecies concerning the "four horsemen of the Apocalypse." The first horse, white, represented false prophets and religious deception. The red horse was for warfare. And the black horse followed with famine. Unprecedented famine was also predicted in Ezekiel 5:12: "One third of you will die by plague or be consumed by famine...."

Got to Keep Hope

It's not a pretty picture, is it? But is there hope? Of course. With God there is always hope. Not only does our Lord offer believers a special escape hatch (more on that later), but He also offers us special protections here on Earth during times of trial and tribulation.

"Behold," we are told in Psalm 33:18-19, "the eye of the Lord is on those who fear Him, on them who hope for His lovingkindness; to deliver their soul from death, and to keep them alive in famine."

To experience this kind of protection we are commanded by Jesus not to be frightened, but to have faith in Him. We are told to be prayerful and to follow His way of life.

"And the Lord shall guide thee continually, and satisfy thy soul in drought," Isaiah 58:11 (KJV) instructs us. We must be alert and prayerful at all times, "in order that you may have the strength to escape all these things that are about to take place, and to stand before the Son of Man" (Luke 21:36).

Another Green Revolution?

Years ago I interviewed Dr. Norman Borlaug, one of the preeminent scientists in the world when it comes to agriculture. He has been called "the father of the Green Revolution." The man responsible for so many great technological advances in farming today says there is little hope for similar breakthroughs in the future.

"I think it's folly to expect science to pull a rabbit out of a hat in the 11th hour to solve the food production problem," he said. He added that he believed the anticipated "hunger and misery of millions would provoke a great global holocaust." [16]

It is folly to put our hopes in man and science at times like this. The Bible says that these are signs of the times that signal to us to look heavenward as His redemption draws near.

References

[1] *L'Express*, September 2, 1993

[2] *Los Angeles Times*, December 15,1992

[3] Ibid.

[4] Ibid.

[5] Ibid.

[6] Ibid.

[7] Ibid.

[8] Ibid.

[9] Associated Press report in the *San Francisco Chronicle*, Nov. 8, 1993

[10] Ibid.

[11] Reuters report in the *San Francisco Chronicle*, July 18, 1993

[12] Ibid.

[13] As reported in the Buffalo (NY) *News*, April 1, 1996

[14] Reuters report in the *San Francisco Chronicle*, July 18, 1993

[15] Ibid.

[16] Dr. Norman Borlaug, interview with author

Chapter 8

ISRAEL—CENTER OF WORLD DESTINY

And Jerusalem will be trampled under foot by the Gentiles until the times of the Gentiles be fulfilled.
—LUKE 21:24

And you will come up against My people Israel like a cloud to cover the land. It will come about in the last days that I will bring you against my land...."
—EZEKIEL 38:16

On a recent trip Israel, it was the talk of the town. Israelis everywhere were expecting to soon be inundated with another massive wave of immigration—one that would fit perfectly into the biblical prophetic endtimes scenario.

Why are the Israelis expecting another major influx of Jews from around the world? Several reasons. First of all, the dramatic events taking place in volatile, topsy-turvy Russia could spur the remaining remnant of Jews there to make the pilgrimage to the Holy Land. Natan Sharansky, head of the Zionist Forum and a former Russian refusenik, says he thinks a massive *aliya* from Russia is imminent.

"Masses of Jews could decide to come to Israel before the flames spread," he said. "The government must be ready to set aside resources to absorb a mass *aliya* (a permanent emmigration to Israel). This is the time to show the Jewish people and the world that Israel is the only safe and open home for the Jewish people."[1]

Why Jews Leave Russia

Not only is the political situation in Russia unstable, but there has been a tremendous resurgence of anti-semitism, particularly among the opponents of Boris Yeltsin.

"The scene in Moscow on Sunday, Oct. 3, [1993] looked like something from a film on czarist-era pogroms: wild men in ragtag uniforms carrying guns, sticks and metal rods and waving monarchist and Communist flags careened through the streets in stolen army trucks, on their way to attack Russia's main TV studio," reported journalist Alexander Lesser. "For about 12 hours that day, these men ruled Moscow. And few here doubt that had they succeeded in consolidating their grip on power, some would have turned their attention to the Jews."[2]

Israeli sources estimate there may be as many as 1 million Russian Jews vacillating about moving to Israel. Though Yeltsin has improved the political climate for these people, they fear his grip on power is tenuous at best.

"Rutskoi [Yeltsin's chief rival] would not have encouraged attacks on Jews, but in the circumstances he could not control the forces of the city," explained Anatoly Shabad. "Pogroms would have begun immediately. I saw leaflets inciting people to kill Jews. I was shocked—we've had plenty of anti-Semitic material here, but I had never seen such direct incitement before. One leaflet showed a Russian child pleading, 'Daddy, kill a Jew for my future.'"[3]

But it is most important that God predicted through Jeremiah that this is exactly what would happen in the days leading to Messiah's return, *"'Therefore behold, the days are coming,' declares the Lord, 'when they will no longer say, As the Lord lives, who brought up the sons of Israel from the land of Egypt,' but, 'As the Lord lives, who brought up and led back the descendants of the household of Israel from the north land and from all the countries where I had driven them' Then they will live on their own soil"* (Jeremiah 23:7,8).

Where Else They Come From

It is in such a climate that Sharansky and others in Israel believe another big wave of Russian emigration is coming soon. But Russia isn't the only place Jews will be coming from. God says in Ezekiel 39:27-28 that before He is finished, He will leave none behind. The restoration of the Jewish homeland will be complete in the latter days—our generation.

"When I bring them back from the peoples and gather them from the lands of their enemies, then I shall be sanctified through them in the sight of the many nations. Then they will know that I am the Lord their God because I made them go into exile among the nations, and then gathered them again to their own land; and I will leave none of them there any longer."

Where else will they be coming from? Another interesting report circulating in Israel these days indicates that the Jewish state will soon be seeing waves of immigrants not only from Russia but from Africa and Asia as well.

Who Are the Shinlungs?

Right now, in Israel, the first members of the Shinlung tribe from the Indian-Burmese border are undergoing conversion and assimilation. Here's their amazing story. In the early 1950s, a farmer named Chala had a dream. God told him, he believed, that his people were really a lost Israelite tribe and it was time for them to return to their homeland.

Inspired only by the dream, a group of tribespeople, led by Chala, began walking to Israel. They were stopped by police and sent home. But they didn't give up. They wrote letters to Israel officials and pleaded for help. Meanwhile, thousands of the tribespeople began practicing Judaism, which they learned from Jews in Bombay.

In the summer of 1994, the first 36 young Shinlung were flown to Israel. And about 5,000 more are eagerly awaiting more flights. But the tribe totals more than 1 million. And some Israelis don't consider it far-fetched that the great majority of them will eventually come.[4]

These could well be descended from the ten northern tribes that were driven into dispersion by the Assyrians in the 8th century B.C.

Millions More Want to Come

But that's only the tip of the iceberg. In fact, there are tens of millions of other obscure tribes like the Shinlung who claim to be descended from the original ten lost tribes of Israel. The leader of 4 million Ethiopians recently petitioned Israeli authorities for recognition as descendants.[5]

It seems the Ingathering of the Exiles is more a reality than ever before. Miracle? Yes. But why should that surprise us? It's exactly what the Bible told us would happen. There is no place on Earth where we see prophecy being fulfilled as dramatically and spectacularly as in Israel.

This is one reason Israel today is quite literally at the very center of the world stage—just the way you would expect it in the last days. And the stage lights are only going to get brighter in the days ahead. Do you know that the Bible indicates Israel is destined to become the center of world affairs in the last days? Just read Zechariah 12-14 if you have any doubts.

Will Israel Discover Oil?

But, I believe, along with this greater power and leverage must come increased economic clout. Reuters reported an oil strike near the Dead Sea in mid-1995. Unfortunately, the oil is hidden below a thick salt crust, making drilling—for the moment—economically unfeasible. Pinhas Dror, the former Israeli Economic Ambassador to Israel, said last year that problem may only be temporary. In an interview, he said that the only other place on earth where oil has been successfully extracted through a salt crust was in Siberia. He said some of the Russian scientists involved in that project are now in Israel. According to his sources, he said, there is a "lot of oil down there."[6] I think there is some biblical evidence to suggest that great oil deposits may be hidden beneath Israel's soil.

However, it's possible Israel could achieve that level of prosperity without oil—but with high technology. In 1993, my news journal *Countdown* literally scooped the international media with a report on a new technology Israel hopes will revolutionize the way the world produces electricity. It's called "Snap," and later, even the *Wall Street Journal* reported on its great potential.

Here's an excerpt of that report: "A wind dissipated the flood in Noah's day. Another wind parted the Red Sea for the fleeing Israelites. And now a wind may once again play a role in the history of Israel—only this time it would be a man-made wind blowing inside a tower more than half a mile high.

What Is 'Snap'?

"The wind tower is the serious proposal of a team of Israeli scientists, engineers and architects who believe they have found a cheap method of generating electricity. Situated in the desert near the sea, the generating station would consist of a hollow cylinder 3,300 feet high—twice the height of New York's World Trade Center—and 1,500 feet in diameter.

"The idea works like this: Sea water is pumped to the top of the tower and sprayed into the center, where it rapidly evaporates in the dry desert heat. As the air is cooled by the evaporation, it grows denser and heavier and begins falling, plunging even faster down the tower interior. By the time the cold air hits the tower bottom, it's traveling at 50 miles an hour.

"If the water is sprayed continuously, the result is a powerful downdraft that can be piped into tunnels to drive wind turbine electric generators. By one calculation, such a wind tower built in the Negev desert and drawing water from the Red Sea, could produce 40 billion to 80 billion kilowatt-hours of electric energy a year.

"The energy's cost would be a mere two cents a kilowatt-hour, less than one-fifth the cost of generating a kilowatt hour in, say, California. And, in some versions the tower could also desalt sea water, providing cheap water for desert farming."[7]

Israel is indeed on the threshold of something miraculous. Basically, Snap will produce electricity from dry desert air and clean water from sea water.

Imagine the Applications

"If put into application this clean power from dry desert air and sea or brackish water will have a significant impact on the world economy and the environment and will create hundreds of thousands of direct jobs worldwide when commercialized," says Dr. Zaslavsky. "Indirect jobs created, including economic growth spawned by Snap, would have to be estimated in the millions and over time perhaps in the tens of millions, as it will allow development of now poor countries by supplying low-cost electricity and water."[8]

Zaslavsky and others involved in the project predict environmentalists will embrace the process because it uses a renewable resource and is basically non-polluting. If fully developed it could provide a virtually limitless supply of power and fresh water to a developing world.

"When the Snap technology is demonstrated successfully, the chances for real peace in the Middle East and other areas will be significantly enhanced," says Dr. Zaslavsky. "The abundance due to Snap will be endowed to lands which are now poor in water and often poor in other resources. Snap will turn the desert predicament into its asset."[9]

What about Feasibility?

In actuality, the Snap process doesn't really involve new technology—just a new theory of what can be done with existing technology. Building the tower "would be a piece of cake," according to Wendel R. Wendel, president of Starnet International Corp., an engineering construction concern in Longwood, Florida. He estimates it could be built in two years or less at a cost of $300 million. Israel, however, plans to first build a $25 million pilot version of the plant to test the theory.[10]

We know that in the last days Israel is going to become the center of attention in the world. We already see that happening politically, religiously and geostrategically. Now, with "Snap," there is strong reason to believe Israel is about to move center stage in the scientific and economic realm.

Israel—Under the Microscope

But, no matter what, Israel is certain to get more than its share of media attention because it is always—quite literally—under a microscope, not only from the press in the United States, but internationally as well.

"Picture a map of the world on which the countries are drawn not according to their actual size, but proportional to the amount of attention they receive in the American press," writes Israeli journalist Ze'ev Chafets. The United States would be, by far, the biggest nation on the map. Russia would be next. And then the third largest nation, according to media scrutiny, would be Israel. "Although it has a population smaller than Los Angeles and occupies an area no larger than Massachusetts, Israel is one of the most prolific news centers in the world. More than 200 full- and part-time resident Western foreign reporters and news personnel are stationed in Jerusalem and Tel Aviv— certainly the highest per-capita concentration of foreign corre- spondents permanently based anywhere. Moreover, they are augmented each year by as many as 2,500 visiting correspon- dents who come to Israel on assignment for brief periods."[11]

Moreover, not only does Israel get far more coverage than any nation of its size in the world, but it also gets much more negative coverage—especially in the all-important western press. The result is that the Israelis always seem to wear the black hats in the media. Thus, they have been universally con- demned even by many former friends in the United States and around the world. As is usually the case, especially with the broadcast media, the problem is not so much what the cameras show as what they fail to show.

What Media Don't Show

For instance, countless hours of television and hundreds of thousands of column inches of newspaper stories have been devoted to the Palestinian uprisings in Israel. But why haven't we seen such coverage of incidents resulting in far more casual- ties in other countries, especially in the Mideast? Here are a few examples of some real atrocities in that region:

- In September 1970, King Hussein's army attacked Palestine Liberation Organization guerrillas based in Jordan, killing at least 4,000.

- In 1977, Egyptian police and troops in one day killed 200 people who were rioting over the availability of food.

- In 1982, Syrian President Hafez Assad crushed a religious uprising in Hama. An estimated 20,000 Syrians—mostly unarmed civilians—were killed in the massacre.

- In 1987, Saudi Arabian security forces in one day killed about 400 Muslim pilgrims in Mecca during a riot provoked by Iranians.
- In 1988, the Iraqi army launched a gas attack on Kurdish civilians, killing about 5,000.

Why the Bias?

While each of these incidents received some news media attention, the coverage of all of them combined has been dwarfed by the scrutiny of the overblown *intifada*. Why the double standard? There are several reasons.

Because Israel is a pro-Western, democratic nation committed to the ideals of free speech and press, there is good access for journalists. Jerusalem, therefore, is covered by far more reporters than any other Middle East city and by more American reporters than any foreign city besides Moscow. And because Israel is a staunch U.S. ally, it is always under the microscope of the American press.

Israel—like other beleaguered pro-Western nations in the world—is the target of a great deal of disinformation and unfair reporting. Largely because it has been a dependable friend and ally to the United States, the Jewish state is another victim of the "blame America first" liberal bias in the media.

As Chafets points out, the Middle East is an enormous region—roughly the size of Europe—and, except for the state of Israel, is covered by only a handful of American journalists. Fewer cover all the Arab nations combined—about 30—than the number of reporters who cover sports for the *New York Daily News*. And of those few reporters actually on the scene, only a tiny minority of them speak Arabic or can even read the local newspapers. [12]

It's a Matter of Access

On top of that problem, add the fact that most of the Arab countries are closed societies that are selective about the reporters they allow in and carefully supervise their visits and access. With the exception of Egypt, most of the Arab world is cloaked in reportorial darkness—both in terms of indigenous press and foreign media.

This kind of distortion and bias has placed Israel center stage in the court of world opinion and helped to make the Jewish state something of a pariah nation. Funny, how that's just what the Bible predicted for Israel in the last days.

Even Napoleon Understood

And throughout the last 2,000 years, people have always seemed to recognize that Israel and the Middle East represented something more significant than a strategically located land mass the size of Europe. Even Napoleon Bonaparte, living in a time when Jerusalem was little more than a dusty old artifact, understood it: "No empire can ever be wrought without the peace of Jerusalem at its center because that is the hinge of history," he said. "But then, no empire can ever be wrought with the peace of Jerusalem at its center because such peace is humanly unattainable. It is an impossible mysterious mistress."

Bonaparte, a student of the Bible, knew what others have known throughout the ages. The prophets had stated clearly that when the nation of Israel was reborn, as it was in 1948, this historic event would mark the beginning of the end. It would signal that the Second Coming of our Lord and Savior was very near.

"Now learn the parable from the fig tree," the Lord Himself tells us in Matthew 24:32-34. "When its branch has already become tender, and puts forth its leaves, you know that summer is near; even so you too, when you see all these things, recognize that He is near, right at the door. Truly I say to you, this generation will not pass away until all these things take place."

Many biblical scholars have pointed to the fact that a generation in the Bible is generally regarded as 40 years. Some people point out that 40 years has already passed since the rebirth of Israel and Jesus has not returned.

Well, folks, we simply don't know for certain how long a

biblical generation is. In addition, we're not certain when that final countdown began. Did it begin in 1948 when Israel was reborn? Or could it have begun in 1967 when Jerusalem, the apple of God's eye, was recaptured and reunified under Jewish control? We simply don't know and that is the way God wants it. The Bible repeatedly warns against date-setting, and even Jesus Himself, when He walked on the Earth in human form, said He did not know the precise hour of His own return. God wants there to be some mystery involved in this process.

Jerusalem, O Jerusalem

My recent study of Daniel 9:24-27 has convinced me that the capture of Jerusalem in 1967 may be a more prophetically significant event than the rebirth of the nation. Think of it. In June of that year, the Jews recaptured Jerusalem and re-established a lasting sovereignty over it for the first time since the Babylonian destruction in the 6th century B.C.

Indeed we have witnessed something extraordinary in Israel in the last 40 years and, in particular, in the last 25. The Jewish state has faced unbelievable odds and risen to the occasion to survive. Israel is still there. And the very existence of Israel is a testament to the truth of the prophets and the fact that God keeps His word.

Why is that true? Because, by all rights, the tiny speck of a nation known as Israel should never have been able to stand up to the onslaught of attacks it has faced over the years from its hostile Arab neighbors. It is, quite simply, a miracle. Everything from the rebirth of the nation, the victory in six days in 1967, the reuniting of Jerusalem, to the way the small nation has withstood diplomatic, military and media pressure for all these years is simply inexplicable in strictly human terms.

How Israelis Live

Just consider a few realities modern Israelis live with every single day:

- The Arab nations now have tremendous military strength. Syria alone is roughly on a strategic par with Israel. Damascus commands 4,500 tanks; Iraq has 6,500; Jordan, 1,000; Saudi Arabia has 1,000, Egypt has 3,300. Israel does not even have one-quarter of this total.

- The Iraqis, following their long war with Iran, now have lots of battle experience. They have learned how to conduct long-range air attacks that involve mid-air refueling. And they have demonstrated their ability to employ chemical weapons against civilian populations.

- Iraq has used its rocket technology to launch a satellite. It now has missiles with a 900-mile range. They have long worked on nuclear capability as well as chemical and biological arms.

- The Syrians have Scud missiles with a range of 275 kilometers, enough to hit any population center in Israel. And Syrian missiles can be equipped with chemical warheads.

- Saudi Arabia has purchased missiles with a range of 2,800 kilometers.

- Israel is faced with new threats from the Iranian-backed guerrillas in Lebanon, who have concentrated their efforts against the Israeli-backed South Lebanon Army. The attacks on this security zone are part of a long-range plan to begin full-scale assaults on Israel's northern border.

- And remember the Gulf War? It wasn't that long ago that Scud missiles were raining down on Israel, which showed the utmost restraint by not responding to the attacks.

Security Jeopardized

And, despite all of these facts, Israel has still agreed to give up more occupied land in the Gaza Strip and Jericho and is discussing turning over more strategic territory in Judea, Samaria and the Golan Heights. This series of developments was enough to make even the most confident warriors scared.

"During the last 40 years, I've been in so many complicated, difficult situations—on the battlefield...and I never lost my self-confidence," explained Israel's gutsy general, Ariel Sharon. "I don't think I've ever been as worried as I'm worried now. What brings me to worry is the combination of events taking place outside Israel and events taking place inside Israel."[13]

Even though God's hand of protection is without a doubt on the nation of Israel, it is understandable that Israeli leaders should be concerned about the future. Not only is Israel a tiny island in a sea of hostility, but there is no question, in reviewing Bible prophecy, that a cataclysmic, apocalyptic war will engulf the Mideast prior to the return of the Messiah. This isn't just a belief of evangelical Christians, mind you. Most Muslims also agree that Jesus will return amid a second advent holocaust. But even many Orthodox Jews get similar readings from their Old Testament prophets.

Jews Look for Messiah

"Indeed, one of the most decisive, divisive and dynamic dialogues taking place in the Jewish world today is whether or not we are living in the era of the 'beginning of the sprouting of the Redemption'—and if so, how that should affect Israel's political policies and national decisions," explains Rabbi Shlomo Riskin, dean of the Ohr Tora institutions. [14]

Since the dawn of the nuclear age, it has been easy to assume that the mass annihilation discussed in Scripture preceding humanity's redemption might be the result of a nuclear exchange.

For instance, Ezekiel predicts that fire will rain on Magog (Russia) after it attacks Israel. Because the Bible talks about mass destruction by fire, the nuclear scenario seems to make sense. But today, we see new weapons of mass destruction under construction and ready for deployment in the Mideast and elsewhere. Germ warfare, biological weapons and chemical warheads are all part of our vocabulary after the Iran-Iraq war and the Persian Gulf conflict. The world is now entering an era of unprecedented nuclear proliferation. Even renegade nations like North Korea, Libya and Iraq may soon have the potential they need to launch World War III.

Israel Backed into a Corner

Is it hard to imagine Israel, faced with such threats, launching a nuclear response? Israel is a very tiny country in a giant land mass known as the Middle East. The Jewish state is less than half the size of San Bernardino County in California. Its Jewish population is about 3.5 million—roughly the size of Iowa. Compare that to the 22 Arab states, armed to the teeth, and virtually all of them in a constant state of war with Israel. Together, they have more than 140 million inhabitants and a land area larger than the United States. That is the reality that Israel faces every day.

On Oct. 6, 1973, the Egyptian army attacked Israel from across the Sinai Desert. On the same day Syria invaded from the Golan Heights. It was Yom Kippur, the Day of Atonement, and the holiest day on the Jewish calendar. To say the Israelis were surprised would be an understatement.

In the early days of the war, there were unprecedented and stunning victories for the Arabs. Israeli casualties were very high. Hardened and confident combat units were so outnumbered and outflanked they were fleeing in disarray. The clash resulted in the loss of 500 tanks and 49 aircraft in the first three days.

The modernized Egyptian forces used missiles and electronic defenses to blast its way to the eastern bank of the Suez Canal. Israeli counterattacks by three tank divisions were repelled. The Syrians used 1,400 tanks to roll through the Israeli defenses on the Golan and moved to the edge of Galilee and Israel's heavily populated valleys. Only a handful of Israeli tanks stood in their way.

Arming the Doomsday Weapon

Israeli Defense Minister Moshe Dayan, for one, thought it was all over: "This is the end of the Third Temple," he said. "The situation is desperate. Everything is lost. We must withdraw." On Monday, Oct. 8, 1973, Israel called its first nuclear alert and began arming its nuclear doomsday weapons.[15]

What Israelis have code-named the *Samson Option* was almost launched. And like Samson of old, Israel would have taken down all their enemies with them in cloud of nuclear dust.

Only some heroic bluffing by an Israeli tank commander and some surprise hesitation by the Syrian forces prevented what could have been a nuclear holocaust in the Middle East. That's a real-life historical scenario worthy of consideration. That's how easy it would be to get involved in a nuclear exchange in the Middle East.

Israel is facing world pressure like never before. Because the Arab world has been successful at framing the debate over the Middle East as a struggle between downtrodden Palestinians and powerful, heavily armed Jews, Israel has moved precipitously close to compromising its own security needs.

Land for Peace

"Land for peace!" is the cry heard 'round the world. In 1993 we saw Israel bullied and blackmailed into turning over more lands to the Arabs—this time to its sworn enemy, the terrorist Yasser Arafat. Objective military and intelligence people say any more land concessions would be strategically foolhardy.

"The absolute minimum territory Israel requires to deter war is the territory it is controlling today," concludes intelligence expert Joseph de Courcy.[16]

Way back in 1967, when the level of military technology and sophistication available to the Arab states was much lower, a Pentagon study found that Israel needed control of the land just east of Jerusalem, the central West Bank of the Jordan River and part of the Sinai including Sharm esh Sheikh. Israel can overcome its frightening security problems and territorial inferiority only by maintaining a strong deterrence factor.

In the late 1970s, Israel agreed to give up the Sinai peninsula to Egypt in exchange only for a peace treaty. Many military and intelligence experts agree that further land concessions would leave Israel with indefensible borders and no effective *conventional* deterrent against attack. The world should take note that if it stands by and lets Israel be overrun, the *Samson Option* is still very much in readiness.

Notice the emphasis on the word *conventional*. Because Israel still has its non-conventional form of deterrent—nuclear weapons. Does the world really want to force Israel to rely exclusively on nuclear weapons for its defense? Tragically, that seems to be where things are headed in the Middle East today.

This Is Peace?

The peace process as it is unfolding between Israel and the Palestinians is an object lesson in Middle Eastern politics. To begin with, we have Arafat, a lifelong terrorist and architect of some of the most brutal terrorist attacks ever perpetrated against the Israeli population. Only two years before, Arafat was playing kissie-face with Saddam Hussien during the Gulf War. Remember, 98 percent of the PLO's funding at the time came from Saudi Arabia and Kuwait—both victims of Saddam's aggression. Why would Arafat bite the hand that feeds him? One reason only. Because Saddam was raining Scud missiles down on Israel. That demonstrates the depth of Arafat's hatred for Israel as of 1991.

By September of 1993, Arafat was Israel's friend, holding out his hand in friendship to Prime Minister Yitzhak Rabin. The world marveled at the prospect of peace at last for the Middle East. Rabin, Shimon Peres and Arafat shared the Nobel Peace prize. Who could have anticipated such an event? So infatuated with the prospect was the world's press, that they 'overlooked' anything that might tend to cast doubt on Arafat's sincerity. Especially Arafat's own words. Some quotes from this great man of peace, Yasser Arafat:

- "Israel shall remain the principal enemy of the Palestinian people, not only now, but in the future"[17]

- "Within five years, we will have six million to seven million Arabs living on the West Bank and in Jerusalem. [This] will cause a mass emigration of Jews. We

Palestinians will take over everything. We will eliminate Israel and establish a purely Palestinian state"[18]

• "I have no use for Jews. They are, and remain, Jews"[19]

• "We now need all the help we can get from you in our battle for a united Palestine under total Arab-Muslim domination."[20]

Note the dates of these various quotes. These are comments made after the famous handshake of peace.

In October, 1995, Prime Minister Yitzhak Rabin was murdered by a Jewish assassin, Yigal Amir. Amir claimed his intention was to derail the peace process. His actions had the opposite effect. Instead, the average Israeli began to link right-wing extremists to anyone who opposed the peace process as it was developing. In the emotional aftermath of Rabin's assassination, his successor, Shimon Peres, enjoyed unprecedented support. Peres and Arafat put together one deal after another, and peace truly seemed possible.

Then came the suicide bombing attacks in Tel Aviv, Jerusalem and Gaza in early 1996. The bombings were orchestrated by Hamas, who, like Yigal Amir, wanted to see the peace process derailed.

War-weary Israelis are finding very little difference between the current state of peace and the previous state of war. According to the *Jerusalem Post*, "the peace process, if not dead, is certainly on life support."

One thing not clearly understood in the West is the actual base of support for the Peres peace plan within Israel. Although 51% of Israeli citizens supported the peace process, that majority included a substantial population of Arab Israeli citizens. Without the nine Knesset seats held by Arab Israeli citizens, the Peres government would lose its majority. In other words, remove them from the equation, and the majority of Israeli Jews are actually opposed to the agreement.

In addition, keep in mind that since 1991, the population of Israel doubled with the influx of emigrants, primarily from the Soviet Union. That further diluted the voice of those Israelis who lived under constant threat of war for five decades. There is still plenty of opposition, and many in government who recognize the strategic importance of the land over which they are bargaining.

Why Israel Needs Territory

In the 1990s, it is more critical than ever that Israel hold on to the strategic lands it captured in 1967. Why?

- As weapons of mass destruction become more widely available in the region, the area needed to wage war expands.

- Topography and control of the high ground has become more important in an age when all sophisticated weapons require the transmission of electromagnetic radiation and guiding sensors and antennae deployed from line-of-sight locations.

- The speed of modern aircraft calls for greater warning space.

- The precision and destruction capabilities of modern weapons systems require the dispersal of military airfields, emergency depots and other military facilities.[21]

Intelligence experts point out that if Israel withdraws to its pre-1967 borders, every military airfield will be covered by enemy radar and be within reach of modern artillery. In addition, Israel's major population and industrial centers would be within range of conventional artillery, not to mention missiles.

The Fire Next Time

If the Arab states, with their superior numbers, deployed a massive attack including tanks, conventional artillery and ground-to-ground missiles, Israel would literally have only one choice—go nuclear.

As de Courcy puts it: "The choice which will face Israel's decision-makers if Israel retreats to indefensible borders is between two options: (a) They can respond to the mobilization of Arab forces by a risky conventional pre-emptive strike and be condemned by the rest of the world as aggressors. (b) They can wait until the Arabs attack and depend on the use of nuclear weapons for survival."[22]

There is no question, in reviewing Bible prophecy, that a cataclysmic, apocalyptic war will engulf the Mideast prior to the return of Jesus Christ. In this nuclear age, it makes sense to us that the mass annihilation we read about might be the result of a nuclear exchange. Because the Bible talks about mass destruction by fire, this scenario seems to make sense.

"And I will send a fire on Magog [Russia]," Ezekiel recorded.

If faced with annihilation you can count on Israel to protect its civilian population by any means necessary. But now that the Arab states are deploying weapons of mass destruction, are we certain they will hold them in reserve? All the evidence we have indicates that Syria and Libya would look for an opportunity to fire them.

Is there anyone who doubts that the Syrians are willing to push the button to launch surface-to-surface missiles carrying chemical warheads into Israeli population centers? The Syrian leadership has shown no compassion for human life and has, in fact, destroyed thousands of its own civilians when faced with rebellion. Given what you now know about the long history of Islamic jealousy and hatred of the Jews, is it difficult to imagine a decision being made in Baghdad or Tebran to fire a nuclear warhead at Tel Aviv?

But when we bring Iran and its rapidly developing nuclear missile capability into the equation, the situation becomes truly apocalyptic. There is no question as to whether they will use them as soon as they get sufficiently prepared.

It's clear that the Bible can't be talking about any other time in history but today. No man knows the day or hour this dramatic climax is going to occur. But there can be little doubt that this is the generation. It could start tomorrow. We are on the brink of some startling prophetic development.

Never before has the world stage been set for the climax of history as it is today. Pray for God's intervention. The "times of the Gentiles" are rapidly drawing to a close.

References

[1] Natan Sharansky, *Jerusalem Post Weekly Edition*, Oct. 2, 1993

[2] Alexander Lesser, *The Jerusalem Report*, Nov. 4, 1993

[3] Ibid.

[4] Yossi Klein Halevi, *The Jerusalem Report*, Sept. 9, 1993

[5] Ibid.

[6] In an interview with John Kinsella, May, 1995

[7] *Wall Street Journal*, June 6, 1993

[8] Ibid.

[9] Ibid.

[10] Ibid.

[11] Ze'ev Chafets, *Double Vision*, William Morrow & Co., New York, 1985, pages 217-218.

[12] Ibid., page 14

[13] Ariel Sharon in a speech in September, 1991

[14] Rabbi Shlomo Riskin, *The Jerusalem Post International Edition*, Jan. 9, 1993

[15] Seymour M. Hersh, *The Samson Option*, Random House, 1991, pages 222-223.

[16] *Intelligence Digest*, July 29, 1992.

[17] In a speech read for Arafat by PLO Justice Minister Freih Abu Middein, Gaza, May, 1995.

[18] From a speech delivered by Arafat in Oslo, Norway, January 31, 1996

[19] Ibid.

[20] Ibid.

[21] Ibid.

[22] Ibid.

Chapter 9

THE RUSH TO REBUILD THE TEMPLE

Behold, I will make Jerusalem a cup of drunkenness to all the surrounding peoples, when they lay siege against Judah and Jerusalem. And it shall happen in that day that I will make Jerusalem a very heavy stone for all peoples; all who would heave it away will surely be cut in pieces, though all nations of the earth are gathered against it.
—ZECHARIAH 12:2-3 (NKJV)

Therefore when you see the abomination of desolation which was spoken of through Daniel the prophet, standing in the holy place (let the reader understand), then let those who are in Judea flee to the mountains; let him who is on the housetop not go down to get the things out that are in his house; and let him who is in the field not turn back to get his cloak.
—MATTHEW 24:15-18

Right now, as you read these words, religious Jews in Jerusalem's Old City are studying ancient priestly rites to prepare for the day that King Solomon's Temple is rebuilt to usher in the coming of the Messiah. Near the site of the Temple, the seminary of Aterat Kohanim (Glory of the Priests) is reviving an extinct class of Jewish priests and their servants known as Levites so they will be ready when the ancient prophecies are fulfilled and the Temple, twice destroyed, is rebuilt.

Jewish law says the Temple must be rebuilt on the site of its ruined predecessors. But the 35-acre Temple Mount is now occupied by two of Islam's holiest shrines—the Dome of the Rock and the Al Aqsa Mosque.

Two religions, Judaism and Islam, thus are on a collision course with global and heavenly repercussions. For Muslims, the Temple Mount represents the third holiest shrine on Earth—the place that the prophet Muhammad last touched before ascending into heaven. To the Jew, there is no place on Earth as holy and central to the essence of Judaism. Of the Torah's 613 commandments catalogued in the Talmud, approximately one-third refer directly to rituals that can only be performed in the Temple rebuilt on its official site.

Today, there seems to be an insurmountable problem regarding the city of Jerusalem. Islam will never accept Jerusalem as the undivided capital of the Jewish state, and Israel will never agree to give it up. This is the intractable, insoluble crisis that will soon result in the climax of world history.

The Most Disputed 35 Acres on the Planet

Even more specifically, within Jerusalem is the area that both faiths so covet—the Temple Mount. But it is also the most sacred real estate in the world to the Jews. This is the spot on which God asked Abraham to sacrifice his son. This is the place where the Lord established His name forever. At the Temple Mount now sits the Dome of the Rock. And where Solomon's porch once stood, there is the Al Aqsa Mosque.

It is this Temple Mount that will serve as the center stage for the final countdown to Armageddon. Right now, as you read this, preparations are being made to rebuild the Third Temple—an act that almost certainly will set off massive protests, gnashing of teeth and lamentations in the Muslim world.

For the last 19 centuries, devout Jews have prayed three times a day for the rebuilding of the Temple: "May it be Thy will that the Temple be speedily rebuilt in our days," they say.

The importance of the Temple Mount site in Jerusalem to two faiths make it the most strategic and potentially explosive piece of real estate on the face of the Earth.

Nobody's Laughing Anymore

Since the 1960s, I have been writing and saying that the single most important key to prophecies yet to be fulfilled involve rebuilding the Temple. Twenty-five years ago, the whole idea of Jews actually rebuilding their holy Temple seemed quaint—even far-fetched. Today, nobody's laughing about the notion. Here are some of the events that have given new hope to religious Jews and caused consternation among Muslims:

- Two Talmudic schools are training nearly 200 descendants of Levi in the demanding details of Temple service.

- 38 intricate vessels required for animal sacrifices in the Temple have already been painstakingly recreated. Only 65 more are needed.

- The uniforms of the high priest and a number of attending priests have been made according to the precise formula of the Torah. Even the flax was spun by hand according to the prescribed design.

- Hundreds of musical instruments of biblical times that are necessary for Temple worship have been built.

- A group from the Temple Institute approved by the Chief Rabbinate scouted through Europe to find pure red heifer cattle so that the requirements for cleansing the priests for Temple service demanded by Numbers 19:1-10 may be fulfilled when the time comes.

Sitting and Waiting

Ateret Kohanim is a mystic offshoot of the Gush Emunim, or Bloc of the Faithful, a grass-roots movement that seeks to reclaim biblical title for all Jewish lands in Israel. It has helped to spearhead Jewish settlement in Judea and Samaria and purchased property from Arabs in Old Jerusalem.

In the early 1980s, some Gush Emunim activists were accused of plotting to blow up Muslim shrines to make way for the rebuilding of the Temple. But Rabbi Shlomo Aviner says that kind of activity was "a mistake that was harmful to the Temple Mount and to our people."[1]

"It is bothersome that the Arabs are defiling the Temple Mount, but we must sit and wait," he adds. "Messianism is a belief in a better world. It won't happen in one day. First we have to build the land of Israel, reach a higher level of morality and justice."[2]

Ateret Kohanim, one of at least three Jewish seminaries in the Old City, teaches students all of the priestly rituals including animal sacrifice, a practice that disappeared from Judaism after the Romans razed the second temple in 70 AD. Today, the seminaries are building altars, weaving priestly robes and manufacturing all the instruments necessary to revive these ancient traditions and rituals.

The Importance of the Rituals

Why is all this so important? The prophet Daniel predicted that three and a half years before the Messiah's coming, sacrifice and offering would be stopped by the treachery of the future Roman Antichrist. (Daniel 9:27). The Lord Jesus confirmed this prophecy and emphasized that there would be an abomination that causes desolation set up in the Holy Place of the Temple (Matthew 24:1-5). That abomination will occur when the infamous Man of Lawlessness—or Antichrist—takes his seat in the Temple of God (II Thessalonians 2:3,4).

Of course, for Temple rites to be stopped in the last days, we know they must be restarted. The words of Jesus Himself in Matthew 24:15 require that a new Holy Place be built and a complete sacrificial system re-instituted. And since only a consecrated Temple can be defiled, this prophecy shows that the physical Temple must not only be rebuilt, but a functioning priesthood must begin practicing once again.

'Renew Our Days'

For years prophetic teachers puzzled over how the Temple could be rebuilt. The first major stumbling block was overcome on June 7, 1967, when the Jewish people recaptured the site of the Temple for the first time in nearly 2,000 years. It didn't take long for speculation to begin about rebuilding the Temple, even in the most secular sources.

"Since the destruction of Jerusalem by the Romans in AD 70, Conservative and Orthodox Jews have beseeched God four times a week to 'renew our days as they once were'—a plea for the restoration of the Temple," wrote *Time* magazine just weeks after the Six Day War. "Although Zionism was largely a secular movement, one of its sources was the prayers of the Jews for a return to Palestine so that they could rebuild a new Temple. Learned Jewish opinion has long debated when and how the Temple can be rebuilt. The great medieval philosopher Maimonides, in his *Code of Jewish Law*, argued that every generation of Jews was obliged to rebuild the Temple if its site was ever retaken, if a leader descended from David could be found, and if the enemies of Judaism were destroyed."[3]

A Look at the Logistics

Nearly all Jews—religious or not—would like to see the Temple rebuilt. But the big question for years after Jerusalem was reunified under Jewish control was how this could be done without destroying the Muslim shrines and potentially setting off a major religious war. It seemed a major stumbling block to seeing this important prophecy fulfilled—so much so that, as I mentioned earlier, some fanatics even sought to blow up the mosques on the Temple Mount.

The problem seemed destined only for a miraculous solution. Even Rabbi Aviner, ever the optimist, told interviewers in the mid-1980s: "That is a problem we leave for God to handle."

Well, God handled it. He provided a solution to the irreconcilable problems. Actually, the solution was there all along—just waiting for man to discover it.

New Information about Site

After years of study, Dr. Asher Kaufman, an eminent Israeli archaeologist and a professor at Hebrew University, has offered convincing evidence that the Temple was not built on the site now covered by the shrine. The most reliable records all indicate that the Temple's centerline ran due west from the center of the Eastern gate of the Temple wall. Using this coordinate, Kaufman discovered the actual northwest cornerstone of the inner court for the Temple of Jesus' day.[4]

Dr. Kaufman's investigations show that the original Temple site appears to have been approximately 330 feet north of the Dome of the Rock. In my book, *A Prophetical Walk Through the Holy Land*, I demonstrate in detail how the Temple can be rebuilt with its inner court wall and still clear the Dome of the Rock by 26 meters. This fits exactly with the cryptic prophecy of Revelation 11:1,2. The Angel who measures the Tribulation Temple is told not to include the outer court with its wall because it was given to the Gentiles until the Messiah Jesus comes.

It Shall Be Rebuilt

I remember my whole body tingling with excitement when I measured the distances on the Temple platform and realized that

God had left out the outer court because it allowed for the Gentile temple to remain alongside the rebuilt Jewish Temple during the Tribulation. Folks, the footsteps of our Lord and Savior, Jesus Christ, can already be heard as He approaches the doors of heaven to return. The Temple is the last sign that needs to fall into place before events irreversibly speed toward the return of Jesus.

And I am more convinced than ever it will be rebuilt—in our lifetimes! Imagine the ramifications. If you have any doubts about the seriousness and magnitude of such an event, just consider a series of incidents that took place in December 1992 between Hindus and Muslims in India. Tens of thousands of frenzied, militant Hindus stormed and destroyed a 16th century Islamic mosque and plunged India into the gravest political crisis since the nation's founding. In the days that followed, rioting by Hindu and Muslim mobs resulted in hundreds of deaths and anarchy throughout much of the nation.[5]

Keep in mind that the Indian mosque in no way compares in spiritual and historical importance to the Islamic shrines in Jerusalem. Yet, the reaction to the assault resulted in hundreds of deaths, rioting, looting and plunder of untold proportions. Rebuilding the adjacent Jewish Temple—even without physically affecting the Islamic shrines—would be perceived as a much more serious assault on the Islamic religion. And rebuild it they will.

The Psychological Issues

Although the Jews now control the entire city of Jerusalem, Israeli authorities have permitted the Muslims to maintain the Temple Mount. Anyone who has visited Jerusalem knows how the Dome of the Rock and the Al Aksa Mosque tower over the Western Wall and the rest of the city, imposing a constant visual and psychological incentive to devout Jews to rebuild the Temple.

The Muslim authorities in Jerusalem have resisted all attempts by Israeli archeologists and scholars to study the site and uncover important artifacts. They view any such inquiry as the precursor to the inevitable reconstruction of the Temple. And they are right.

Interestingly, even though today many Arab leaders call for the internationalization of Jerusalem and insist that all they really want to see is a city open to all three great monotheistic faiths, much damage has been done to Jewish antiquities while under Muslim control. King Hussein of Jordan, who, until 1967, presided over Old Jerusalem, now says the city belongs equally to Christians, Jews and Muslims.

"The holy places of Jerusalem should be moved out of the orbit of the attempts of any to impose sovereignty over them," he said. "That alone belongs to Almighty God. The rights of all should be equally recognized. A dialogue should produce the kind of meeting of the followers of the three monotheistic religions, aimed at forging a peace, which has not been our fortune far too long. The Holy City should be separated from any temporal sovereignty, which I hope will represent the coming together of the Palestinians and Israelis on this question."[6]

A Double Standard

But that's not the way the king wanted things prior to 1967, when many Jewish properties under Jordanian control—both ancient and modern—were destroyed or defaced. In addition, even today Muslim authorities who are permitted to watch over the Temple Mount have participated in covering up and removing ancient remains of archeological and spiritual significance.

"There seems to be a deliberate attempt to destroy any evidence of a past Jewish presence on the Temple Mount," wrote my Christian friends Chuck Missler and Don Stewart, who have thoroughly investigated the prospects for a rebuilt temple. "Asher Kaufman listed 16 different Jewish antiquities that were destroyed by the Waqf in recent years or buried under dirt and concrete."[7]

As the Bible tells us, the dispute over Jerusalem and Israel's borders will never be settled by any peace agreements nor any whiz-bang diplomatic breakthrough. Jerusalem, the Bible says, will be a stumbling block for the entire world. And now you know why. But, nevertheless, Jews can never forget about rebuilding the Temple. Number 20 of the 613 commandments in the Torah calls for the building of a Temple in Jerusalem if one does not exist and orders the maintenance of the Temple if it does exist.[8]

Israel's Spiritual Calling

This is the driving motivation behind an act that will serve as one of the most important fulfillments of Bible prophecy. Remember, rebuilding of the Temple is significant not only because of the potential firestorm it will create between Jews and Muslims in the Middle East and the significance of that conflict spiritually. But the Bible also makes it clear that in the last days the Antichrist will establish his reign in the Temple of Jerusalem. Therefore, the Temple must and will be rebuilt.

Think, for a minute, about all the reasons Israel has for rebuilding the Temple. First, of course, is the fact that religious Jews have been longing for this dream for 19 centuries. From the time of the destruction of the Second Temple, there has really been no spiritual center for the Jews. They have not even been able to perform their religious rites without a Temple. Synagogues are no substitute. They are merely places of prayer and teaching. The priesthood, an integral part of Jewish worship, has been inactive since Jerusalem's fall in 70 AD.

A Bonanza for Tourism

That's the spiritual calling. But there is also the natural human desire so many have to relive the greatness of Israel's earlier history—something we know the Jews will do in the last days. But let's think even more practically. Not only would the Temple become a unifying force for Israel's diverse and pluralistic society, it would also, without doubt, become the greatest tourist attraction in the world.

It's basic economics. Imagine what a new Temple would do

for the Israeli economy, which relies so heavily on tourism. The Temple would also serve to attract more Jews from all over the world—and, as we have already discussed in this book, the Bible tells us that eventually all of the dispersed will return to their homeland. The Temple would serve as a kind of spiritual magnet.

This, too, would fit into the prophetic scenario, which indicates that Israel is destined to play a major role in the world and experience vast wealth, power and prestige in the last days. Why else would the Antichrist choose to set up his throne in Jerusalem unless Israel had moved center stage in the world's political and economic picture. That's just what this future world leader does: *"Who opposes and exalts himself above every so-called god or object of worship, so that he takes his seat in the temple of God, displaying himself as being God,"* we read in II Thessalonians 2:3,4.

Imagine the Firestorm

It is hard to imagine a scenario in which the wealthy and powerful Islamic nations just sit back and watch as Israel rebuilds its Temple in Jerusalem. Perhaps this "man of perdition" uses that throne to establish a false peace between Islam and the Jews. You know, though there is nothing monolithic about Islam, there is one thing that unifies all Muslims—from the most fundamentalist to the most secular. That one thing is a vision of "liberating Jerusalem from the infidels."

"And this, from the point of view of world stability, is the critical point," concludes Joseph de Courcy, editor of *Intelligence Digest.* "If the Arab world achieves some form of nuclear parity with Israel [via the ex-USSR or China], an Islamic coalition will in all probability unite behind one more attempt to regain Jerusalem by force. That is the cliff-edge the world seems destined to face sometime in the middle years of this decade [the 1990s]."[9]

In Luke 21:24, the Bible tells us that "Jerusalem will be trampled under foot by the Gentiles until the times of the

Gentiles be fulfilled." We are literally witnessing the end of the times of the Gentiles. The whole world has its attention riveted on Israel and the struggle for Jerusalem.

I remember saying to myself a little over 13 years ago while writing the book, *The 1980s: Countdown to Armageddon*, that if the Lord doesn't come by the mid 1990s, we'll be able to see the end more clearly from there. And now that we're here, wow, can we see it!

"These are extraordinary times." That's a phrase we hear repeated frequently these days by everyone from presidents to political commentators. Even the most seasoned newsmen who have "seen it all" are in awe of the world developments of the early 1990s. All of them realize that something unique in the history of the world is happening today. And what's most stunning about it all is the breathtaking rapidity of these developments.

We see it in the crumbling of the Eastern Bloc of Europe and the Communist Empire. We see it in the disintegrating Soviet Union economy. We see it in the failing eco-system of planet Earth. Even though we see it all so clearly, it's still difficult to comprehend. What does it all mean? How does it all fit together?

The only way to understand the big picture is to look at the various categories of signs that the Bible predicted would come together just before the return of Christ. The key to understanding is in some familiar scriptural passages. Jesus Himself gave us the best insight shortly before his execution on the cross.

How Jesus Explained It

In Matthew 24:3, the disciples are described as coming to Jesus and asking: *"Tell us, when will these things be, and what will be the sign of Your coming, and of the end of the age?"* The question was in the context of Jesus' prophecy that Jerusalem and the Temple would be destroyed prior to His return.

Note that the disciples actually asked three questions:

(1) When will these things be?

(2) What will be the sign of Your coming?

(3) And, what will be the sign of the end of the age?

The disciples didn't realize how complex their questions were. They assumed that the destruction of Jerusalem, the return of the Messiah and the end of the age would all occur about the same time.

But look how carefully and precisely Jesus answered the questions. In Luke 21:24, Jesus addresses only the first question about the destruction of the state of Israel and the ensuing Diaspora.

"And they will fall by the edge of the sword, and will be led captive into all the nations; and Jerusalem will be trampled under foot by the Gentiles until the times of the Gentiles be fulfilled," Luke recorded.

Here we see clearly that the destruction of Jerusalem and the Temple is not connected directly with His Second Coming. This event has already occurred in 70 AD, when the Roman 10th Legion under Titus destroyed the city and Temple. That was the second destruction of the city. The Babylonians destroyed it first. Jerusalem would remain under foot until the times of the Gentiles were fulfilled, Jesus said.

The Times of the Gentiles

Now how would we know when the times of the Gentiles would be fulfilled? We would know when Jerusalem would *begin to be* delivered from under the foot of Gentiles. When did that begin? June 5, 1967.

Let's remember that in 1948, the Jews recaptured a small part of their land. But it wasn't until 1967 in the Six Day War that Jerusalem was retaken. Since then the Jews have maintained sovereign control over the city for the longest period since the Babylonian exile some 2,500 years ago.

As I have restudied the Book of Daniel recently, I have begun to see that the recapture of Jerusalem was much more important than even the taking and re-establishing of the nation of Israel.

The focus of Daniel's prophecy about the last seven years before Christ's return is on Jerusalem. Daniel 9:24 speaks of the allotment of time *"decreed for your people and your holy city."* During this allotted time, all prophecy up to and including the Messiah's coming as it relates to the Israelites and Jerusalem— are to be fulfilled.

Jerusalem is the key to all of the Second Coming prophecy. That's why it was such an important development when the city was taken in 1967. It is also relevant that we see so much turmoil taking place in Israel and the Middle East right now concerning control of the city of Jerusalem.

Only after Jesus answered that first question about the holy city did He address the broader questions about His return and the end of the age. And what He said as it was recorded in Matthew 24 and Luke 21 is the key to understanding the days we are living in today.

Now that most things have been made to facilitate the restoration of Temple worship, the actual building of the Temple cannot be far away. It takes more faith than I've got to say this is all just a coincidence! It's much easier to say it's all fitting exactly into God's predicted endtime scenario.

References

[1] Rabbi Shlotno Aviner, Associated Press report, Nov. 24, 1984

[2] Ibid.

[3] *Time*, June 30, 1967, page 56

[4] *Biblical Archaeology Review*, March-April 1983

[5] *Los Angeles Times*, December 7, 1992, page 1.

[6] King Hussein of Jordan, *New Perspectives Quarterly*, excerpted in the *Los Angeles Times*, Oct. 28, 1993

[7] Don Stewart and Chuck Missler, *The Coming Temple*, Dart Press, 1991, page 137

[8] Ibid, page 104.

[9] *Intelligence Digest*, January 24, 1992.

Chapter 10

THE NEW ISLAMIC THREAT

And he will be a wild donkey of a man,
his hand will be against everyone,
and everyone's hand against him.
—GENESIS 16:12

They have said, 'Come, and let us wipe them out
as a nation, that the name of Israel be
remembered no more.
—PSALM 83:4

I'm going to say something now that is dangerous to say publicly. It's even more dangerous to put in print. But I'm going to say it anyway because it's true—and because someone needs to say it.

The greatest threat to freedom and world peace today—is Islamic fundamentalism. Whether we in the West care to admit it or not, we are already at war. The media, our diplomatic and political establishment and even our military planners have been tardy in recognizing the danger. In fact, tragically, the world's sole remaining superpower—the United States—has responded to this monumental threat by embarking on a suicidal, unilateral demilitarization process of unprecedented speed and recklessness. Like the Scriptures warn, the West is blithely saying "Peace and safety" and talking about "peace dividends." Yet the free world today is facing danger greater than anything since World War II.

Here's how the reliable *Intelligence Digest* assessed the situation: "Over the rest of this decade, the divide between radical Islam and the industrial democracies will become the most destabilizing factor in world affairs." [1]

Successor to Communism

Still ignored by most so-called experts and the media, the rise of Islamic fundamentalism threatens most Middle East regimes, sponsors uprisings in many other nations and is spreading rapidly throughout the world. While many in the West are still congratulating themselves on the defeat of Communism in the Soviet Union and its satellites, there is a quiet new menace growing stronger every day—a force more explosive and dangerous than totalitarianism of the right or left. In fact, Islamic fundamentalism is actually billing itself as the successor to Marxism as the main agent of change in the world and the No. 1 challenge to the Judeo-Christian world order.

And what is its "Grand Design?" Iranian President Akbar Hashemi Rafsanjani says the movement's goal is to unite all of the Islamic nations under the leadership of a coalition led by Iran and Syria. The first effort will focus on driving the West out of the Middle East and "liberating Palestine." The second goal of this unholy alliance is to replace the Judeo-Christian world order with an Islamic world order.[2]

Now, maybe you're sitting there puzzled over just how religious zealotry in a far-off land could threaten you. Perhaps you are wondering just how fundamentalist Islam could really replace Communism as the greatest danger to world order and peace. Please stay with me. First, let me demonstrate that these folks have the motives to fill this role. Then we'll talk about whether they have the means.

Means, Motive and Opportunity

In a meeting presided over by Rafsanjani, the Iranian leader told Arab political and religious leaders that Islam has replaced Marxism as the No. 1 ideology and power in the world to destroy Western civilization. Here's how he put it: "Our plan is to overthrow all Western influence in the Middle East and then overthrow the Judeo-Christian world order," he said.[3]

Because of this radical agenda, a few keen military and intelligence observers believe the Islamic threat is the most important security issue for Israel and the West. Here's the way one Israeli general explained it to me: "Stopping the Iranian-Syrian axis and their lead over the Islamic world is the most important issue of this decade. It is even more important than it was in 1939 to stop Adolph Hitler. And remember I'm a Jew saying this."[4]

The first strategic objective of the Damascus-Tehran alliance is to unite all of the Islamic countries of the world—from Indonesia, Malasia and Bangladesh to Pakistan, Afghanistan and Turkey to the six former Soviet Islamic republics to Saudi Arabia, Egypt and Libya to all of the nations of Africa. Islamic fundamentalism will lead all of them into holy war, or jihad. Iran will be the great spiritual leader and Syria, the main military power.

Islam's Grand Design

But Islamic unity and control of Middle East oil fields is only the first stop in Iran's plans for conquest. The real prize is Jerusalem. In 1992, Iran's spiritual leader, Ayatollah Ali Khamenei, met leaders of Lebanon's terrorist party Hezbollah and endorsed its jihad against the Jewish state. Khamenei congratulated Hezbollah on its recent terrorist and electoral victories in Lebanon and "stressed the need to combine jihad with political activities."[5]

Iran has made little secret of its support for international terrorism. Groups like Lebanon's Hezbollah and Hamas, the Islamic fundamentalist Palestinian Liberation Organization rival, have been completely underwritten and directed from Tehran. Such groups—like the one that directed the deadly truck-bombing of the U.S. Marine barracks a few years ago — have demonstrated that their first and foremost concern is not the here and now but the hereafter. Muslim terrorists have been deluded into believing that if they die in the service of Allah they will immediately go to heaven and have eternal life. Therefore, Islamic fundamentalism draws on a vast potential army of fanatics who are more than willing to give their lives for the cause.

Faulty Assumptions

Imagine what that kind of zealotry could mean in the nuclear age—in the time when weapons of mass destruction can easily fit into a suitcase. It is this easy acquisition of nuclear, chemical and biological warheads in the post-Soviet world that more than any other factor makes Islam the greatest threat to peace the world has ever known.

The recent "peace" agreements between Israel and the Palestine Liberation Organization were founded on the faulty assumption that the primary cause of conflict in the Middle East is the dispute between Palestinians and Jews in Israel. Conventional wisdom presupposes that if Israel would only withdraw to its pre-1967 borders, the Arabs would be satisfied and peace could be achieved through compromise. While this kind of thinking has pervaded Washington for years, only recently has it also begun to infect the highest levels of government in Israel as well.

This view is wrong and I will prove it to you. Wars have been raging in the Middle East since the beginning of time. The worst of them—Iran-Iraq, the Persian Gulf War, Afghanistan, etc.—have had nothing to do with Israel. And, if indeed the Arabs' main concern was achieving a Palestinian state and returning Israel to its pre-1967 borders, why did they attack the Jewish state three times before that? If the Arabs were seriously committed to the idea of a Palestinian state on the West Bank, why didn't they institute one when that land was under their control?

Unfortunately, the mood around the world—and even the current political climate in Israel—seems to be in favor of these so-called "land for peace" swaps. What this will mean, however, is that Israel may be forced into a position in which its borders are indefensible in conventional warfare. If attacked in a concerted way by several aggressors, Israel may well be forced to "go nuclear" to defend itself against annihilation, as I mentioned previously.

Indefensible Borders

"Most Israeli strategists are convinced that a return to pre-1967 borders would make Israel indefensible by conventional means," says de Courcy. "They contend that without control over the Golan Heights, the air space over the West Bank, the passes up to the West Bank watershed, and the Jordan Valley, Israel would be forced, in a period of extreme tension, to defend itself through a pre-emptive nuclear strike. This may sound like special pleading, but it is irrefutable that the risk of a nuclear exchange is heightened not diminished if Israel's borders become less defensible by conventional means."[6]

What Islam Is Up To

The Middle East is a powder keg, all right. But it's not because of Israeli policies. Islam, with its grand and global ambitions—not Israel—is the culprit. Here are just some of the recent critical developments in the Islamic world:

- Iranian crews are being trained by Russia in the Baltic to command the Islamic republic's new submarine fleet. With the acquisition, Iran will be the region's only serious naval threat in the Persian Gulf.[7]

- Christians have increasingly become subject to attack in Islamic nations. Similar atrocities are on the increase in Pakistan, Egypt, Indonesia and throughout the Islamic world.[8]

- The Saudis purchased the second most important English-language news agency in the world—United Press International—and made no bones about the fact that they would like to influence news coverage in the West.[9]

- Iraq's Saddam Hussein is still in power—and, according to some reports, growing stronger than ever. The Iraqi ruler is blithely ignoring one of the key elements of the cease-fire imposed on him after the Persian Gulf War. [10]

- Muslim zealots are gaining power around the globe. From the Persian Gulf to Morocco, Islamic die-hards are using any means necessary—from ballots to bullets—to take over nations. Lebanon, Algeria, Egypt, Jordan, Tunisia, Sudan—and even in Israel-Islamic fundamentalists are clamoring for power.[11]

- Five former Soviet republics have formed an economic

bloc with Iran. The vastly expanded regional grouping will cover 5,040,700 square km (1,886,345 square miles) and include about 300 million people. [12]

The Islamic Bomb

On top of those awesome developments, more and more Islamic states now possess weapons of mass destruction. Syria, Egypt, Iraq and Libya are all producing chemical and biological warheads.

The April, 1996 issue of *Time* reported that Libya's Muammar Gaddafi is developing another nerve gas plant near the town of Tarhunah. His new plant, according to the CIA, is built into the side of a mountain, hidden from the prying eyes of spy satellites and protected from American bombers. Using computer models based on what information is available, the CIA concluded the plant is several thousand square feet in size and three stories high. CIA Director John Deutch called it the "world's largest underground chemical weapons plant."[13]

The entrance is wide enough to accommodate two tractor trailers, but, less than 100 feet inside, the lanes split around a giant rock wall. Even a smart bomb could not navigate itself through the tunnel to destroy any equipment inside. Moreover, the Pentagon, having studied the Tarhunah layout, determined a commando raid would be a suicide mission. This is how *Time* sums up the situation: "The White House now believes the factory could be operating by the end of the decade." "You never stop anything like this," a U.S. intelligence source says. "You only slow it down and buy time." When time runs out, as the CIA harriers fear it will, an unstable international outlaw will have the means for limitless manufacture of weapons of mass destruction." [14]

You have only to see a movie like *Executive Decision* to get some idea of what a Muslim fanatic like Khaddafy could do with the lethal nerve gas he is intent on producing.

But as potentially destructive as those weapons are, they are viewed in Iran and elsewhere in the Middle East as "poor men's nuclear weapons." The emphasis in more than half a dozen Islamic nations is on buying a nuclear capability.

Russian President Boris Yeltsin confided in President Bush in 1993 that "certain Islamic states" did indeed try to buy tactical nuclear weapons from the former Soviet republic of Kazakhstan. Russia, at the same time, is being linked closer to this emerging new Islamic world than ever before. Iran, the leader of the new Islamic world order, is looking forward to a time when the Islamic world can draw Russia into an alliance against Israel—or, as the Bible describes it, places "the hook in the jaw of Magog" (Ezekiel 38:1-8).

The Prophetic Connection

The rise of Islamic fundamentalism and the threat it poses to the whole world, and especially Israel, reinforces the idea that we are seeing the scene set for the fulfillment of Ezekiel's prophecies about a future invasion of the Middle East by a coalition of Russian and Arab forces.

But am I overstating the case against Islam? Is it really big enough and powerful enough to threaten not only Israel but the entire free world?

Let's take a closer look: Islam is the fastest-growing religion in the world. A survey of the largest religions in the world showed Roman Catholicism first with 622 million followers, Islam second with 555 million, Hinduism third with 462 million and Protestantism fourth with 370 million. Today, Islam has catapulted into first place with more than 1 billion adherents! [15]

Of the world's 5.2 billion people, 20 percent are Muslims. Though Islam is Arab in origin, only one-fifth of the world's Muslims live in Arab countries. There are 400 million in Pakistan, Bangladesh and India. Iran and Turkey have about 110 million. Africa, too, has large populations of Muslims. According to demographic estimates, by the year 2025—if the Lord hasn't returned yet and straightened things out—there will be 8.3 billion people in the world and one-quarter of them will be Muslims.

The Power of Islam

But to appreciate the growing power and influence of Islam, you must look beyond the population figures. Muslims now control, to some extent, about 50 of the world's most important countries—from Indonesia in the East, through the oil-rich states of the Middle East, to Senegal on the Atlantic.

A total of 70 of the world's 184 countries are considered part of the Dar al Islam, or house of Islam. It is a religion practiced in the jungles of Africa, the sands of the Sahara, the oil fields of the Middle East, the mountains of Asia and the islands of the Pacific. Islam is also making its impact felt in traditionally Christian parts of the world. In England there are now more Muslims than Methodists. There are even more Muslims than there are evangelical Christians.[16]

"Funded by the vast resources of Arab oil money, the Muslims are buying abandoned Anglican churches and turning them into mosques at such a rate that some Muslims claim that England will soon be the first Muslim European country," says author Robert Morey. About 10 years ago there were an estimated 150 mosques in England, today there are more than 1,100.[17]

Islam is also growing rapidly in Australia, Canada, Germany and the United States. There are now more than 500 Islamic centers in the U.S. and more Muslims than Episcopalians or Presbyterians, and, by the year 2000, Islam may well surpass Judaism as America's largest minority religion.

Israel's Internal Threat

But maybe the biggest surprise of all is the rapid growth of Islam within the borders of the state of Israel. The faith is uniting Arabs in Judea, Samaria and Gaza in a way that simple politics—like the kind practiced by Palestine Liberation Organization leader Yasser Arafat—never could. This makes it much less likely that any accommodation involving an autonomous "Palestinian" state could ever be worked out.

About 1.9 million Arabs live within the borders of Israel.

About 92 percent of them are Sunni Muslims, while the other 8 percent are Christian.[18] But that Christian minority is shrinking all the time—victims of harassment and persecution by the Muslim majority.

As distasteful as aspects of Islamic life are, the religion is fulfilling a deep spiritual hunger among the people of the Arab world in much the same way that Christianity is advancing in other parts of the world. There is a growing recognition in modern Arab states like Egypt, which have experimented with socialism and secularism, that man does not live by bread alone. There is a spiritual yearning, and materialism—even the kind of vast wealth brought about by the largest oil reserves in the world—cannot answer that need. Though Islam is not a true path to God, it does offer an alternative to the world's reigning deity of moral relativism.

But more than at any time since the Crusades, Islam is posing a serious threat to the Western world. It now possesses the wealth and the weaponry to supplant the old Soviet Union as the greatest challenge to the United States, Israel and the Judeo-Christian ethic. And unlike Communism, which lasted only 70 years, Islam has a long imperial history.

A Little History Lesson

Islam tried to overrun Europe in the eighth century, but was repelled by Charles the Hammer and the Franks at the Battle of Tours. In the 12th, 13th and 14th centuries, Christianity and Islam clashed again in the Crusades, and the Muslims renewed the attacks in the 15th and 16th centuries as the Ottoman Turks took Constantinople, invaded Italy and besieged Vienna. Europe's imperialism in Africa and Asia put a halt to Muslim expansionism in the 19th and 20th centuries.

But it was not until Islam developed untold wealth through oil, that its military might has been revived. The only thing standing in the way of the Muslim nations achieving some degree of parity with the West is their tendency to fight among themselves. But, as we have seen in earlier chapters, there is one cause that has the potential to rally them together—hatred of the Jewish state.

And in recent years Israel's qualitative military superiority over the Arabs has significantly declined. The Arab states have managed to buy some of the most sophisticated weaponry in the world. Keep in mind, in Israel's last all-out war with a combined Arab force, it took—depending on your point of view—either luck or Divine Intervention for Israel to fight and win. Even so, there were two nuclear alerts called during the 1973 Yom Kippur War.

The Arab Arsenal

Take a moment to appreciate the potential of the massive Arab arsenal:

- It is now almost certain that Iran has purchased several nuclear warheads. Tehran and other Islamic powers will almost certainly have the capability to produce their own nuclear weapons within a few short years.

- Together, Syria, Iraq, Jordan, Saudi Arabia and Egypt have more than 16,000 tanks. Israel, by comparison, has fewer than one-quarter that number.[19]

- Syria's immediate military aim is to achieve strategic parity with Israel. To that end it has spent more than $19 billion in recent years on the most advanced fighters, missiles, air defense and chemical weapons.[20]

- Syria, Iraq and Saudi Arabia are now all equipped with missiles that can hit targets at ranges of between 275 and 2,800 kilometers. Many of these weapons are equipped with chemical warheads and can be fitted with nuclear warheads when they become available.

- A $1 billion contract has been signed between Tehran and the Russian Federation. It will provide the Iranian armed forces with 400 T-72 tanks. The Russians are providing training as well. Moscow has also contracted to supply Iran with 500 BMP-2 armored fighting vehicles, each equipped with anti-armor laser-guided missiles. Last year, Iran spent $5 billion with China, $4 billion with Russia and $3 billion

with North Korea for the best weapons money can buy.
• Since 1973, the Arab states have imported more than $170
  billion worth of modern weapons. The Arab states at war
  with Israel have spent a total of $450 billion on their mili-
  taries since that time—about $30 billion annually compared
  to Israel's defense budget of $5.7 billion. Iran alone spends
  more annually than Israel.[21]

Plenty of Money to Burn

How can the Islamic world continue to spend such exorbi-
tant sums of money on armaments? Simple. The Muslim nations
have an almost limitless source of cash—the oil-producing
nations of Saudi Arabia and Iran.

Iran is back in the oil business in a big way, after its long
slump following the overthrow of the Shah and its decade-long
war with Iraq. After that war, southern Iran had eight rigs pump-
ing oil. Today there are 50. The country is now producing 4 million barrels a day, making it the fourth-largest producer in the
world. In 1992 alone, Iran took in $20 billion in oil revenues.[22]

As if Iran and Syria and the other hostile Islamic nations of
the Middle East didn't have enough financial resources individually to accomplish their ends, there is growing evidence of
strategic economic alliances between key Muslim nations. One
such bloc involves Iran and the former Soviet republics. Five
former Soviet republics and Afghanistan have now joined the
Economic Cooperation Organization (ECO) of Iran, Pakistan
and Turkey, creating what Pakistani officials say will a formidable economic bloc.

"The ECO had been inching along at a snail's pace for
years, but now it will be forced to develop very quickly,"
Minister of State for Economic Affairs Sardar Asif Abmad Ali
said in an interview.[23]

Unholy Alliances Shaping Up

Five Central Asian republics—Turkmenistan, Kyrgyzstan,
Tajikistan, Uzbekistan and Azerbaijan—as well as Afghanistan

all joined in late 1992. Oil-rich Kazakhstan, the largest of the Central Asian states stretching from China as far west as the Urals, has opted for observer status while it tries to gain entry to the European Community, Ali said. The vastly expanded regional grouping will cover 372 million square miles and include about 300 million people.[24]

"No other religion poses such a challenge to the West at this time," says G.H. Jansen, an expert on Islam. "Islam has confronted the West militarily for 1,300 years. Now, in addition to the military confrontation of the past, an economic confrontation has been added."[25]

The goal of Islam from the days of Muhammad has been to unite all followers in a common brotherhood for the purpose of waging jihad, or holy war, on the Judeo-Christian and nonbelieving world. In Muhammad's original revelations, the Arabic word for jihad meant basically a "struggle" for the cause of Islam. It was then expanded to embrace self-defense. And very quickly took on a different, more aggressive denotation—offensive, military action.

Looking Long-term

Islam is a philosophy that looks and thinks long term. It is a world view that encourages taking two steps forward and one step back, if eventual goals are more likely to be achieved. Westerners think in terms of today or tomorrow. Islamic leaders are thinking about the future 10 years, 20 years, 100 years from now.

That's why it was a pity that Israel chose to recognize, negotiate and compromise with sworn enemy and terrorist Yasser Arafat in an effort to defuse its more serious problems with the rising tide of Islamic fundamentalism. It was a risky tactic—one fraught with danger not only for the Jewish state but for the entire world. The stage is now set for the kind of explosive developments students of Bible prophecy have long anticipated.

What the Israelis have actually done by establishing autonomous Arab states in Jericho and Gaza is to create the kind of bridgehead in Israel Arafat has, until now, only dreamed about. The record of Arafat and the PLO is stained with the blood of innocent Jews, Arabs, women, children and anyone else who got in the way—schoolchildren in Avivim, Ma'alot and Antwerp, Jewish athletes in Munich, synagogue worshipers in Istanbul, a child and his pregnant mother in Alfeh Menashe and a mother and her children in Jericho.

How Soon They Forget

Arafat was the man who ordered innocent Arab brothers in Nablus hanged by their chins on butcher hooks until they were dead, he says. He was the man who ordered the bellies of pregnant Arab women split open while their husbands looked on; he was the man who ordered the hands of Arab children cut off while their parents watched in horror. Remember, the PLO was created in 1964 with one objective in mind—destroying the Jewish state.

So why did Arafat change his tune and resort to peace talks? Arafat chose negotiations as his latest tactic because he was on the ropes—deprived of funding from the oil-producing states, losing popular support to the Muslim extremists and undercut on the world stage by the end of the Cold War.

But the big problem with the agreement between Yitzhak Rabin and Arafat is that it won't achieve its desired results. Clearly this was a treaty based on the realization that both the PLO and Israel now face a common enemy—radical Islam. The problem is, Arafat and the PLO are powerless against this new threat.

Not only is the PLO now a toothless tiger—deprived of its power by the surging popularity of Islamic fundamentalism—the organization also makes no bones about its ultimate goals in "Palestine." The new slogan is "Gaza and Jericho First." And that is not difficult to understand. These territories, under Arab control, represent a mere foothold that will be extended later through whatever means are necessary—violence or diplomacy. The final objective is still the same—the end of the Jewish state and the beginning of a new Arab one.

The suicide bombings in early 1996 by radical members of Hamas demonstrate just how little influence Arafat retains over the radical elements within the Palestinian people. Forced by the court of world opinion to crack down on Hamas, Arafat has ordered the arrest and detention of hundreds of Muslim radicals. Despite Arafat's private assurances that the peace deal is just a tactic paving the way for the eventual Muslim takeover of all Israel, Hamas and other radical elements just don't care to go along with the program.

The Strategic Bridgehead

So, instead of dividing and conquering two enemies, Israel is still facing two implacable foes—one dedicated to wiping Israel off the face of the earth immediately and the other over time. The only difference is that those enemies now have a strategic bridgehead in the Jewish state.

Now let's take a look at how Israel's sworn enemies are using their oil resources, military might and strategic positioning to lure Russia into a coalition that will result in the worst holocaust in human history.

References

[1] *Intelligence Digest*, January 24, 1992

[2] Primary intelligence sources

[3] Ibid.

[4] Ibid.

[5] Tehran Radio report monitored by Middle East News Service, 1992

[6] *Intelligence Digest*, June 3, 1992

[7] Reuters, May 18, 1992

[8] Reuters, May 14, 1992

[9] *San Francisco Chronicle*, June 26, 1992

[10] *The Washington Post*, July 20, 1992

[11] The Associated Press, Aug. 31, 1992

[12] Reuters, Nov. 27, 1992

[13] *Time*, April 1, 1996: "Target Gaddafi, Again"

[14] *Time*, April 1, 1996: "Target Gaddafi, Again"

[15] *Los Angeles Times*, "U.S. Struggles to Deal With Global Islamic Resurgence," January 26, 1992, page 1

[16] Robert Morey, *The Islamic Invasion*, Harvest House Publishers, 1992, pages 55-56.

[17] Ibid., page 5.

[18] *Los Angeles Times*, Ibid.

[19] Ariel Sharon, *Wall Street Journal*, February 22, 1989, page A-17.

[20] *Facts and Logic about the Middle East*, report, San Francisco, 1992.

[21] Sharon, Ibid.

[22] *Wall Street Journal*, "Iran's Oil Production Is Soaring," November 25, 1992, page 1.

[23] Reuters, November 27, 1992

[24] Ibid.

[25] Reuters, October 27, 1992

Chapter 11

THE HOOK IN MAGOG'S JAW

Son of man, set your face toward Gog of the land of Magog, the prince of Rosh, Meshech, and Tubal, and prophecy against him, and say, "Thus says the Lord God, Behold, I am against you, O Gog, prince of Rosh, Meshech, and Tubal. And I will turn you about, and put hooks into your jaws, and I will bring you out, and all your army, horses and horsemen, all of them splendidly attired, a great company with buckler and shield, all of them wielding swords; Persia, Ethiopia, and Put with them, all of them with shield and helmet; Gomer with all its troops; Beth-togarmah from the remote parts of the north with all its troops—many peoples with you.
—EZEKIEL 38:2-6

And you will come from your place out of the remote parts of the north [the extreme north], you and many peoples with you... a great assembly and a mighty army; and you will come against my people Israel like a cloud to cover the land. It will come about in the last days that I shall bring you against My land....
—EZEKIEL 38:15-16

It was a shock Western diplomats should never forget. Russian Foreign Minister Andrei V. Kozyrev got up to the podium at a forum of European diplomats in Stockholm and threatened to re-form the old Soviet Union under Moscow-dominated leadership.

Russia, he said, is determined to defend its interests in the entire territory of the former Soviet Union, "using all available means, including military and economic means." Kosyrev accused the West of meddling in the internal affairs of Yugoslavia and called for an end to all sanctions imposed by the U.N. Security Council on Serbia.

The Cold War, it appeared, was back. The U.S. secretary of state said the speech gave him "heart palpitations." The Russian bear had awakened, and the West had a new reason for nightmares.

But, shortly after delivering the speech, the Russian diplomat returned to the podium to explain that he was just kidding. Never mind, he said. It was all a dramatic ploy to bring attention to the fact that progress and reforms in Russia could evaporate in a split second if, once again, power changes hands in Moscow.

Russia Is Wildly Unstable

It was a warning the entire world should heed. In the old days of the Soviet Union, the world watched the Kremlin balcony for personnel and hierarchy changes that could signal new policies and direction. In today's Kremlin, the impending changes are less subtle. There are shouting matches in the Congress of People's Deputies. There are angry demonstrations in the streets. There are even occasional gunfights and artillery battles between government forces and rebels. The Soviet Union is gone. The Cold War is over. But the Bible tells us Russia is going to play a critical role in the final moments of history. And the world stage is clearly being set for that drama.

What Happened to the Soviet Union?

In 1991, we saw the Soviet empire literally implode upon itself. It just fell apart. Some of the old hard-liners tried to take the reins of power and return to an era of despotism and totalitarianism. But they achieved the very opposite of what they set out to do.

The KGB and the army blinked. And when the people saw that, they threw off the shackles of repression and dictatorship. For that we should truly thank God. It was truly the answer to prayer for millions of people. But if you think the world is a safer place because of Communism's collapse in Russia, I've got a bridge I'd like to sell you.

The USSR no longer exists and the Russian Republic alone doesn't represent a threat of total world conquest. Nevertheless, Russia still poses a real danger to the United States, with its modernized nuclear force which took decades to build aimed at our nation like a gun to our head.

Russian Military Capability

You don't hear much about some of the most awesome parts of that arsenal. For instance, where are those 34 Red October-style Typhoon submarines right now as you read this? Any idea? Each one carries 200 nuclear weapons and every warhead is capable of ionizing a major U.S. city. Multiply 200 by 34 and you have some idea of the destructive capacity of those subs. Add to that the Backfire bombers that were built in the late 1980s. They are fast enough to outrun most of our interceptors. And, despite recent disarmament agreements, they still have uch of their inter-continental ballistic missile arsenal. That's just some of what Moscow has under its control.

But what about those Soviet nuclear weapons outside of Russia? Keep in mind that just one of the Islamic former Soviet republics, Kazakhstan, has within its borders enough missiles to be the fifth leading nuclear power in the world. The other Muslim republics all have nuclear weapons as well and represent a real threat to world security. All of these nations are building bridges to the radical, fundamentalist Islamic world—led by Iran.

Two factors make sales of missiles and nuclear technology by these former Soviet Islamic republics to their Muslim brothers almost a certainty: (1) their need for hard currency and (2) the subliminal influence of their Islamic religious faith.

The Russian-Islamic Alliance

Russia, too, is being linked more closely than ever before to this Islamic world. Why do you suppose Iran decided not to recognize any of the former Soviet republics as independent Islamic states, preferring to link them with Russia and the Commonwealth of Independent States? Iran is looking down the road. Individually those states would have little political influence over Moscow. But together they have great sway over Russia.

Iran is looking forward to a time when the Islamic world can draw Russia, along with its Muslim satellite nations, into an alliance against Israel. Does that sound like a scenario you have heard before? Does Ezekiel 38 come to mind? In addition, because of its topsy-turvy, uncertain internal political climate, Russia is more unstable than ever. Who knows who will be ruling this nation a year from now—or even next week for that matter?

The Soviet Union may be gone, but Russia—despite dramatic moves toward democracy and freedom—is, in this increasingly volatile world, more dangerous than ever. We must never forget that Russia and its former Republics represent a paradox of history. They have a third-world domestic economy and standard of living linked to a world class military-industrial complex. The one thing they have to sell to a dangerous and lucrative Mideast market is the best weapons of mass destruction that money can buy.

This is the kind of environment—combined with the remnants of this colossal military infrastructure—that breeds military take-overs.

Sizing Up the Threat

Yes, the Evil Empire may be gone, but Russia's role in the endtimes scenario remains the same. The mainstream media may not be tracking developments in Russia with much scrutiny and depth or giving them the attention they deserve, but, behind the scenes, there are momentous and profound events taking place in Moscow. The great bear may not look as dangerous as it once did, but looks can be deceiving.

But, Hal, you might ask, weren't you surprised by the crumbling of the Soviet Union? Isn't that an event that runs counter to Bible prophecy? Hasn't the Soviet Union's power been somewhat diminished?

Let me answer that this way. I am not a prophet. I have never claimed to be. In fact, over and over again I have tried to explain that I am simply a student of the Bible. What I know about the future is limited to what I can glean from the pages of a book whose predictions have proven to be 100 percent accurate. So, of course, I could never have imagined the precise scenario that led to the end of the Soviet Union. However, let me ask you to consider the following. Read the next few paragraphs about the decline of a nation and decide if this word picture looks familiar.

An Historical Parallel

"General prosperity hid signs of trouble. Governing the society was a costly business, especially paying military expenses. When the wars ended, the government no longer had money to pay expenses so it raised taxes. Leaders tried to limit costs by reducing the size of the military budget. But such cutbacks merely weakened defenses.

"The economy suffered because more goods were imported than exported. Money, especially gold, flowed out to pay for imported luxuries. To increase the supply of money at home, leaders issued new coins, mixing lead with the gold. The addition of lead devalued the coins because their value had been based on gold content.

"Since the devalued coins were worth less than older coins, merchants demanded more new coins for the same product— that's, they raised prices. Higher prices, in turn, meant that more money was needed. An increase in the money supply followed by an increase in prices created inflation."

Do these troubling signs of an empire in decline ring familiar? As the famous 19th century philosopher Georges Santanyana observed; "Those who fail to learn from the past are doomed to repeat it."

All Human Systems Temporal

The fact of the matter is that this scenario was not written about either the United States or the Soviet Union—though it certainly could have been. It is actually excerpted from a high school textbook in a section describing the beginning of the end of the Roman Empire. [1]

The most important lesson we can learn from the dramatic decline and fall of the Soviet empire is that all human political systems are temporal. No matter how wisely they are crafted, no matter how much terror might be employed to keep them together—all man-made governments will eventually crumble under their own weight.

And as any high school history textbook can illustrate for us, there are familiar signs that we can look for when analyzing the health of any empire. Sometimes, though, even the experts are fooled. Such was the case with the rapid fall of the Soviet Union.

"Never before has the end come so quickly," wrote one

observer. "It began as the Russian Empire of the czars, who centuries ago proclaimed Muscovy as history's 'Third Rome.' It later became the Soviet Empire, heralded by Lenin and Stalin as the logical extension of history's vanguard. On Christmas Day, it simply ceased to exist."[2]

No one, but no one, could have predicted just how quickly the Soviet empire would fall.

"Historically, empires tend to linger for decades, sometimes centuries, past their prime," said a historian. "Consider the Romans, who were expelled from their capital by barbarian invaders in the year 410. But the lights were not put out in the Western Empires provisional capital of Ravenna until 476, with the capitulation of Romulus Augustulus, the absurdly named last emperor. And the Eastern Empire held on until 1453, when another barbarian onslaught broke down the walls of Constantinople and obliterated the 'Second Rome.'"[3]

The Decline and Fall

While history has seen more than a few empires come and go, no one can recall one as relatively powerful as the Soviet empire falling so quickly and virtually nonviolently. Literally, it seemed, the Soviet Union was the dominant military power on earth one day, and the next it had self-destructed. But despite the rush of events, what happened in the Soviet Union is indicative of a pattern of expansionism, stagnation and decline that has affected every empire throughout history.

The end usually comes, say historians, when an outside force exposes the imperial structure as a facade, corrupted and directionless within and vulnerable to almost any external challenge. The decline and fall of Rome is still the basic model. And, though the decline took many, many years, the end of the Roman Empire came as surprisingly as in the Soviet Union. Often, when empires fall, it seems as if God's hand is directing history.

When Constantine marched on Rome in 312 AD, his forces were badly outnumbered. For six years he had fought many rivals for control of the western part of the empire. Although he was the master of most of that territory, he had not yet fought the ultimate battle for the city of Rome. On the day before the crucial battle, Constantine looked up at the noon sky and saw what he described as a cross of light above the sun with these words: "Conquer by this."[4]

"At this sight, he was struck with amazement, and his whole army also witnessed the miracle," recalled Eusebius, a Christian bishop and friend of Constantine, who later converted to Christianity. "And while he continued to ponder its meaning, night suddenly came on; then in his sleep the Christ appeared to him with the same sign and commanded him to make a likeness of the sign that he had seen in the heavens and to use it as a safeguard against his enemies."[5]

At dawn, Constantine ordered his artisans to shape "a long spear, overlaid with gold" into a cross. Above the cross was a "wreath of gold and precious stones" around the first two letters of Christ's name. Constantine ordered his soldiers to inscribe the same two letters on their shields.[6]

Constantine's army carried the jeweled cross into battle and triumphed. He became the emperor of Rome and proclaimed Christianity to be the state religion of the Roman Empire. But before the city fell that fateful day, there were years of decline and decay beginning late in the Second Century.

Collapsing Under Its Own Weight

"The decline of Rome was the natural and inevitable product of immoderate greatness," wrote Edward Gibbons. "Prosperity ripened the principle of decay; the causes of destruction multiplied with the extent of conquest; and as soon as time or accident had removed the artificial supports, the stupendous fabric yielded to the pressure of its own weight."[7]

Rome lasted longer than any other Western empire, and its pattern of slow decline has been repeated throughout history. The Persian empire founded by Cyrus the Great in the Sixth Century BC dominated Asia Minor and the Middle East for 200 years. The Ottoman empire controlled all Asia Minor and much of northern Greece and eastern Balkans by the 14th Century, reaching the peak of power 200 years later. The Ottoman empire did not really end until after World War I.

The Mystery of the Soviet Fall

Why did the Soviet Union go down so quickly, while these other empires declined over many years? Some say it is the fact that the Communist state relied on a single, rigid, failed doctrine.

"It was an attempt to rule a country under the principles of Marxism-Leninism, and it just was not possible," explains Sino-Sovietologist Gaston Sigur, a George Washington University professor. "It was not an empire in the classical terms, with a dynasty like the Hapsburgs or the Romanoffs giving it legitimacy, accepted by the people. The dictatorship of the proletariat was never accepted by the people." [8]

In any case, the Soviet Union is no more. It has been replaced by the Commonwealth of Independent States. While the new union seems to be stumbling toward democratic reforms, free enterprise and a more open society, it is a very unstable time in a land with little history of freedom and *more intercontinental ballistic missiles than it knows what to do with.*

God vs. Moscow

During the late 1980s and early 1990s, I often wondered aloud many times: What is God going to do to prevent the Soviet Union from conquering the world? It was obvious to me that the Soviets were well on their way to achieving that objective.

Had the Soviets kept on the Gorbachev course, he would have been able to drive the U.S. out of NATO. Western Europe was ripe for this move. Anti-Americanism prevailed, and those states were about to break with the United States. That would have left Europe no match for the Soviet military machine. By using only the threat of military intervention, the Soviets could have achieved hegemony over all of Europe. Gorbachev flat out stated in 1989 that he was seeking the "Finlandization" of Europe.

It was all very close to happening. But it could never have happened. Why? Because it would not have been in line with the prophetic scenario detailed in scripture. Scripture clearly indicates, as I have said many times in recent years, that the Soviet Union could not achieve hegemony over Europe, nor conquer the world. That's not the prophetic scenario we see just before the return of Jesus Christ.

So what is the meaning of the developments in Russia? I believe what we have witnessed in the early 1990s is the result of the direct intervention of God in the hearts and minds of some men in the Kremlin. You can read in Scripture how God would move the hearts of kings to do utterly stupid things. That's just what we have witnessed again in Russia.

God Still Reigns

We have seen a paradigm shift in the centers of world power because God has said: "It is my time to make certain things happen." If there is anything that these events prove it is that God still reigns supreme.

The collapse of the Soviet state was absolutely necessary to the fulfillment of biblical prophecy. The old Soviet Union was on a collision course with world domination. Only the unforeseen internal breakup of the Soviet Union could have prevented that eventuality. But world domination—as Ezekiel makes clear—*was never in the script for Russia!*

Ezekiel 38:8 describes modern-day Israel, after the Jews have returned from many nations and "are living securely." Today, the Jewish population of the former Soviet Union and East Bloc nations has moved to Israel in record numbers. There they believe they are living more securely than ever before—especially following peace agreements with Egypt, the Palestine Liberation Organization and other Arab countries.

In fact, Ezekiel 38 forecasts a period of pseudo-peace for the world. Then God is going to cause the Russian leader—whomever it may be—to make a great tactical error. He is going to side with the Muslims against Israel and attack. As a result, the whole world will be engulfed in the greatest holocaust in history.

There is no question, in reviewing Bible prophecy, that a cataclysmic, apocalyptic war will engulf the Mideast prior to the return of Jesus Christ. In this nuclear age, it makes sense to us that the mass annihilation we read about might well be the result of a nuclear exchange. Because the Bible talks about mass destruction by fire and brimstone (melted earth), this scenario seems to make sense.

"And I will send a fire on Magog [Russia]," Ezekiel recorded.

But how could this be? Isn't Russia moving away from its aggressive and bellicose foreign policy of the past? Isn't the Russian leadership talking about scrapping its nuclear weapons?

The Real Story in Russia

I won't pretend to know all the answers to these questions. But in the interest of truth and accuracy, it's important to know what's really going on in Russia today. Here's something I don't think you will read anywhere else, folks. But it should be on the front page of every newspaper in the United States.

As President Clinton and the European powers offer Russian President Boris Yeltsin a virtual blank check to help revitalize his suffering economy, Moscow continues to spend billions modernizing its strategic nuclear arsenal.

Yes, I know. You've been told that the Russians are scrapping their nuclear weapons and that's why we need to encourage them with foreign aid. Well, let me tell you, Russia's nuclear weapons are as well-positioned to destroy the United States in a first strike as they have ever been. And it is the United States, not Russia, that is unilaterally disarming at a dangerous pace.

Let me be clear about something. I am not suggesting Yeltsin is anything but a true reformer who wants to move

Russia toward market economics and democratic reforms. However, he is one man. He may not even have total control over the military in Russia. And he is literally surrounded by men who more closely resemble the hard—line, Communist totalitarian leaders of the old Soviet Union.

In mid-March,1996, the Russian Duma called the breakup of the Soviet Union an "act of treason." The Communist Party has infiltrated the Russian parliamentary body, while Russia and the rest of the world slept. The Duma voted 250-98 to accept the resolution, which blamed Boris Yeltsin for the breakup.

Stung by the criticism, Yeltsin accelerated his plans for re-unification with some of the former breakaway republics. Russia, Belarus, Kyrgyzstan and Kazakhstan formally entered into what amounts to a re-unification treaty on April 3, 1996. The treaty makes provisions for integrating currency as well as providing for the free movement of goods, services, labor and capital. Russia has made overtures toward the remaining breakaway republics as well. The situation in Russia presents a classic dichotomy. Russians long for a return to the superpower status—and its attending prestige, while hoping to avoid the evils of Communism—apparently by re-inventing Communism from the ground up. As Boris Yeltsin expressed the sentiment; "The person who does not regret the dissolution of the Soviet Union does not have a heart…But the one who wants to reproduce it in full does not have a head."[9]

The Russian effort to rehabilitate Communism fits precisely into the prophetic scenario. Russia's first three converts, Belarus, Kyrgyzstan and Kazakhstan have heavily Muslim populations. They have entered into an alliance precisely in concert with the promises of Scripture for the last days.

Russia's Nuclear Arsenal

The way the nuclear weapons modernization program continues at full speed in Russia should, therefore, give every American, every Israeli and every free citizen of the world reason to be alarmed. With the MIRV (Multiple Independently-targeted Re-entry Vehicle) ICBMs due to be eliminated under the terms of START and START II, Russian modernization efforts are concentrated on single warhead missile systems like the SS-25. Intelligence reports suggest that by the end of this decade the Russians will deploy three new strategic systems, an SS-25 mobile, a silo-based version of the SS-25 and a new missile to replace the SSN-20 on the Typhoon class submarine.

Reports also indicate that the modernized versions of the SS-25 will have larger throw-weights and much greater accuracy. Keep in mind, this modernization and improvement of the Russian nuclear arsenal is being done at the very time that the U.S. has basically halted much of its own strategic modernization program and is proceeding unilaterally in many respects to dismantle the existing strategic systems in advance of entry into force of either START I or START II treaties.

The modernization effort is not a violation of any treaty with the United States. START restricts the size of the strategic forces but not their capabilities. So the Russians are accomplishing more with less.

"The continued deployment of Soviet mobile ICBMs [such as the SS-25] will give the [Russians] a monopoly on a survivable, land- based strategic reserve," says Lawrence Fink, a Soviet and defense analyst writing in *Defense News.* [10]

Why Modernize? Why the Cover-Up?

The modernization effort began long before the Soviet Union collapsed. U.S. intelligence experts have been predicting it would come to a halt for several years, but it continues unabated.

"The SS-25's modernization has been ignored by the media, while aid to Russia has dominated the headlines, as well as the administration's policy," stated *Defense Media Review.* [11]

The West Is Vulnerable

The most disturbing part of this revelation, however, is the fact that the U.S. is leaving itself totally vulnerable to whatever fate dictates for Russia. After spending $32 billion developing a strategic defense, the U.S. program was virtually abandoned by the Clinton administration.

No strategic defense. No modernization effort. Combine that with the massive military cutbacks and you have a prescription for disaster.

In addition, Russia has abandoned its long-time public relations position against launching a nuclear first strike. Russian military officials have hinted that they are concerned about the Russian army's ability to repel a possible Chinese invasion without the use of tactical nuclear weapons. [12]

Other Unconventional Weapons

But it's not just China that Russia has in mind. In fact, according to U.S. defense and strategic—weapons experts, Russia's military continues to conduct large exercises that include mock nuclear attacks on the United States.[13]

Also of prophetic significance is the revelation by a defecting scientist that Russia has developed extremely deadly biological weapons that could produce a "superplague" capable of wiping out tens of thousands of people within a week. [14]

I was among those who warned about the dangers posed by the old Soviet Union for years. Were we right? According to newly discovered documents in East Germany, were we ever! In 1993 we learned that the Soviet Union and East Germany were planning a full-scale invasion of West Germany "so detailed and advanced that the Communists had already made street signs for Western cities, printed cash for their occupation government and built equipment to run eastern trains on western tracks."[15]

The former head of the Soviet nuclear forces recently admitted that they had over 45,000 nuclear warheads in the mid-1980s instead of the 30,000 our best intelligence estimated they had. This proves that I, along with few in the news field, was right in contending that the Soviets were masterfully deceiving the West as to their true nuclear capability. And who's to say that they are not still doing the same thing today? The hundreds of tunnels in the Ural mountains could be hiding a doomsday arsenal of mobile ICBMs.

Don't Trust Disarmers

When Western officers took over Eastern bases after the reunification of Germany in 1990, they found more ammunition for the 160,000-man East German army than the West Germans had for their 500,000-man force. They said the operational planning was far more advanced than anything Western intelligence had ever envisioned.

Could it be that certain forces in Moscow are still preparing for the goals they had established for over 70 years? Wouldn't it be better to be safe than sorry?

The Bible tells us that Russia will play an important military role in the last days. Though all of the talk these days is about Russia disarming, it is clear she is still well-equipped to play out that final endtimes role scripted for her in prophecy.

In Ezekiel 38, the Bible describes the way Russia fulfills that role. Russia seems to be led into this conflagration almost against her will. I believe it will be the strong Islamic influence on Moscow that places those "hooks into the jaws" of Magog.

The Armageddon Coalition

What the Bible is talking about here is an alliance of Arab, African and Islamic nations with the republic of Russia. Today Russia is being linked more and more closely to this emerging new Islamic world order than ever before. Iran, the leader of this Muslim confederation, is looking forward to a time when the Islamic world can draw Russia into an alliance against Israel.

I remember the skepticism I drew in 1970 when I wrote in *The Late Great Planet Earth* that Iran (ancient Persia) would turn against the West and together with Russia would become one of the main powers that starts the world's last war by attacking Israel. At the time, the Shah of Iran was the United States' key ally in the Mideast, and also a friend of Israel. But Ezekiel proved to be right.

Interestingly, even reformist-democrat Yeltsin seems to be yielding to a new foreign policy that places a priority on strong relations with the Islamic world, especially Iran, and the central Asia republics. Back in 1992, Yeltsin made it clear to all those who were listening just what his intentions were when he said: "Now we will move in the East."[16] By this, Yeltsin explained that he meant closer ties with Islamic nations like Iran.

My intelligence sources, who have not been wrong so far about this area, tell me that Russia has already signed an accord with Iran that *will commit them to fight on the side of Islam in the next Islam-Israeli war.*

Turkey has noticed this foreign policy trend and has been alarmed by it.

"Russia is returning to the policies of the czar," charges Vakul Erkul, a Turkish diplomat. "Russia wants to create a belt of semicolonial states along its southern belt."[17] Is Russia putting together the alliance of *"many nations"* that will sweep across the Middle East in the last hours before the return of Jesus Christ?

It's clear that the Bible can't be talking about any other time in history but today. No man knows the day or hour this dramatic climax is going to occur. But there can be little doubt that this is the generation. It could start tomorrow.

References

[1] *World History: Patterns of Civilization*, Prentice Hall, Englewood Cliffs, N.J. 1991, page 115

[2] Oswald Johnston, *Los Angeles Times*, Jan. 3, 1993

[3] Ibid.

[4] *World History*, Ibid., pages 118-119

[5] Ibid.

[6] Ibid.

[7] Ibid.

[8] *Los Angeles Times*, Ibid.

[9] CNN, March 17, 1996

[10] *Defense News*, October 1993

[11] *Defense Media Review*, October 1993

[12] *Sacramento Bee*, Nov. 4, 1993

[13] *Washington Times*, Sept. 14, 1993

[14] *Washington Times*, Jan. 22, 1993

[15] *Human Events*, March 27, 1993

[16] *Intelligence Digest*, July 22, 1992

[17] *Washington Times*, Sept. 25, 1993

Chapter 12

ASIA'S MARCH TO ARMAGEDDON

And the sixth angel poured out his bowl upon the great river, the Euphrates; and its water was dried up, that the way might be prepared for the kings from the east.
—REVELATION 16:12

L ike the Soviet Union, China has an important and terrifying role in the endtimes scenario. And never before has the giant power of the East seemed more prone to assuming its fateful place in premillennial history.

The Book of Revelation predicts that "the Kings of the East" will move across the Euphrates River, the ancient boundary between the Middle East and the Orient, and travel southwest into the war that will rage around Israel. According to prophecy, this Asian army will number "200 million" soldiers (Revelation 9:16). Besides 20th-century China, no other nation in the history of the world could assemble such numbers. Yet the Bible foretold this development 20 centuries ago.

There's only one specific reference to the nations of Asia in the prophetic word. But it is a very important reference—one that shows they will play a momentous role in the final great war. It's found in Revelation 16:12-16. This is a clear reference to the nations of Asia, because in the original Greek, "east" is literally translated as "Kings of the sun rising."

The Ancient Dividing Line

The Euphrates River is significant, too. Ancient historians used that river as the dividing line between Asia Minor—what we call the Middle East—and Asia, or the Far East. Asia, to the people of the Middle East, was this vast unknown world.

Asia has always been something of a mystery to the Western mind. As we look back in history, we find that one of the first great ancient civilizations was China. When my ancestors were still painting themselves blue and worshipping demons in Scotland, the Chinese were already a very advanced civilization.

India and the nations in the subcontinent have also had their great moments in history.

Home of Sophisticated Paganism

But these great civilizations of the East, as vast and as talented as they have been, were always inhibited by false religion. Paganism found its deepest roots in Asia. Even though the Chinese invented gunpowder, rocketry and other great breakthroughs, they still only advanced to a certain level in the modern world. The Japanese remained a separate society until Admiral Perry sailed in and persuaded them to open up for trade. They wanted to be a closed society and still are to a great extent. India has been held back by a religiously imposed caste system and the worshipping of many gods and idols. False religion has been an inhibiting factor for all of these great nations.

In the Book of Acts, the apostle Paul writes about how he tried relentlessly to take the gospel into Asia, but the Holy Spirit wouldn't let him. He was to go first where the Gospel would be received readily—westward. The apostles Thomas and Matthew, however, did go to Asia. Both died as martyrs there. We think Matthew got all the way to China, because there are some ancient translations of the Gospel that have been found. We know that Thomas got to India, and even today there are churches named after him in that Hindu land.

Some received the Gospel, but, relatively speaking, very few. The organized level of false religion in these countries was far beyond what existed anywhere else in the world. There was false religion in the West, but it wasn't as organized and deceptive as Buddhism, Hinduism and Shintoism.

The Sleeping Giant

Nevertheless, the Bible tells us that in the last days, the people of the East will become a great and formidable people. As we look at how things have developed in the 20th century, China has been a real sleeping giant. For centuries it had been in decline. But when Communism took root there in the 1920s, it wiped out the feudal system and the warlords and united the people past the barriers of religion and culture. As brutal as it has been, central control really turned China into a nation again and brought the people into the industrial age. The sleeping giant has awakened.

Recently, the Chinese leaders realized they could never feed 1.2 billion people with a centrally controlled economy. China is, thus, moving against its will toward a market economy. It's really a natural for the Chinese. They may be the most naturally capitalistic people in the world. With this move is coming a real economic powerhouse. The Japanese economists, some of the most astute in the world, have predicted that China will soon become the world's leading financial giant by the year 2025. (I've got news for them: We probably won't get there. The world will most likely be under new management by that time.)

Japan Curries Favor

The Japanese, however, feel so strongly about what's happening in China and believe so much in its potential, that they have even sent their Emperor to Beijing to apologize officially for atrocities committed in World War II. This is unprecedented in Japanese history. But Japan is committed to establish stronger economic ties with China because the Japanese understand what an economic colossus China will become.

China has barely begun to scrap its Communist bureaucracy and apparatus, but already it is experiencing boom times financially. Its economic growth defies statistics. While the western world considers 3 percent annual growth to be good, China's economy has been growing at an annual rate closer to 28 percent. But even that figure is considered conservative because the central government has had trouble keeping up with the private sector's 16 million new private businesses.[1]

Boom Times for Asia

India, with 800 million people, is also moving toward greater free enterprise and free trade. Foreign investment is pouring in, and China and Japan are making strong alliances with it as well. When you connect China and India, you have 40 percent of the world's population right there. And when you link Japan, you connect Asian know-how and Asian capital to go along with Asian interests. Japan has always wanted to develop this kind of Asian trading bloc. Now it's falling together as if some invisible Hand is at work. And I believe that invisible Hand is the providence of God.

Interestingly, my intelligence sources tell me that the Chinese leadership had to promise its military that a large sum of the revenue raised through China's prosperous transition into capitalism will go directly into the military forces. That was one of the compromises that needed to be made to minimize opposition to departing from the Marxist-Leninist path. In fact, they promised that the military will be built up to the point where it is second to none!

India also is making huge investments in its military. India's main concern for the moment is a regional one—Muslim Pakistan. But later, in an alliance with China and Japan, India's forces could well be involved in a World War.

The Deadliest Invasion

The Bible predicts this coalition will have great destructive power. When this 200 million-man army begins to march, Revelation 9 states that it will wipe out a third of the population of the world. Today, of course, China is a major thermo-nuclear power with intercontinental missiles capable of hitting anywhere in the West. China also has intermediate-range nuclear weapons and nuclear submarines. It is a real power with first-class bombers and fighter planes.

India is also a nuclear-capable power with intermediate-range missiles. Pakistan, of course, has nuclear weapons and is moving toward missile capability. It was the first Muslim nuclear power and gets its funding from the oil-rich Islamic nations. North Korea, too, will soon be a nuclear power.

Japan, because of its technical mastery, could probably

become a nuclear power practically overnight if it wanted. And there is every indication that Tokyo is moving in a more militaristic direction after nearly 50 years of resistance.

"The government is trying to create a full-fledged army," warns 71-year-old Takeo Yamauchi, a veteran of the bloody fighting on Saipan in 1944. Japanese "won't have the courage to resist."[2] Rest assured that if Japan begins to militarize and develop nuclear weapons, Taiwan and South Korea would quickly follow suit.

China's Hand in Mideast

Asia is no longer a backward sleeping giant. It is awake. And it is awake at the very moment that the entire prophetic scenario is being fulfilled. Asia, which has until now played a minimal role in the history of the Middle East, has suddenly become an active player.

According to some intelligence sources, Iran already has at least four nuclear warheads, from the former Soviet republic of Kazakhstan. Iran reportedly plans to fit the warheads to Chinese Silkworm missiles. And, yes, China has admitted supplying missiles to several Islamic states. [3]

Meanwhile, the Central Intelligence Agency says that whether or not Iran has been able to *procure* nuclear weapons from other sources, it will be able to *produce* them by the year 2000. According to the CIA report, Iran's Rafsanjani has put together a team of nuclear experts, many of them American-educated, to direct a nuclear program.[4]

Iran is not relying solely on the republics of the former Soviet Union for technical expertise in its quest for weapons of mass destruction. Another key strategic ally for the Islamic world in this regard is China.

In the spring of 1991, Leonard S. Spector of the Carnegie Endowment for International Peace told a congressional subcommittee that China was helping Algeria in the development of a nuclear weapons program.[5]

No Holds Barred on China

"This is a supplier [China] that seems to be operating without restraint and a recipient [Algeria] that seems to be operating as though this was the norm," Spector testified. "[Algeria] is a country that doesn't even have the security problems of, say, Pakistan or Israel. It seems as though a country has entered into a nuclear weapons program rather lightly. It's almost gratuitous."[6]

Intelligence sources say China has already supplied at least some sophisticated nuclear technology to both Iraq and Iran. How sophisticated? According to the best intelligence experts, China *"is supplying nuclear weapons technology and military advice on how to match nuclear weapons to various aerial and missile delivery systems."*[7]

And what does China have to say about these reports? Yes, China admits again, it has provided nuclear technology to Iran and other nations in the Middle East. But it was all intended strictly for "peaceful purposes."[8]

Iran has also purchased a 300-megawatt reactor from China despite U.S. efforts to block the deal, and may be negotiating to buy another. Washington thwarted an earlier attempt to buy a reactor from India. Tehran hopes Russia will honor a 1989 agreement by the former Soviet Union to provide two 450-megawatt nuclear plants despite Moscow's expressed intention to abide by international controls. Years will be needed to build the Chinese reactor, but when completed, it will be the first in Iran capable of producing weapons-grade uranium. Once that is available, experts say, building a bomb is only a step away.

Iran's Best Friend?

"Any country that can run a nuclear reactor is able to make enriched or purified uranium," said Frank Barnaby, a nuclear weapons expert based in London. He said fissionable material could be obtained as little as six months after a reactor becomes operational. The Iranians have acquired military nuclear tech-

nology from China and Pakistan, as well as a vast range of
equipment from the West, despite international controls.[9]

Tehran is building its conventional military forces as rapidly
as it is developing and deploying its nuclear assets. On October
25, 1992, one of three Russian Kilo-class submarines purchased
by Iran sailed through the Suez Canal on its way to the Persian
Gulf. [10]

Further news of Iran's continuing arms buildup comes
almost daily, reports *Intelligence Digest*. There are reports that
North Korea has shipped to Iran one hundred 300 km-range
Scud missiles (half of which may be due to be passed on to
Syria). This shipment is said to be in addition to 250 missiles
already received from Russia, North Korea and China. [11]

By 1997, Iran plans to have acquired some 2,000 missiles,
intelligence sources say. There are also reports of a massive
arms deal imminent between China and Iran that will provide
Tehran with "an enormous quantity of arms" including:

- 38 warplanes that will join the 115 combat craft acquired
  from Iraq during the Persian Gulf War;

- 10 ballistic missile systems, including five Silkworms;

- 50 armored vehicles designed for riot control;

- 400 tanks;

- 400 medium-range 120mm and 122mm artillery pieces;

- A range of light military equipment, including shoulder-
  held armor-piercing missiles, radars and other surveillance
  systems. [12]

China's Possible Motivations

Why would China be so interested in helping the Islamic
world in its struggle against the West? There are two main reasons—one financial and the other ideological.

The most obvious reason for its weapons sales in the Middle
East is China's desperate need for foreign currency. For several
years China has been dumping massive numbers of missiles and

nuclear technology into the powder keg of the Middle East. Saudi Arabia has received between 50 and 60 ballistic missiles from China since 1988, according to intelligence sources. Iran has imported more than 170 Chinese and North Korean missiles and is eager to buy more.

But there is another factor that makes China and Islam natural allies.

Fundamentalism and Totalitarianism

The comparisons between Islamic fundamentalism and totalitarian political mindsets is worthy of some consideration in these days when Communism seems to be winding down in influence. The totalitarian left, losing heroes around the world, seems to be identifying more closely with Islam than ever before.

That's the ideological component of the alliance between the last great bastion of totalitarianism in the world today and the anti-Western Islamic world. China and radical Islam now have one overriding objective, according to a reliable intelligence source: "the diminution of Western economic and cultural hegemony. Neither democracy nor economic development will alter the deep-seated anti-Westernism of China and radical Islam. China will continue to arm the most anti-Western elements in the Islamic world and use them to divert pressure from China."[13]

China has become the leading arms dealer for Iran and much of the rest of the Islamic world since the demise of the Soviet Union. In 1992, Iran spent $5 billion with China, $4 billion with Russia and $3 billion with North Korea for the best weapons money can buy. [14]

The Spiritual War

Now, what does Revelation tell us about this China connection and this Asian march toward Armageddon?

You know, the closer you walk with the Lord, the more you

become aware of the spiritual warfare going on around us.

Behind the scenes in this conflict are angels. They play a vital role in history. In Revelation 9:13-21, the Bible tells us that one angel, apparently one loyal to God, is ordered to release four other fallen angels, or demons, who are bound at the Euphrates River.

These four angels are extremely powerful demons who, at some point, stepped over their authority and were limited to influence on the Eastern side of the Euphrates. For centuries they have been restricted from using their influence on the western side of that great river—God hasn't permitted it.

But at this point in history, Revelation tells us these four demons will be unchained, unshackled and permitted to torment man beyond the Euphrates. And listen to how precise God is about his timetable on all this. Revelation 9:15 says: "And the four angels, who had been prepared for the hour and day and month and year, were released, so that they might kill a third of mankind."

What John Witnessed

Now, how are they killed? Before you read the explanation, understand that this description was written by John after he was actually transported to be a living witness of this endtimes battle, which I believe is coming in this decade or the next. Repeatedly he describes things in the first person: "I saw...I heard..."

Imagine: This is a first century man permitted to witness a 20th or 21st century, high-tech war and asked to describe it to people in the first century. John had to take from phenomena with which he was familiar and try to match it with things of which his world had never even dreamed. That's what we're reading when we read Revelation. No wonder it's hard to understand. But here's what he says about the battle in Revelation 9:17-19.

> And this is how I saw in the vision the horses and those who
> sat on them: the riders had breastplates the color of fire and of

hyacinth and of brimstone; and the heads of the horses are like the heads of lions; and out of their mouths proceed fire and smoke and brimstone. A third of mankind was killed by these three plagues, by the fire and the smoke and the brimstone, which proceeded out of their mouths. For the power of the horses is in their mouths and in their tails; for their tails are like serpents and have heads; and with them they do harm.

Interpreting the Vision

Now, are these real creatures in nature? No. John was trying to illustrate with first century phenomena weapons of a very advanced age. Clearly we are reading about some kind of destructive vehicles. I believe they are firing missiles. When he talks about fire, smoke and brimstone, I think he's talking about nuclear war. It kills a third of the population in very short order, and this destruction does not come from God. It comes from the attacking army.

Why are they attacking? And whom? Let's back up for a moment and look at our world in the 20th century again.

Do you know what caused the great split in the Communist world between the old Soviet Union and China? It occurred because of a rivalry between two power-hungry, egomaniacal, bloodthirsty dictators—Josef Stalin and Mao tse-Tung—each of whom believed he deserved to be sole, undisputed leader of the world communist movement.

Even after both had died, however, the antipathy and distrustfulness between these two giant powers of Asia continues. It continues still, even though the Soviet Union is no longer and both Moscow and Beijing have all but renounced Communism.

China's Ambitious Goals

But now that Russia no longer openly aspires to take over the world and to foment international revolution, the hard-line totalitarians in China are only too eager to fill the void for leadership in the Third World. China is especially interested in seeking closer ties to the Arab world.

When you examine all of the prophetic scriptures that deal with this great endtimes clash, I think it's clear that this great Asian military force enters the Middle East only after Russia and its coalition has swooped in and invaded Israel and her neighbors. It's a tactical decision by the Asian allies. They don't want to be left out. After all, we know how vital Middle East oil is to the industrialized world. At this point, it's about the spoils of war in a world, quite literally, gone mad.

Some have talked about this being the "battle of Armageddon." That's incorrect. This isn't a battle. It's a war. The Bible never talks about a "battle" of Armageddon. There are several huge battles. And the reason Armageddon is at the center of things in this great conflagration is simply because it is the geographical, strategic center of the land bridge between three continents and a vital link for Asia to the oil reserves of the Persian Gulf.

In this second phase of the war, Asia finishes off the Russian coalition forces and marches in to claim its booty. But they, too, have a surprise waiting for them. In the next phase of the battle between the Asian forces and the combined power of what remains of the Antichrist's western armies, the Bible says the blood will stand up to the horse's bridle in a valley 200 miles long. Now, in Israel there is only one valley that long—the Jordan River Valley, which starts north of the Sea of Galilee, comes south down along the Jordanian border to the Gulf of Eilat.

What we're talking about here is simply the greatest holocaust in the history of the world. For the first and last time, man will be totally released from God's restraint to do what has always been in his heart.

Why Don't They Wake Up?

If the kings of the Earth had any sense at all, they would take heed of this message—not because Hal Lindsey says it, but because this is the Word of God. The Earth is headed for utter destruction for failing to believe in God's Son and because its leaders are throwing off the restraints of God. We're headed there very quickly.

The whole prophetic scenario is in place. We see the Islamic nations united in a mutual hatred of Israel. The dispute has nothing to do with borders or territory. It has to do with the existence of Israel and its claim on Jerusalem. We see Russia as no longer a world threat, but a regional power with a world-class military—exactly what Ezekiel 38 and 39 predicted it would be. We see Asia awakened from a long slumber, coalescing into a major world power.

And last, we see the old Roman culture, which has been divided and balkanized for centuries, uniting. Along with it, the world has found itself in a power vacuum. It's a world without leaders, without answers. Into this breach, a leader unlike any the world has ever known is about to march. Stay tuned.

References

[1] *San Francisco Chronicle*, July 7,1993

[2] *Wall Street Journal*, May 30, 1993

[3] *Intelligence Digest,* October 16, 1992

[4] *The New York Times*, November 30, 1992

[5] *The Los Angeles Times*, April 12, 1991

[6] Ibid.

[7] *Washington Times*, April 11,1991

[8] *Los Angeles Times*, November 6, 1991

[9] The Associated Press, December 13,1992

[10] *Intelligence Digest*, November 1992

[11] Ibid

[12] Ibid

[13] Primary intelligence sources

[14] *Countdown*, December 1992

Chapter 13

THE RISE OF
THE ROMAN EMPIRE II

*And it was given to him to make war
with the saints and to overcome them;
and authority over every tribe and people
and tongue and nation was given to him.*
—REVELATION 13:7

There wasn't much fanfare. No ticker-tape parades. No marching bands. Not even a front-page story in the *New York Times*. But something significant happened the first day of 1993—something that someday may affect every man, woman and child on the face of the Earth.

On January 1, 1993, Western Europe became a single economic market, linking 345 million people in 12 nations and eliminating tariffs and custom barriers. [1]

Something else happened on November 1, 1993, though, you had to look hard for coverage of it in America's major daily newspapers. On that day, those same 345 million people became citizens of the new "European Union."

Welcome to the United States of Europe

With the Maastricht Treaty ratified and in place, German Chancellor Helmut Kohl said Europe would move into "an ever closer community, not just a free-trade zone." He also indicated that Europe would move quickly ahead to adopt a common currency. Here's the timetable for further unification efforts:

- The European Community (EC) created the European Monetary Institute on January 1, 1994. The Institute, located in Frankfurt, Germany's financial center, is scheduled to become a central bank no later than 1999, issuing a single currency.

- The EC is to forge common foreign and security policies with decisions made by consensus, unless all parties agree to vote on a joint action. Defense issues will be handled by the Western European Union, a group of nine EC states. In 1996, the states will review political cooperation and may turn the WEU into the EC defense arm and create a common defense policy.

• Majority voting replaces unanimous voting at EC meetings. The community is expanding its influence over areas including education, public health, culture, consumer protection, industry, research and development, environment, social affairs and development cooperation.[2]

• The EC is in the midst of a massive public investment project in new roads, rail lines and communications networks that could provide a burst of economic growth and transform the continent's landscape by bringing East and West closer together[3]

Is This the Revived Roman Empire?

For most Europeans, "The United States of Europe" is becoming more of a reality every day. And this emerging entity bears more than a striking resemblance to the revived Roman Empire—the economic and political powerhouse that dominates the world just prior to the return of Jesus Christ.

In the 25 years since I authored *The Late Great Planet Earth*, there has been a dramatic move toward that kind of one-world political system—toward globalism. The European Community is at the center of all such activity. It remains the model for other similar regional communities. And many other nations are eager to cash in on some of the benefits that unification and unrestricted trade and access will bring.

The 15 members of the EC are Austria, Belgium, Denmark, Finland, France, Germany, Greece, Ireland, Italy, Luxembourg, Netherlands, Portugal, Spain, Sweden and the United Kingdom. The European Free Trade Association is comprised of seven nations, some of which have recently been granted full membership in the EU. They include Finland, Iceland, Norway, Sweden, Switzerland, Liechtenstien and Austria.

Meanwhile, in the east, Poland, Czechoslovakia and Hungary are seeking to conclude special association pacts with the EC that will provide them with preferential trade benefits.

Europe's Ambitions

It seems clear that what the world is looking at is one, big European confederation—the greatest economic colossus ever created. This movement started for earnest in 1968 with the establishment of the Club of Rome.

A 1991 report by the Club of Rome looks forward to what it calls a "brave new world." No kidding. *The First Global Revolution*, by Bertrand Schneider and Alexander King, illustrates how Europe is on the ascendancy and the United States of America is in decline due to "stagnation," a crushing burden of debt and financial instability that threatens the whole capitalist world.

The Club of Rome's first report, *The Limits of Growth* issued in 1972, sold 10 million copies in 30 languages. In some ways it was the blueprint for today's bold new economic, military and political union in Europe. It stressed the negative consequences of unregulated economic growth and development and emphasized strict central government controls and regulations.

That is precisely the direction in which Europe—or, one might call it, "the revived Roman Empire"—is moving. Bigger, stronger, more tightly controlled. What is happening there has almost guaranteed the economic dominance of Western Europe in the New World Order.

Who Would Have Thought It?

A generation ago, no one could have dreamed that an empire formed of the nations that were part of old Rome could possibly be revived. But today, as Europe is on the advent of real unity, we see the potential fulfillment of another vital prophecy leading to the return of our Lord Jesus Christ.

The accelerated trend toward unification of Europe should be taken very seriously as a political and economic threat to the United States, as well as a prophetically significant development. Not many years ago, it was difficult to see how the Bible prophecies of a revived Roman Empire could be fulfilled. It was certainly a challenge for people when *Late Great* was published. Even though Bible believers knew it was inevitable that Europe would unite to set the stage for the era of the Antichrist, it was hard to see evidence of that happening through modern world events. That is certainly not true anymore.

The Bible shows us that the Roman Empire will be revived shortly before the return of Jesus Christ to the earth. Written before Jesus' time, Daniel chapter 7 was known by the scribes as the greatest chapter in the Hebrew Scriptures. Jesus and His apostles referred to it many times. But still, some of it remained obscure until today.

The Biblical Case

Daniel had a dream in which he saw four great beasts come up out of the sea. The first beast was like a lion, but had eagle's wings. The second beast was like a bear; the third beast was like a leopard, but had four heads. The fourth animal was *"dreadful and terrible"*—it had iron teeth and 10 horns. Angels explained to Daniel that the great beasts were *"four kingdoms, which shall arise out of the earth."*

The first kingdom was Babylon, which became a world empire in 606 B.C. when it conquered Egypt. Nebuchadnezzar took over the empire from his father and made it a world kingdom. The second kingdom was the Media-Persian Empire. The Babylonian empire was conquered by the Medes and the Persians about 530 B.C. A few hundred years later, the Greeks became the third empire, when Alexander the Great conquered the Persians.

Around 68 B.C., the fourth and greatest kingdom seized world power. Rome was not given the name of any animal, but it was described as fierce. In phase 1, this kingdom gained world authority, then it disappeared, and, just as the Scriptures predict, it will rise again just before Jesus returns to establish the Kingdom of God.

In phase 2 of the fourth kingdom, Rome will be in the form

of a 10-nation confederacy. Therefore we can expect five nations to withdraw from the CE or we can expect to see some mergers of nations.

"And of the ten horns that were in his head, and of the other one which came up, and before whom three fell; even of that horn that had eyes, and a mouth that spake very great things, whose look was more stout than his fellows," it says in Daniel 7:20 (KJV).

The Future Fuehrer

And heading up this 10-nation confederacy will be a man of such magnetism and power that he will become the greatest dictator the world has ever known. He will be the Antichrist. The Antichrist will be a messianic-type figure who seems to have answers to the world's problems. He will be extremely charismatic, attractive and beguiling. He will dazzle the world with miracles produced by Satan's power.

It may take a figure like this to bring Europe into its final confederated state. And it will take this figure to lead the world to the brink of destruction before Jesus Christ returns to redeem the planet.

For years I've been telling you to keep your eyes on Europe. That's where much of the prophetic scenario remains to be played out before the very near return of our Lord and Savior Jesus Christ.

Germany Is Calling the Shots

While there has been much upheaval in Europe in recent years, it has been difficult to assess it all from a biblical perspective. What does it all mean? It seems like it has been two steps forward and one step back for the European Community. Will that economic and political union provide the framework for the 10-nation confederacy and a revived Roman Empire described in the Bible as precipitating a period of world tribulation? Or is Europe still on the verge of some major new shakeout that will lead to that union under a powerful leader still to emerge?

Intelligence sources have now confirmed a revelation I first discussed some time ago: that the Soviet Union and Germany signed a super-secret pact in Geneva, the details of which are now becoming known. This agreement not only laid the foundation for much of the upheaval we have seen in Europe in the last several years, it could also provide the backdrop for the dramatic developments we all anticipate in the fulfillment of Daniel chapter 7.

The Secret Agreement

Here's what Germany and Russia agreed to, according to the best intelligence sources available:

- There would be no opposition to a split of Czechoslovakia.

- The Czech Republic would become part of the German sphere of influence, with the eventual aim being the regional political incorporation into Germany in 12 to 15 years.

- Germany would compensate Russia for the economic damage suffered in the loss of influence in Eastern Europe.

- Hungary would be allowed to pursue its aim of regaining territory it lost after World War I. In a 1920 treaty, Transylvania was incorporated into Rumania, part of the Ukraine and the Danube went to Czechoslovakia, and other former Hungarian lands went to Yugoslavia.

- Germany would increase economic aid to Hungary so that living standards would be higher than in Czechoslovakia, thus making negotiations for a greater Hungary more attractive.

- Russia agreed not to object to the division of Yugoslavia, with Croatia and Slovenia entering Germany's sphere of influence.

- Germany agreed not to get involved in entanglements with the Ukraine and the Baltic states.[4]

The New Face of Europe

This was the rough outline of the agreement that many intelligence operatives have had some sketchy knowledge of since

1990. Only now, however, are we able to see how critical this pact was for reshaping Europe and the former Soviet Union in less than five years.

First of all, people are wondering why we have had the problems in the Balkan states following the dismemberment of Yugoslavia. President Clinton and others have seemed puzzled as to why the major European powers don't want to settle such matters and stop the bloodshed and the ethnic cleansing taking place in Bosnia. Well, folks, here's the answer: It was all part of a geo-strategic plan between Berlin and Moscow from the get-go.

Second, analysts have remained quizzical about why Russia ever allowed Eastern Europe to break away from its domination without bloodshed—really without opposition at all. This agreement explains it. Strapped for cash, Moscow opted to trade Eastern Europe for some sort of compensation, probably cash as well as other geo-political considerations from Germany.

But, most important, the agreement also illustrates that Germany, the force between the two World Wars fought this century, still has enormous global aspirations. For instance, the taking of Czechoslovakia was one of the key objectives for Berlin in World War II. Now we see that Germany has not forgotten about this strategic imperative.

Germany Again?

Germany, apparently, has merely switched its tactics. Rather than rely on brute military strength to reach its imperial goals, it has, like Japan, decided economic power can be more persuasive. Germany appears to be moving very quickly now toward becoming, once again, the dominant power in Europe—and Europe is moving rapidly toward becoming the dominant power in the world.

Consider that Germany has managed to pull all this off without the benefit of a great, charismatic leader. Helmut Kohl is hardly Machiavelli. But what Germany lacks in creative leadership, it makes up for in national will and ambition. Just imagine what Germany would be capable of if a real charismatic leader should emerge in the next several years. I believe very strongly that Germany could well become, in the very near future, the dominant force that gathers together the 10 nations under the power and leadership of the Antichrist.

Meet the New Boss

Kohl himself has become Europe's leading cheerleader for unification. And when cheerleading doesn't achieve the intended results, he resorts to threats and intimidation. In August 1993, Kohl expressed dismay with the pace of European unification efforts. In a television interview he stated that such a union was the only way to avoid war on the continent.[5]

"War in Europe is only avoidable through European union, and for that reason, political unity is...most important," Kohl said. "The important thing is indeed that something is happening in this century which no one in the previous 90 years of this century believed possible—that after two world wars...it's possible to really build this Europe."[6]

No Place for America

What should be frightening about this trend for Americans is the very hostile attitude of the new Europe. The European Community is *anti-American*. There is simply no other way to put it and still be accurate.

France is the ringleader in downplaying the role America has played historically in keeping Europe free and peaceful for the half-century. The socialist leaders of France see the U.S. only as an economic aggressor. They are pushing for a United States of Europe to be protectionist—especially when it comes to Japan and the U.S. Their goal, however, is not *to divide* the world, but *to conquer* it.

The masterminds of the anti-U.S. feeling in Europe believe they can strangle America and Japan and force them to submit to European leadership on economic matters. They want nothing less than to be the world's lone economic colossus.

Big Step Toward World Government

What the Maastricht Treaty spelled out more clearly than any previous document was that European union meant the end of national sovereignty, leadership by French socialist Jacques Delors and the first big step toward world government.

Sage foreign affairs expert Hilaire Du Beirier reminds us that way back in 1918, Russian Communist Leon Trotsky wrote in *Bolshevism and World Peace*: *"The task of the proletariat is to create a United States of Europe, as a foundation for the United States of the World."*

The EC Game Plan

According to my own intelligence sources, here is what the EU plans to do to keep the plan for European unity on track:

- NATO must be destroyed. The defense of Europe will be handled by the Western European Union. The United States must be isolated and excluded from all meaningful participation and cooperation with Europe.

- The powers of Europe will attempt to impose their will on weaker member states. Witness what is happening in Yugoslavia right now.

- The president of the EC—currently Jacque Santer—will automatically become the president of Europe. At Delors insistence, the 518 members of the European Parliament will ratify this choice to give the whole proceeding the appearance of democracy.

- The president of the EC will have more power, with at least some meetings of national cabinet ministers in Brussels, which decide national laws, to be under the jurisdiction of the new president.

- The present system, under which presidency of the commission rotates among the 15 national leaders and their governments every six months, will be abolished.

- The right to veto will he scrapped, leaving the group in power with the ability to impose its will on the continent. This will be a real shock to the people of Great Britain, which will lose its sovereignty even in the most sensitive issues of foreign policy.

- Europe will adopt a Kruggerand-style gold coin as its standard of currency. To mollify nationalistic concerns, at first the coin will be imprinted with a national insignia. Later, as Europeans become more comfortable with the idea of unity, the national insignias will be discarded.

Europe's Grand Dreams

"Europe will be a bigger country than the U.S. soon," declared former French President Giscard d'Estaing at a small dinner the Kissingers held at their home. "Despite the difficulties and setbacks, the Common Market is moving steadily, inevitably toward a unity of markets, productivity and currency. By the year 2010, the entity that is Europe will be number one in the world's economy. The U.S. will be second, China third and Japan fourth."[7]

Europe is also rapidly escalating its military cooperation and strengthening the Western European Union, the military arm of the EC. WEU is frowned upon by the United States, which is excluded and fears it will hurt the NATO alliance. It will. Established more than three decades ago, the WEU—whose members include Britain, France, West Germany, Italy, Belgium, the Netherlands and Luxembourg—had been almost completely inactive before being revived by the French. Now the WEU is playing a much more important role than most people realize.

Who Can Pull It Together?

The Bible shows us that the Roman Empire will be revived shortly before the return of Jesus Christ to the earth. While it would have been difficult to imagine such a revival a few short decades ago, the EC offers a convenient vehicle for such an economic and political resurrection.

Heading up what will evolve into a 10-nation confederacy will be a man of such magnetism and power that he will become the greatest dictator the world has ever known. He will be the Antichrist.

The Antichrist will be a messianic-type figure who seems to

have answers to the world's problems. He will be extremely charismatic, attractive and beguiling. He will dazzle the world with supposed miracles. It may take a figure like this to bring Europe into its final confederated state. And he is alive today.

He's Alive Today

There is a potential dictator waiting in the wings somewhere in Europe who will make Adolph Hitler and Josef Stalin look like choir boys. Right now he is preparing to take his throne, inflaming his soul with visions of what he will be able to do for mankind with his grand schemes and revolutionary ideas.

He is called by various names in the Bible: King of Babylon, Little Horn, Man of Sin, Son of Perdition, Beast and Antichrist. He will be the ultimate humanist, believing so passionately in mankind's ability to solve problems that it becomes part of a religious obsession. He'll believe he is doing a good thing when he brings repression on believers, and he'll be able to convince most non-believers, as well.

One of the important factors that will set the stage for the acceptance of the powers and supernatural aura of the Antichrist will be the world's acceptance of the occult and New Age philosophies.

Everything that is happening in Europe today—and, indeed, throughout the rest of the world—indicates that this religious and political fuehrer is about to make a dramatic entrance onto the world stage.

The world is now divided into four spheres of political power, in exactly the pattern predicted by the prophets just before the climax of history and the coming of the Messiah.

Look at the Alliances

Thousands of years ago, the prophets predicted this alignment of power would take place following the rebirth of the state of Israel. The four spheres of power are:

- the Arab confederacy or the king of the south;
- the great confederacy of the north headed by Russia, the sons of Magog;

- the sons of the sun rising, the kings of the East including China and Japan;
- and the revival of the Roman Empire.

We can now see all four of these alignments developing right before our eyes.

What is the future of this Western alignment? Daniel prophesied that there would be four successful world empires. He also warned that the fourth empire—which was Rome—would go into a period of decline before reviving as a 10-nation confederacy just prior to the return of Jesus.

Bible Imagery

Daniel chapter 2 and chapter 7 showed the panorama of these four great empires coming onto the scene. In chapter 2, it was depicted by the image of a giant man—the head of gold was Babylon, the arms and breasts of silver was Media-Persia, the torso of bronze was the Greek-Macedonian Empire and the legs of iron represented the first phase of the Roman Empire. The feet and 10 toes of iron mixed with clay represents the Roman Empire in phase two.

In the final phase of Gentile power, the empire is represented as a mixture of iron and brittle clay. Daniel indicates that the empire will be brittle, but it will have in it the strength of iron. That appears to be exactly the kind of situation that is arising in the European Community.

Many have tried to put together the Roman Empire since it crumbled politically in 476 AD. While it continued to exist as a religious empire—the Holy Roman Empire—others tried to re-establish the political force. Charlemagne tried and failed. Napoleon tried and failed. Bismarck tried and failed. Hitler tried and failed.

Some nearly succeeded, but it wasn't God's time. What these great conquerors could not do militarily has been done in our lifetime by economics. Jean Monnet of France is called the father of the European Common Market. His vision has always been that it would ultimately be a United States of Europe.

He knew that military force alone couldn't bring unity. And he theorized that the only way to bring the nations of Europe together was to merge their industries and monetary systems. The coal and steel pact was the very first step.

Even 10 years ago, it appeared that nothing could bring these intensely nationalistic people together. Yet, in recent years we've seen quantum leaps taking place toward unity.

But there is still great diversity in Europe. There are different languages, customs and nationalities. Could this be represented by the clay feet and toes in Daniel? But there is also the great power of the old Roman Empire—that's the iron.

What Europe can produce as a unified system without hindrances is almost beyond comprehension. *Fortune* magazine said if true unity ever comes about, Europe will make Japan look like a backward nation. The economic power will be enormous. But it will also be a formidable military power as well.

Today, the man who will command this economic and military colossus is alive and well on planet Earth. The man who will make a pact with Satan for a few months of glory in this world is planning his ascendancy. Let's go meet him.

References

[1] *New York Times*, Jan. 2, 1993

[2] *San Francisco Chronicle*, Nov. 2, 1993

[3] *San Francisco Chronicle*, Nov. 18, 1992

[4] *Intelligence Digest* and other primary intelligence sources

[5] *Los Angeles Times*, August 10, 1993

[6] Ibid.

[7] *Forbes* magazine, April 25, 1988

Chapter 14

THE COMING FALSE PEACE

And you will be hearing of wars and rumors of wars; see that you are not frightened, for those things must take place, but that is not yet the end.
—MATTHEW 24:6

For when they say, "Peace and safety!" then sudden destruction comes upon them, as labor pains upon a pregnant woman. And they shall not escape.
—1 THESSALONIANS 5:3 (NKJV)

The century now entering its final years has been the bloodiest in the history of mankind. Two great World Wars killed millions of combatants and innocent civilians alike. The Nazi Holocaust claimed the lives of at least 7 million. Meanwhile, Communism, over the last three-quarters of a century, claimed perhaps 100 million in the gulags of the Soviet Union, China, Cambodia, Cuba, Ethiopia and dozens of other totalitarian police states.

In the 1980s we saw the casualty toll rise as the Soviets invaded Afghanistan, killing as many as 1 million Afghans. The prolonged conflict between Iran and Iraq resulted in hundreds of thousands of deaths. And all over the globe, insurrectionary movements—led by both communists and anti-communists— fulfilled what Jesus predicted in Matthew 24: *"For nation will rise against nation, and kingdom against kingdom...."*

But perhaps the most striking development of the 1990s is the absence of any full-blown conflagrations in the world and the hope that has emerged for a period of great and lasting peace.

Is This the End of History?

This hope, inspired mostly by the breakup of the Soviet Union, the rejection of Communism in Eastern Europe and the peace agreements between Israel and some of its Arab neighbors, was epitomized by a report written by Francis Fukuyama of the U.S. State Department, called, appropriately, *The End of History.*

"What we may be witnessing is not just the end of the Cold War, or the passing of a particular period of post-war history, but the end of history as such," Fukuyama wrote in the widely hailed report. "That is the point of mankind's ideological evolution and the universalization of Western liberal democracy as the final form of human government."[1]

The war between western values and political systems was over, he said. Democracy had won. Communism had been defeated. And, on the surface, the assessment seemed to have some merit. After all, the Berlin Wall was in the process of coming down. The Soviet Union was breaking apart and Russia and some other republics were moving toward democracy and free enterprise. The Russians withdrew from Afghanistan and called their invasion a mistake. Czechoslovakia, Poland and other East Bloc nations seemed to be on the road toward freedom. East Germany reunited with West Germany. Even China seemed to be acknowledging that Communism didn't work.

The Russian Checkmate

The changes in Russia were the most profound. For years I have been saying that something had to be done to keep the Soviet Union from conquering the world. They were well on their way toward that end. And I don't mean to suggest that today they are some kind of benign power. They are still a formidable force—certainly one of the mightiest military powers in the world.

There are still plenty of people in the Kremlin who have not given up their dream of world domination. However, they have been thwarted for now. This is a major setback. This has stopped them temporarily from their headlong drive toward conquering the world. This development had to happen because prophecy is clear about the fact that Russia will not take over the world.

Meanwhile, the dramatic changes in Eastern Europe have generated an unprecedented level of euphoria in the West. Coinciding as the developments do with the steps toward unification of Western Europe, many observers believe they are witnessing the continent's renaissance.

The Rebirth of Europe

"We optimists—some would call us dreamers—believe we are witnessing Europe's rebirth," says Dominique Moisi, editor of the French publication *Foreign Affairs*. "A 75-year period is ending as Europe emerges from a long, dark tunnel created by its near suicide of 1914, repeated in 1939."[2]

Throughout Europe and the rest of the world there is a kind of euphoria of peace. So what's the prophetic connection? It's interesting that in I Thessalonians 5:1-3, it talks about a time when people say, "'[There is] peace and safety,' then sudden destruction comes upon them...and they shall not escape."

The Bible is very clear that there will be a period of time in the last days when the whole world lets down its guard. It will be a time of great hope, but it will be a very false hope and false peace.

Such a development would have seemed far-fetched just a few years ago. The Soviet Union was still the Evil Empire and Europe seemed hopelessly divided. So dramatic is this breakout of "peace," that the *Bulletin of Atomic Scientists*, notorious for its doomsday clock which inched toward oblivion every year or so, has actually begun pushing the hands of the clock back several minutes every year.

The Decline of the U.S.

The world is dividing into regional coalitions just the way the Bible predicted it would in the last days. And, sadly, as I have discussed earlier in this book, that also means the decline of the United States. While this is difficult for me to say as a patriotic, flag-waving American, the signs are all around us. It's undeniable.

And this fact should be alarming not just to Americans, but to the entire free world. Because the United States, with all of its faults, has been the No. 1 supporter of efforts to bring freedom and peace to the world. The U.S., in fact, has been so committed to helping others around the world that, after World War I,

World War II, Korea, Vietnam, etc., it has literally exhausted its resources and will to fight. The U.S. has gone from being the leading economy in the world to being the leading debtor nation. Those the U.S. has helped the most have withdrawn from America as they have become more prosperous.

Japan, therefore, is looking for new markets. The expanding European Community is looking elsewhere—even to the point of excluding America from meaningful trade agreements and cooperation. The United States is being isolated and frozen out of economic alliances.

This may be encouraging news to America-haters in Europe, Russia, Japan and Arab nations, but it is certainly not good news for Americans or for constitutionally governed free-trade-oriented nations of the English-speaking world.

The Road to Holocaust

And because an EC-Moscow-Tokyo axis will seek to appease radical Islam, an American surrender of world leadership will make ultimate catastrophe inevitable—a thermonuclear war in the Middle East. Today, my friends, that's not just the opinion of a somewhat grizzled student of Bible prophecy, it's also the opinion of the keenest minds in global intelligence. We're heading into a much more dangerous world than we have ever known. But, yet, there is an illusion of peace.

Into the leadership vacuum left by the decline of the United States races a united Europe. Soon, once again, Rome will be at the center of power in the world. But, right now, France and Germany are calling the shots in Europe. And the policies dictated in Bonn and Paris are anti-American indeed.

Today's Franco-German Europe is socialist, protectionist and has a tendency to appease the Islamic world and Russia. When Europe finally arises as the dominant power in the world, the United States will no longer be able to protect Israel, and Europe will be strongly pro-Arab in its foreign policy.

Looking for a Leader

Do you know what has been holding Europe back from being a great power again? Two things: nationalism and bureaucracy. History shows us that there is only one way to overcome such drawbacks—great leadership. It will take what I called in *The Late Great Planet Earth* the "future fuehrer."

The Bible predicts that the last great power of the West that will, for a short while, control the whole world will be a revived form of the ancient Roman culture and people. Ten nations that derived from that cultural ancestry will be merged by a great leader who is about to come on the scene.

The world will receive this man as the answer to all of its problems. He will have super-human intelligence and abilities that will mesmerize people. He will be followed blindly as a benevolent messiah figure. More than ever, Europe is ripe for receiving a leader like this.

The Next Mideast Crisis

And look what's happening in the Middle East—ground zero in the endtimes events. With its all-consuming desire for peace at any price, Israel has now placed itself in an indefensible position. Can you imagine what will happen now if the Muslim nations mount another attack like they did in the Yom Kippur War of 1973? What could the United States do? What could Israel do? It would take the U.S. six months to mobilize enough troops and arms to be a factor. Israel knows this. Israel is also aware of the way America has too often sold out its closest allies. The Arabs are just as well aware of this fact.

Do you think Israel would wait six months—as Kuwait did— to be liberated by Americans? No way. But they wouldn't be able to defend themselves with conventional weapons alone anymore. So what are they going to do? They will be forced to go nuclear.

This latest phony peace deal in the Middle East thus only

ensures that eventually there will be a thermonuclear holocaust in the Middle East. And as we've already discussed, this seems to parallel predictions in Revelation and elsewhere almost to a T. Mark my words. It will happen.

The New Protectorate

But first, I suggest, Israel will place itself in the hands of another protectorate. Israelis understand that they are now dependent on foreign powers for their security. And that pushes them right toward Daniel 9:27, where they will sign a covenant with the Antichrist of Europe guaranteeing their security.

Meanwhile, check out Russia's increasing linkage to the Islamic world. Some people mistakenly thought that when the Evil Empire known as the Soviet Union collapsed that Ezekiel 38 and 39 were no longer relevant to our times. Not true. Russia now fits the bill better than it ever has. Who were the descendants of Magog? They were not all the different nationalities that made up the Soviet Union. They were, instead, quite precisely the people of Russia—ethnic Russians.

And just as Ezekiel foresaw, Russia is throwing its lot in with the Arab nations—with Islam. Why? For one thing, Russia is afraid that if it doesn't side with Islam, the fundamentalists on their borders will cause much trouble. Russia has the longest contiguous border with Islamic nations in the entire world. To appease them, Russia has strengthened its ties with the East.

Russia Threatened by Europe

In addition, Russia realizes that it cannot be a part of the emerging United States of Europe. So its only alternative is to ally itself with the third world Islamic nations—a bloc that happens to be the most anti-western alliance in the world today.

Russia has signed an agreement with Iran, the spiritual leader of this Islamic bloc. In effect, it is a mutual defense pact. In exchange for Iran agreeing not to cause trouble within Russia or the old Soviet republics, Moscow has agreed to provide

Tehran with the latest technology of mass destruction and the technical advisers they need to learn how to use it.

This is a done deal. I first heard about it in 1991. You may not have read about this secret pact anywhere else, but I can assure you this has been confirmed for me by some of the top intelligence sources in the world.

Russia's Last Resort

The Russians still have, of course, the fruit of a 72-year, all-out drive for weapons of mass destruction. They have an arsenal still second to none in the world. Even though the Russians are in a shambles domestically, they still have a world-class military machine capable of unimaginable destruction.

A friend of mine came back from a tour of anti-submarine warfare duty as a reserve Navy pilot in the Arctic. He took a bunch of books with him, because he expected a nice quiet time.

"I never got a chance to open a book," he said. "In fact, I hardly got a chance to sleep. The whole time we were there I was in the air flying in perilous situations, trying to keep track of *missile launch maneuvers* being constantly conducted by the Russian submarines under the polar ice cap."

The subs were practicing missile launches from under the ice. These subs are much like the one described in Tom Clancy's *The Hunt for Red October*. They are silent. Our detection systems that depended on sound are virtually useless in tracking them. There are 34 of these Typhoon class subs prowling around the world. They each carry 200 thermonuclear warheads. They were built for one purpose: launching a surprise attack on U.S. cities.

All the Pieces Come Together

Why are they still practicing launches today? Because Russia has not given up on its idea of seizing world power. But they are not alone in this dream. China, too, has global ambitions as it has ever since they were awakened by Mao tse-Tung in the 1930s.

Beijing, too, sees advantage in linking up with Islam—now the most dangerous organized movement on Earth. Because the Muslims hate the West, China has entree with them and leverage. China has always believed that the enemy of my enemy is my friend. And, as we have diagnosed in previous chapters, Beijing is only too happy to provide Islam with the latest technology in ballistic missiles and nuclear weapons. Other Asian nations, including North Korea, are doing the same thing.

Meanwhile, look at Japan's growing influence in Asia. Tokyo has the know-how and the economic clout to pull Asia together into the kind of powerful regional alliance envisioned in Revelation 16:12-16. Japan is investing billions of dollars in China.

So there you have the power lineup as it stands right now. Doesn't it sound oh so familiar? We've just discussed the way the Bible describes the centers of power in the last days. We're almost there right now. Do you hear me? Can you see it?

Jerusalem the Key

But it doesn't end there. Because all of these new alliances and regional powers are going to be motivated by one thing in the last days—the struggle for Jerusalem. Is this shaping up? Is it ever. Only now it's not just prophetic teachers pointing it out. Anyone who reads the newspaper can see it for himself. And the most insightful intelligence sources understand that this ancient city of no particular strategic value has more potential for setting off a global clash than any other site.

"Jerusalem is without doubt the most intractable of world problems," writes Joseph DeCourcy, editor of *Intelligence Digest*. "Israel's attachment to Jerusalem, including East Jerusalem, cannot be exaggerated...The Arab-Israeli dispute cannot be solved with concessions over the West Bank and Golan Heights because the real problem lies in Jerusalem and neither side will ever compromise. The only fact that keeps the peace at the moment is Israeli military dominance. But the West is determined to undermine this by pressing Israel to give up the

Golan Heights and the West Bank. Furthermore, China is arming the Arabs with nuclear technology and once Israel's nuclear deterrent is neutralized, then the path is clear for the Arabs to strike once more at Jerusalem. Once an Islam-appeasing European Community has consolidated its power in Europe, radical Islam has taken over North Africa and pro-Islamic Russia has reverted to its historic role of defender of the third world interests against the West, then the radical Arab camp will almost certainly attempt to reverse a half-century of humiliation at the hands of the Jews—*they will attack.*"[3] (Emphasis mine.)

There couldn't be a more perfect modern-day description of what was predicted hundreds of years ago in Zechariah 12-14. There it tells us that the last war of the world will be started by a dispute over Jerusalem. We've got that dispute right now. As a matter of fact, the West helped guarantee the world a dispute over Jerusalem by forcing the Israelis into a pact with the Palestinians. But this is just step one. What's next? Now the expectations are that Israel will give up Judea and Samaria and the strategic Golan Heights.

Soon will come the time when Israel has no alternative but to use all or part of its nuclear arsenal—conservatively estimated at some 200 warheads. That doesn't even count its neutron bombs.

The Euphoria of Peace

But the world isn't thinking about any of this right now. It is still caught up in the euphoria of a false peace. I don't believe this is the false peace spoken of in the Bible, however. That is still to come. It will be manufactured by the Antichrist himself. But what we're experiencing today should give us a glimpse of what it might be like.

The Bible tells us that when the Lord returns it will be as a "thief in the night." No one will expect the great holocaust that envelops the world and precipitates the Second Coming. It will come on a wave of great peace.

It may very well be that the Antichrist will come in on this wave of peace euphoria. More likely, however, he will emerge in times of trouble—providing the glue to hold Europe together and answering, at least temporarily, the riddle of the Middle East. That's why the reunification of Western Europe happening at almost the same time as the breakup of Communism and the foment over Jerusalem is very significant from a prophetic standpoint.

Messiah-mania in Israel

But nowhere is the peace euphoria more delirious than in the Middle East, where it seems to many that ancient rivalries may finally be giving way to reason and common sense. Some Israelis are so caught up in the peace trappings that they are actually hearing the footsteps of the Messiah!

"Prepare yourself for the Messiah," reads a popular bumper sticker in the Jewish state. "Welcome King Messiah," announce signs on buildings around Jerusalem.

"We want Moshiach now!" chant the Chabad faithful. "Prepare yourself for the coming of the Messiah!" The messianic fervor intensified so dramatically in the early 1990s that the Lubavitcher clan members began claiming that their rabbi, the 90-year-old Menachem Mendel Schneerson of Brooklyn, who had never set foot in the Holy Land, is actually the chosen one.

The enthusiasm is understandable in the context of historical events of the last 25 years. Think of it. First there was Israel's dramatic victory over combined Arab forces in the 1967 war, then the miraculous triumph in the Yom Kippur War. Then came the unexpected fall of communism and the world's movement toward disarmament.

Most Israelis and even some Lubavitchers, however, remained uncomfortable with the idea that Rabbi Schneerson, partially paralyzed and barely able to speak following a stroke and gall bladder surgery, was really the Messiah. But, nevertheless, even many of the skeptics were convinced as never before that they are living in the messianic era. And, of course, they are right.

The messianism of the Jews in Israel and around the world is unprecedented. While Christians throughout the last 2,000 years have frequently believed they were living in the general time of the Second Coming, Jews have never in history been as expectant about the Messiah as they are today, according to Ravitzky.

"Indeed, one of the most decisive, divisive and dynamic dialogues taking place in the Jewish world today is whether or not we are living in the era of the 'beginning of the sprouting of the Redemption'—and if so, how that should affect Israel's political policies and national decisions," says Rabbi Shlomo Riskin, dean of the Ohr Tora institutions and chief rabbi of Efrat.[4]

Rabbi Riskin, too, cites the Six Day War, the liberation of Jerusalem, the Ingathering of the Exiles from all parts of the world and the fall of the Soviet Union as key signs that make "even the secular wonder." He further states that "the dream of ultimate Redemption must be understood as the cornerstone of our faith."

"In the Amida prayer, which we recite thrice daily, we speak of Jerusalem and the Ingathering as preceding the rebuilding of the Temple and the Messiah's rule," writes Rabbi Riskin. "When we read the prophetic visions and see the renaissance and development of a lush and inviting Jewish homeland, we cannot but be inspired by the signs."

Looking for the Right Messiah?

But while the Jews are eagerly anticipating a messiah, it is also clear from listening to the modern Jewish scholars that they are looking for a very different kind of messiah than their Old Testament Prophets predicted. They clearly forecasted that the Messiah would be the human descendant of David, But He would also be called *"the Mighty God, the Father of Eternity and the Prince of Peace"* (Isaiah 9:6,7).

The Prophet David, under the inspiration of God's Spirit, also called Him Lord, *"The Lord says to my Lord, 'Sit at my right hand until I make your enemies a footstool for your feet'"*

(Psalm 110:1 NIV). Now, if David called his own son by a title of Deity, how can He also be his son? Of course the only answer is that God's Spirit was predicting that the Messiah would be both truly man and fully God united in one person.

Solomon was also guided by the inspiration of God's Spirit to raise this profound question, "Who has ascended into heaven, or descended? Who has gathered the wind in His fists? Who has bound the waters in a garment? Who has established all the ends of the earth? What is His name, *and what is His son's name*, if you know? (Proverbs 30:4 NKJV). This beyond question asserts that the Creator God has a Son equal with Himself.

But the messiah most Jews are looking for today is a very human messiah—*more of a natural peacemaker than a supernatural God-man.*

"Ultimately, the job of the Messiah is to gather the nations under the banner of the One God, and to bring the world to peace," says Rabbi Riskin. "If a gathering of the nations for the sake of peace is an explicit description of the messianic period, it clearly suggests something natural, human and recognizable. Maimonides likely had this verse in mind in composing his *Laws of Government*. In Chapter 11, Law 3, he writes that we shouldn't think that the King Messiah will have to perform 'miracles and wonders, and create new things in the world, or cause the dead to rise.'"[5]

Instead, he says, the model of the Jewish messiah is "a human being involved in human activities, dependent upon the military expertise and ethical religious accomplishments of the nation." They are expecting the natural order of the world to continue, except that peace will reign.[6]

"Everything is the same, except that Israel will not be subservient to other nations," explains Maimonides. The proof that one is the messiah, Maimonides writes, is that he brings Israel national sovereignty and the world peace.[7]

This mindset, of course, is one that could easily lead to the acceptance of a false messiah—the very kind prophesied in the Bible—who will make a peace pact with Israel and rule the world for a time from Jerusalem until the real Prince of Peace returns to Earth with a shout and sets up His millennial kingdom.

Maybe Francis Fukuyama is right. Maybe we are nearing the "end of history." But if we are, it's not because of the triumph of peace and liberal democracy. It's because all the signs indicate the Messiah is indeed returning soon. Yes, we must be very near that time. If you listen closely enough, you can almost hear the true Messiah's footsteps. And you can also sense that the False Messiah is in the wings, ready to come on stage.

References

[1] Francis Fukuyama, "The End of History", *The National Interest*, Summer 1989

[2] *Foreign Affairs*, Paris, France, Summer 1989

[3] Joseph DeCourcy, *Intelligence Digest*

[4] *Jerusalem Post*

[5] Ibid.

[6] Ibid.

[7] Ibid.

Chapter 15

THE FINAL CONFLAGRATION

For then shall be great tribulation, such as was not since the beginning of the world to this time, no, nor ever shall be. And except those days should be shortened, there should be no flesh saved: but for the elect's sake those days shall be shortened.
—MATTHEW 24:21-22 (KJV)

And the slain of the earth shall be at that day from one end of the earth even unto the other end of the earth: they shall not be lamented, neither gathered, nor buried; they shall be dung upon the ground."
—JEREMIAH 25:33 (KJV)

He that dasheth in pieces is come up...
the chariots shall be with flaming torches in
the day of his preparation, and the fir trees
shall be terribly shaken. The chariots shall rage
in the streets, they shall jostle against one another
in the broad ways: they shall seem like torches,
they shall run like the lightnings.
—NAHUM 2:1,3,4 (KJV)

Behold, the Lord lays the earth waste,
devastates it, distorts its surface, and scatters
its inhabitants...a curse devours the earth,
and those who live in it are held guilty.
Therefore, the inhabitants of the earth
are burned, and few men are left.
—ISAIAH 24:1, 6

L et's talk about World War III. Though there are many theories about the exact alignment of nations and the timing of events, no serious student of the Bible can deny that it predicts terrible conflict in the last days before Jesus returns. How bad will it actually be? Unimaginably bad.

The death and destruction will make the first two World Wars—in which tens of millions died—pale by comparison. Unimaginable, right? But if we examine what the Bible tells us about that final conflagration and take a close look at the world today, we can almost see the handwriting on the wall.

The holocaust will be preceded, as we have discussed, by a hopeful period of false peace. Evidently, for a moment, at least, some sort of agreement will be reached over that stumbling block of stumbling blocks—Jerusalem. And the world will rejoice over the great statesmanship and diplomacy exercised by the brilliant new leader of Europe who makes it all possible.

How Close We Are

Let me ask you at this point: Does this sound like a scenario that could happen in the very near future? Perhaps at almost any minute? You bet it does. In fact, in the 1990s we have seen the kind of rapid-fire, high-stakes Middle East diplomacy that could well serve as a model for a later and larger regional peace agreement—and the kind of false hope that a super-ambitious, would-be world leader could use to make his power move.

But, you might ask, how could this be? On the one hand, I have stated definitively and confidently that radical Islam will never accept a peaceful settlement of the Middle East situation while Jews still control Jerusalem. But, on the other hand, I say there is going to be a false peace imposed on the area by the European Antichrist at the beginning of the Tribulation period.

A Possible Scenario

Let me pose a hypothetical scenario. It's actually easy to understand if only you can learn to appreciate the way things work in the Middle East. Agreements in the Arab nations don't mean the same thing they mean in the Judeo-Christian world. Islam not only has a track record of re-interpreting, denouncing and reversing settlements, such actions are actually encouraged if they further the cause of Allah.

This is a principle known as *Takiya*, the right within Islam to fake peace when you're weak, so you can wait for better timing to conquer your enemy. There's a famous Arab saying: "When your enemy is strong, kiss his hand and pray that it will be broken one day."

A perfect example of the way this works—in fact the model for it—is *Hudayblya*. Whooda what, you say? Let me explain. Don't be embarrassed if you haven't heard of *Hudayblya*. While there is an important lesson in it, very few of today's self-proclaimed Middle East "experts" even understand the significance of it.

Before signing the Camp David accords with Israel, Egypt's leader Anwar Sadat sought the counsel of an important Islamic leader in Cairo. Sadat wanted to know whether it was all right to make peace with the infidel. Was there any precedent? Indeed there was, he was told. The prophet Muhammad made peace at *Hudayblya*.

The Lesson of *Hudayblya*

Hudayblya is a small oasis between Mecca and Medina where Muhammad fought a battle in the early years of Islam. When he saw he was losing the struggle, Muhammad signed a 10-year peace agreement with the people of Mecca. Two years later, when his forces were stronger and the Meccans were living securely and off their guard, Muhammad marched into the city and captured it.[1]

More recently, this strategy was adopted by the Palestine Liberation Organization. The tactic is openly discussed among the Palestinian leadership, but obscured from the outside world. The idea is this: First we negotiate our way into an autonomous state, then we use that territory as a bridgehead to destroy Israel. That's what the Islamic world is thinking.

Listen to What They Say

Perhaps it is time to listen to what the key players in the Middle East are actually saying and take them at their word. Here's how Hashemi Rafsanjani, sometimes described as the "moderate" leader of Iran, boiled the crisis down to its essence: "Every problem in our region can be traced to this single dilemma: the occupation of *Dar al Islam* by Jewish infidels and Western imperialists. Every political controversy, every boundary dispute and every internal conflict is spawned by the inability of the Umma to faithfully and successfully wage jihad. The everlasting struggle between Ishmael and Isaac cannot cease until one or the other is utterly vanquished."[2]

This kind of thinking has been at the root of the Middle East conflict for hundreds of years and it is still prevalent today. The current Grand Mufti of Jerusalem, Sheikh Tamimi, the leader of Islam in Jerusalem, put it this way: "The Jews are destined to be persecuted, humiliated and tortured forever, and it is a Muslim duty to see to it that they reap their due. No petty arguments must be allowed to divide us. Where Hitler failed, we must succeed."[3]

Take Them at Their Word

Yasser Arafat may look like a moderate compared to his rivals in the hyper-fundamentalist group Hamas, but his suggestions—fairly recent ones—for what must be done to the state of Israel are no less blood-curdling: "Our objective is simply the liberation of the Palestinian soil and the establishment of a Palestinian state over every part of it," he said. "Thus, the Jews must be removed and Israel must he annihilated. We can accept nothing less."[4]

And Arafat's fundamentalist Islamic rivals go even further. The terrorist organization Hamas makes it clear in its founding documents that only the extermination of all Jews will satisfy its bloodlust: "The war is open until Israel ceases to exist and until the last Jew in the world is eliminated."[5]

It is clear with such deep-seated, religiously inspired hatred, that the Islamic jihad against the Jews, Israel and their western allies will be the most destabilizing factor in world affairs for the rest of this millennium.

That Phony Peace

But what does all this have to do with the final, bloody days of Tribulation leading up to the return of Jesus Christ? Well, this should answer the question of how a false settlement—a phony peace deal that fools the entire world—can be established, despite Islam's sworn duty to destroy the Jewish state at any cost.

The fact of the matter is that the Islamic world will never truly accept Israel's control of Jerusalem until the millennial kingdom when all people acknowledge the truth of the gospels and the Lordship of Jesus Christ. From now until then, the tension and conflict between Jews and Arabs—Judeo-Christian values and Islam—will shape world events and lead toward the worst holocaust man has ever known or will ever know. This, my friends, is the road to Armageddon. This is why there is no escaping the destiny of the world described by the prophets for thousands of years. And remember, every prophecy they have made has come literally true.

Understanding Armageddon

But what exactly is Armageddon? Is it a battle? Is it a place? Is it literal? Is it figurative? As I mentioned earlier in this book, though we often hear about the "battle of Armageddon," it would more precisely be described as a war. The Bible never talks about a "battle" of Armageddon. But there are several huge battles that take place in this Israeli valley that has been the site of numerous battles since ancient times because of its strategic location as the land bridge between three continents and a vital link for Asia to the oil reserves of the Persian Gulf.

And though the fighting in this area will be so intense that the blood will stand up to the horse's bridle, the violence and death will be a worldwide phenomenon. One-third of the Earth's population will be destroyed and no one alive will escape the terror and torment of the seven-year Tribulation period. In other words, the fighting and the death and destruction is hardly limited to the Middle East.

We're Talking Nuclear War

In preparation of this work, I studied the prophetic scriptures more intently that I ever have before. For me, taking up where *The Late Great Planet Earth* left off was a momentous project— much tougher in some ways than the preparation of the original book. And after careful study and research, I remain thoroughly persuaded that the world will experience a major international nuclear war during this period. Over and over again, the Bible paints a picture of sudden and fiery death in disparate and faraway lands. Let's examine some of those verses.

In Zephaniah 1:15-18, we learn that shortly before the return of the Lord, civilians living in the world's cities will be stricken down quickly and violently. But note that there is no discussion of any attacking army. The destruction is related to a day of darkness and thick clouds.

The Scriptures Describe It

The great day of the Lord is near, it is near, and hasteth greatly, even the voice of the day of the Lord: the mighty man shall cry there bitterly. That day is a day of wrath, a day of trouble and distress, a day of wasteness and desolation, a day of darkness and gloominess, a day of clouds and thick darkness, a day of the trumpet and alarm against the fenced cities, and against the high towers. And I will bring distress upon men, that they shall walk like blind men, because they have sinned against the Lord: and their blood shall be poured out as dust, and their flesh as the dung. Neither their silver nor their gold shall be able to deliver them in the day of the Lord's wrath; but the whole land shall be devoured by the fire of his jealousy: for he shall make even a speedy riddance of them that dwell in the land (Zephaniah 1:14-18 KJV).

Does this not resemble the kind of portrait that would be painted by an ancient prophet transported momentarily into the 20th or 21st century to witness a nuclear attack? But there are many more examples.

Cities Burned with Fire

Listen to the vision Isaiah (1:7-9) recorded for us:

Your country [Israel] is desolate, your cities are burned with fire: your land, strangers devour it in your presence, and it is desolate, as overthrown by strangers. And the daughter of Zion is left as a cottage in a vineyard, as a lodge in a garden of cucumbers, as a besieged city. Except the Lord of hosts had left unto us a very small remnant, we should have been as Sodom, and we should have been like unto Gomorrah.

And listen to Joel 2:30-31 (KJV): "And I will shew wonders in the heavens and in the earth, blood, and fire, and pillars of smoke. The sun shall be turned into darkness, and the moon into blood, before the great and the terrible day of the Lord come."

And then Luke 17:29-30 (KJV): "But the same day that Lot went out of Sodom it rained fire and brimstone from heaven, and destroyed them all. Even thus shall it be in the day when the Son of Man is revealed."

Judgment by Fire

Over and over again, we read about a judgment by fire raining down on earth—and particularly on the world's cities:

• Isaiah 24:6 (KJV): *"Therefore hath the curse devoured the earth, and they that dwell therein are desolate: therefore the inhabitants of the earth are burned, and few men left."*

- Jeremiah 50:32 (KJV): '*And the most proud shall stumble and fall, and none shall raise him up: and I will kindle a fire in his cities, and it shall devour all round about him.*

- Ezekiel 38:19-20 (KJV): "*For in my jealousy and in the fire of my wrath have I spoken, surely in that day there shall be a great shaking in the land of Israel; So that the fishes of the sea, and the fowls of the heaven, and the beasts of the field, and all creeping things that creep upon the earth, and all the men that are upon the face of the earth, shall shake at my presence, and the mountains shall be thrown down, and the steep places shall fall. and every wall shall fall to the ground.*"

- Ezekiel 25:5 (KJV): "*Thou shalt bring down the noise of strangers, as the heat in a dry place; even the heat with the shadow of a cloud: the branch of the terrible ones shall be brought low.*"

- Isaiah (Isaiah 29:4 KJV) sees a time when people will apparently be seeking shelter underground: "*And thou shalt be brought down, and shalt speak out of the ground, and thy speech shall be low out of the dust, and thy voice shall be, as of one that hath a familiar spirit, out of the ground, and thy speech shall whisper out of the dust.*"

Not Just Nuclear

But, in addition to nuclear exchanges, the entire world will be engaged in conventional warfare as well. There are, for instance, allusions in the Bible to what sounds amazingly like invasions by modern armored columns. This from Joel 2:4-8 (KJV):

"The appearance of them is as the appearance of horses; and as horsemen, so shall they run. Like the noise of chariots on the tops of mountains shall they leap, like the noise of a flame of fire that devoureth the stubble...they shall climb the wall like men of war...and they shall not break their ranks....and when they fall upon the sword, they shall not be wounded...."

The Bible is quite specific about some of the areas of the world that will see the worst devastation. Zephaniah 2 states that the heavily populated Arab region of Gaza will be abandoned. It mentions that Moab and Ammon, both ancient lands now comprised by the nation of Jordan, will be like Sodom and Gomorrah. Ethiopia (Hebrew is *cush*, which means all black Africans), which would mean most of northern Africa, will be "slain by My sword." And Assyria and Nineveh, which are ancient names for the lands now known as Syria and Iraq, will also be made desolate during this final great war.

The Bible also makes it clear that Jerusalem—the focal point of the endtimes fighting—will be vanquished by Israel's enemies in the hours just before the Lord comes. In fact, it seems that the destruction of the holy city is the final straw that angers God and provokes Jesus' return. And when He comes and touches His feet down on the Mount of Olives, a great earthquake literally changes the geography of the area surrounding Jerusalem.

The Fate of Jerusalem

"Behold, the day of the Lord cometh, and thy spoil shall be divided in the midst of thee," we read in Zechariah 14:1-4. "For I will gather all nations against Jerusalem to battle; and the city shall be taken, and the houses rifled, and the women ravished; and half of the city shall go forth into captivity, and the residue of the people shall not be cut off from the city. Then shall the Lord go forth, and fight against those nations, as when he fought in the day of battle. And his feet shall stand in that day upon the mount of Olives, which is before Jerusalem on the east, and the mount of Olives shall cleave in the midst thereof toward the east and toward the west, and there shall be a very great valley; and half of the mountain shall remove toward the north, and half of it toward the south."

But when does this entire chain of events begin? Of course, I don't think any of today's believers will be around to witness this (more on that later), but the first major event to kick off the

Great Tribulation period (the last 3½ years) will be the occupation of the Temple by the Antichrist.

Here's the way Matthew describes it (24:15-22): "Therefore when you see the abomination of [that causes] desolation which was spoken of through Daniel the prophet, standing in the holy place (let the reader understand), then let those who are in Judea flee to the mountains; let him who is on the housetop not go down to get the things out that are in his house; and let him who is in the field not turn back to get his cloak. But woe to those who are with child and to those who nurse babes in those days! But pray that your flight may not be in the winter, or on a Sabbath; for then there will be a great tribulation, such as has not occurred since the beginning of the world until now, nor ever shall. And unless those days had been cut short, no life would have been saved...."

What's the Abomination that Causes Desolation?

It's when this pretender to the throne of the world picks up and moves into the holiest place of the rebuilt Jerusalem Temple that all hell literally starts breaking loose on planet Earth. Shortly after this event, Russia and its military allies in the Islamic world sweep into Israel and fight a war that seems to include at least some tactical nuclear weapons. The Bible tells us that in this first major war of the Tribulation period one-fourth of the world's population will be destroyed. (This will continue to escalate until literally all mankind will be at risk of death.)

Then, as we have discussed in a previous chapter, in Revelation 9, when it talks of this power coming from the east of the Euphrates preceded by a salvo of fire and brimstone that will wipe out a third of the population of the world. Now that sounds like another thermonuclear exchange to me. Now already one-fourth of the population is gone, then another one-third of the survivors are killed. That means half of the original population of the earth is wiped out within a space of no more than a few years. Perhaps in only a few months (Revelation 6:7,8 and 9:15).

In today's terms that would mean 2.7 billion people in less than three years.

The Remnant

When all is said and done—after all the battles have been waged and Jesus has conquered Satan and his minions and bound them in Hell—only a tiny fraction of the world's population will be left. Only a remnant will have survived. Many of the Jews would have been killed. And most of the believers who come to believe after the Tribulation began will have been martyred.

Hard to believe, isn't it? These numbers are so staggering it's easy to become numb to them—to discount them and maybe even think of them as exaggerations and the result of some poetic license on the part of the prophets. Think no such thing, my friends. This is reality. This is what the world will be facing in very short order.

And every day, the biblical scenario for these final clashes becomes easier to believe. I know top-flight intelligence experts and sage international analysts who predict much the same scenario based exclusively on events taking place in today's world.

Here's the way *Intelligence Digest* Editor Joseph de Courcy sees it: "If the Arab world achieves some form of nuclear parity with Israel...an Islamic coalition will in all probability unite behind one more attempt to regain Jerusalem by force. That is the cliff-edge the world seems destined to face sometime in the middle years of this decade."[6] For the record, folks, he's talking about the mid-1990s.

Why Such Suffering?

Why would God allow such destruction, such suffering? The Bible makes clear He will do it for only one reason—so that humanity might finally learn its lesson and turn to God's free gift of forgiveness in Jesus Christ.

"As I live, saith the Lord God, I have no pleasure in the death of the wicked; but that the wicked turn from his way and live," we are told in Ezekiel 33:11 (KJV). In other words, this is God's last-ditch effort to redeem a rebellious world. Look how many chances God has given us. Look how many times man has turned from God's way.

God does care about us. And that's why He has made special preparations for all believers so that we might be spared this misery and torment of the final tribulation. Do you want a ticket ride out of here? Stay with me.

References

[1] Isaac Cohen, *Chicago Tribune*, September 23, 1993

[2] George Grant, *The Blood of the Moon*, Wolgemuth & Hyatt, 1991, page 56

[3] Ibid., page 55

[4] Ibid,. page 56

[5] *Wall Street Journal*, December 18, 1992

[6] Joseph de Courcy, *Intelligence Digest*, January 24, 1992

Chapter 16

THE COMING PERSECUTION

The time is coming that whoever kills you will think that he offers God service.
—JOHN 16:2 (KJV)

It's not a pretty subject. But the Bible talks a lot about persecution of believers in the last days. In fact, in II Timothy 3:12 (KJV), we are warned:

All that will live godly in Christ Jesus shall suffer persecution.

In John 15:18,19 (KJV), Jesus warns his followers:

If the world hate ye, ye know that it hated me before it hated you. If ye were of the world, the world would love his own: but because ye are not of the world, but I have chosen you out of the world, therefore the world hateth you.

And Revelation 13:5-6 (KJV) warns of the coming Antichrist system and the persecution that comes with it:

And there was given unto him a mouth speaking great things and blashemies; and power was given unto him to continue forty and two months. And he opened his month in blasphemy against God, to blaspheme His name, and His tabernacle, and them that dwell in heaven. And it was given to him to make war with the saints, and to overcome them: and power was given him over all kindreds, and tongues and nations.

Jesus Himself said, in John 15:20:

If they have persecuted me, they will also persecute you.

The world is ready.

As we approach the new millennium, the world seems poised on the brink of a period of bigotry and persecution that will be unparalleled since the days of the early church. For instance:

- In Philadelphia—the city of brotherly love and the cradle of American liberty—four veteran evangelists were arrested for conducting traditional open-air preaching to passersby on a public sidewalk. When one Christian protests that he has a constitutional right to continue, he is beaten and jailed.

- In San Diego, an attorney for Christians arrested for peacefully blocking the doorway to an abortion clinic is sentenced to nine months in jail for contempt of court for using "prohibited" words in his defense. Among the words: "fetus," "unborn," "recur," "kill" and "holocaust."

- In Adams County, Colorado, the 10th U.S. District Court of Appeals upheld a lower court ruling prohibiting a fifth-grade teacher from keeping a Bible on his desk—a Bible he read only during silent reading exercises.

- In Houston, the head of an anti-abortion group served a four-month sentence on a criminal trespass conviction for handing out pro-life and venereal disease information on public property in front of a high school.

- In Hawaii the governor has signed into law a bill prohibiting any employer—including churches—from discriminating against homosexuals. In addition, no employer or co-worker may openly criticize any sexual orientation, and workplaces must be free of any offensive literature.

It's Christophobia

These are just a few of the hundreds, perhaps thousands, of instances around the country in which the fundamental tenets and practice of Christianity are under attack. There's even a new word for this trend. Coined by Christian movie critic Ted Baehr, it's called "Christophobia."

What's most interesting and disturbing about this wave of bigotry and persecution is that it seems to be aimed primarily at actions and beliefs that have a biblical basis. The Bible itself is often the focus of the attacks.

What's particularly puzzling about this trend in the United States is the way the "establishment clause" of the First Amendment is being so misconstrued as to foster a hideous brand of official censorship that is depriving a generation of Americans intellectually, emotionally and spiritually. Where are the usual group of "anti-censorship" crusaders who grow so agitated whenever parents try to exercise control over the books their children read in school? Where are those folks who are always pleading for more tolerance, diversity and pluralism when the Christian's rights are at stake?

Why Is the Bible So Detested?

Do you know what's really crazy about this war on Christianity and biblical values? You would think that even the humanist—the non-believer—would acknowledge some of the good things and ideas the Bible has inspired. It was, after all:

- The source of over 1,200 quotations used by William Shakespeare;

- The inspiration for literary giants such as Milton, Bunyan, Sir Walter Scott and C.S. Lewis, and it nurtured the development and world view of Charles Dickens;

- The prime motivating force behind the courage of Christopher Columbus, Abraham Lincoln and Mother Teresa;

- The inspiration for Handel's "Messiah," DaVinci's "Last Supper," Michelangelo's "Pieta" and other powerful works of art;

- The foundation for the Protestant work ethic and its virtues of thrift, honesty and hard work;

- The basis for hundreds of common expressions and allusions, such as "all things to all men," "a house divided," "salt of the earth" and "labor of love";

- Recognized by the U.S. Supreme Court as a book "worthy of study for its literary and historic values";

- Described by *Newsweek* as a set of writings which, "by any standard, are essential documents in the tradition of western culture."

Paul Explained Persecution

Now, even if you don't agree that the Bible is the inerrant, literal Word of God, how can you justify withholding such a milestone work from students? Why should such an important cultural landmark be squelched in the public arena? How can such censorship be rationalized?

Paul answered that question in the first century when he told the Ephesians (6:12): *"For our struggle is not against flesh and blood, but against the rulers, against the powers, against the world-forces of this darkness, against the spiritual forces of wickedness in the heavenly places."*

That's right. This is spiritual warfare. And it doesn't have a thing to do with rationality or intellectual debate. When the world comes after you because of your Christian beliefs, know that the source of that hostility is Hell itself.

Just look at the way Hollywood demeans, vilifies and ridicules Christian characters in movies and TV shows. While the entertainment industry is only too eager to hold consciousness-raising sessions with social deviates and ensure they are never portrayed in a negative light, Christians—particularly clergy—hardly ever get a break.

The educational establishment increasingly introduces humanistic philosophical concepts into the curriculum of public schools. Yet, school boards, state and federal governments, courts and teacher unions seem hell-bent on eradicating any vestiges of biblical traditions in public education.

Liberalism and Humanism Abound

Municipalities and state governments are under siege from the American Civil Liberties Union and other radical secularist groups who are determined to rid the American culture of all publicly displayed crosses, Christmas scenes, menorahs, Ten Commandments and Bibles.

The church in America is under an unprecedented assault by the forces of "liberalism" and "humanism." The same individuals and groups that say they promote tolerance and pluralism find themselves in the position of enforcing censorship, restrictions on free expression and blatant anti-Christian bigotry.

Hypocrisy in High Places

In short, it seems like anything goes in our society except that which reflects a Christian commitment or tradition. We're being told it is "censorship" to ask Congress and the National Endowment for the Arts to restrict taxpayer funds from supporting artwork that is blasphemous, sacrilegious and obscene. Yet, dare not let any public funds be spent—directly or indirectly—for something that would place traditional religious beliefs in a positive light.

It is inconceivable that a major public figure—especially someone who controls a vast media empire—could get away with saying the following: "Judaism is a religion for losers."

It is equally inconceivable that a major media trade publication could editorialize as follows: "All signs suggest that the nominee was found and put forward for one reason: to appease the Jews, who have been clamoring for years to have one of their own—or at least a fellow traveler—on the FCC."

It is equally inconceivable that a major musical star could say: "When you see the Star of David symbol on the bumper sticker of the car in front of you, know that is the enemy."

They sound like the public rantings of anti-Semitic zealots like Louis Farrakhan or the sentiments of Klansmen or neo-Nazi skinheads.

A Fashionable Hatred of Christianity

But the sad reality is that with just one noticeable modification these are the bigoted comments of highly influential members of the entertainment industry. Of course, they were not really talking about Jews, they were talking about us—evangelical Christians.

Here are the actual quotations again—this time with attribution:

- "Christianity is a religion for losers." (Media magnate Ted Turner in the *Dallas Morning News*.)[1]

- "All signs suggest that Mr. [Ervin] Duggan was found and put forward for one reason: to appease the evangelicals, who have been clamoring for years to have one of their own—or at least a fellow traveler—on the FCC." (An editorial in *Broadcasting* magazine.)[2]

- "When you see that [Christian] fish symbol on the bumper sticker of the car in front of you, know that is the enemy. (The late rock musician Frank Zappa at a pro-abortion rally in Los Angeles.)[3]

Why is it acceptable in the media to be an anti-Christian bigot? Why doesn't it raise an eyebrow in entertainment industry circles when powerful people malign evangelicals, fundamentalists and Christian believers in general? Would Hollywood be so tolerant of anti-Jewish remarks, anti-homosexual remarks or anti-black comments? I don't think so.

It would be bad enough if Hollywood's anti-Christian bigotry was confined to off-the-cuff remarks, editorials in trade publications and in attitudes that don't manifest themselves in programming. But, tragically, it is in programming—for both movies and television—that the extreme secular, anti-Christian bias is most clearly reflected.

Hollywood Gets into the Act

In the last 10 to 15 years, Hollywood's treatment of traditional religion—once reverential—has dramatically deteriorated, revealing a hostility so deep and open that it ignores even the realities of the box office. That's not only my conclusion or the conclusion of some right-wing Christian fundamentalist, but of the prominent, highly respected Jewish film critic, Michael Medved.

Is there any doubt that long-term anti-Christian prejudice of the kind we have been discussing could have a profound effect on the psyche of our nation and our world? The distortion and bigotry in the media, combined with the intolerance of groups such as the ACLU, Planned Parenthood, People for the American Way, the National Organization of Women, etc., is setting the stage for a potentially dangerous wave of anti-Christian persecution.

In fact, it's already here. There is a growing intolerance in America. Hate crimes are on the rise. The law is being used to stamp out dissent. People are being persecuted for their Christian beliefs.

The Acceptable Hate Crime

But despite what much of the liberal media establishment suggests, the real attacks are not on homosexuals or pornographic artists or radical left-wingers. The real beleaguered minority at risk in America today is the Church of Jesus Christ.

If you doubt it, consider the following:

- Churches are increasingly being attacked and defaced with paint and hateful graffiti. Services are even being disrupted and worshippers roughed up. Most often the culprits are supporters of abortion or homosexual activists.

- Even the liberal churches are getting into the act. To mark the occasion of the 500th anniversary of the first voyage of Christopher Columbus to the New World, the governing board of the National Council of Churches passed a resolution condemning the Italian navigator for "invading" America. Columbus, they said, was responsible for inflicting upon the Indian population "slavery, genocide, theft and exploitation." The fact that Columbus brought the gospel was lost on the arrogant leftist churchmen.

- A student at a New York high school was told by school officials that he would not be allowed to perform his musical act at a school show because it was "Christian" in orientation. So much for free speech!

- Public nativity scenes continue to come under attack each Christmas season. Courts routinely rule that such displays are unconstitutional in America—one nation, supposedly "under God."

- Employees are being fired from their jobs for sharing their faith with co-workers and others. Judges have been sued for opening their courts with prayer. Library patrons are forbidden from praying silently in their tax-supported institutions.

- Some college campuses are considering banning evangelistic efforts on the campus.

- Graduating high school and college seniors have been forbidden from making reference to their faith in valedictory addresses.

- Students have been forbidden from handing out gospel tracts at some high schools.

- The Freedom From Religion Foundation has launched a crusade to get hotel owners to rid their rooms of Gideon Bibles.

- Property owners in several states have been charged with discrimination for refusing to rent to unmarried couples out of religious convictions.

- A church in Ohio was fined for refusing to apply for a state license to operate a school.

- When a 6-year-old brought a "Jesus Loves Me" book to school in Alabama for show and tell, he was told to take it home because it was "against the law."

Is This America?

What is happening in America? Orthodox religious people in the United States are getting into trouble—big trouble—for the following kind of "subversive" activities: Giving their testimony; possessing religious beliefs on the job; witnessing in public; praying in court for justice; possessing religious literature; preaching a pro-life view from the pulpit; writing letters denouncing pornography; singing about God; meeting to read the Bible.

The church in America is under an unprecedented assault from the forces of "liberalism" and "humanism." The same individuals and groups that say they promote tolerance and pluralism find themselves in the position of enforcing censorship, restrictions on free expression and blatant anti-Christian bigotry.

These examples are just a few cases from the late 1980s. Christians and Bible-based Christianity are indeed under attack. But this is merely a foreshadowing of an even worse persecution to come.

It's not just the Christian faith that's under attack, it's Christian values, too. Just think of the way government is crusading on behalf of gays in the military, condoms in the schools and public funding of abortion on demand.

The Media Bigotry

Don't expect any sympathy from the media when you challenge these policies. When Christians jammed the Capitol switchboard with complaints about President Clinton's lifting of the ban on homosexuals in the military, for instance, the *Washington Post* published a story characterizing them as "poor, uneducated and easy to command."[4] Can you think of another group of people who could be so carelessly insulted by a major newspaper?

And consider this statement by ABC's Hugh Downs on the TV magazine show "20/20": "During times of social stress, humanity usually regresses into the family...In the 1920s, the Ku Klux Klan urged the nation to adopt family values and return to old-time religion. Similarly, Adolf Hitler launched a family-values regimen. Hitler centered on his ideas of motherhood. Fanatics in the Ku Klux Klan, the Nazi Party, the Hezbollah, or any other intolerant organization refer to themselves as religious warriors. As warriors, fanatics censor the thoughts of others and love to burn books. In the modern United States, new proponents of family values continue this tradition of fear and intolerance."[5]

With challenges from an increasingly secular government, hostile media and the growing threat of the New Age movement, with its distinct plan for persecution of Christians, the church is facing unparalleled threats. The United States, which for so long has provided a base for evangelism to the whole world, can no longer be counted on to provide a shining example of religious freedom and tolerance.

Is It Time for Mayflower II?

In fact, there are some Christians and other conservatives who are frankly discussing the possibility of seeking out—like the Mayflower Pilgrims did—another land where people of faith and freedom can live in peace and liberty.

"The irony of our age is that the very land the Pilgrims fled to in order to find refuge from social and governmental persecution, is fast becoming a society hell-bent on rooting out all expressions of religion in public life," observes commentator Robert Moeller. "...Given the chill winds of antagonism and ridicule blowing against Christians in our society, we may in our lifetime see the voyage of the Mayflower II."[6]

In fact, one organization is actively recruiting freedom-loving citizens for a proposed floating city in the Caribbean—complete with parks, theaters, schools, shopping, sports facilities and ports for aircraft. The floating city would be the first of a new sovereign nation called Oceania. The idea is called the Atlantis Project and it's getting serious attention in many quarters. That's how bad persecution of believers has become—even in the West.

Persecution Around the Globe

But, let me tell you folks, the kind of bigotry emerging in the West is nothing compared with what believers around the world are already experiencing. Let me give you some examples:

- The Bulgarian government has denied recognition to an alliance of Bulgarian evangelical churches, a move leaders of those churches say will impede united efforts to resist limits on religious freedom.[7]

- The Romanian Parliament is considering a controversial new religion law that would present new restrictions for non-Orthodox minority religious groups—including Baptists and Adventists.[8]

- Greece is adopting laws that would forbid proselytism and impose restrictions on non-Orthodox religious minorities.[9]

- Indonesian authorities have announced new regulations that will allow missionary activity in the country to be conducted only among the small number of Indonesians who are not members of a major world religion. Those "unbelievers" represent only 0.3 percent of Indonesia's 187 million people.[10]

- China continues to persecute not only political dissidents but religious minorities as well. Among the political prisoners in China listed by international rights groups are dozens of Protestant and Catholic evangelists and clergy who refuse to register with the government.[11]

- In Islamic African nations like Ethiopia and Sudan, Christians are routinely attacked and killed by government forces. [12]

- In Bolivia, evangelicals have been prohibited from holding religious services and distributing tracts and religious magazines in the city's major public hospitals.[13]

- In Vietnam, police routinely arrest Christians for holding unregistered meetings and worship services. Church property is often confiscated.[14]

- In Sri Lanka, the Buddhist establishment is calling for the imposition of anti-conversion laws. [15]

The U.N. Joins the Action

And globally, the United Nations is promoting a convention that would restrict religious freedom by limiting the authority of parents over children. The convention has already been adopted by dozens of nations and is under consideration in the United States and other western countries, as well.

This, my friends, is the sad reality of persecution of believers all over the world today. But there is good news for believers, too. Remember that passage from Ephesians I quoted from earlier in this chapter? Well, there is more to that discussion of spiritual warfare. There is hope. Real hope. Read Ephesians 6:13-18 (NKJV):

> Therefore take up the whole armor of God, that you may be able to withstand in the evil day, and having done all, to stand. Stand therefore, having girded your waist with truth, having put on the breastplate of righteousness, and having shod your feet with the preparation of the gospel of peace; above all, taking the shield of faith with which you will be able to quench all the fiery darts of the wicked one. And take the helmet of salvation, and the sword of the Spirit, which is the word of God.

Yes, Jesus gives us hope. He tells us in Rev. 2:10 (KJV): *"Fear none of those things which thou shalt suffer."* Jesus tells us to pray for those who persecute us.

Our Blessed Hope

"Blessed are they which are persecuted for righteousness's sake: for theirs is the kingdom of heaven," Jesus says in Matthew 5:10 (KJV).

And for those of us living in this world today as we approach an age of growing persecution, there's something else to look forward to. For God promises that He will take His flock out of this world just before the persecution becomes most unbearable.

"Behold, I tell you a mystery; we shall not all sleep, but we shall all be changed—in a moment, in the twinkling of an eye, at the last trumpet,' we learn in I Corinthians 15:51-52 (NKJV). "For the trumpet will sound, and the dead will be raised incorruptible, and we shall be changed."

Amen to that. Read on to learn more about this Ultimate Trip.

References

[1] Joseph Farah, *Between the Lines*, February 1990

[2] *Broadcasting* magazine, Nov. 27, 1989

[3] KNBC TV report, January 20, 1990

[4] *Washington Post*, February 1, 1993

[5] *Mediawatch*, January 20, 1993

[6] *News Network International Review*, November 1993

[7] Ibid.

[8] Ibid.

[9] Ibid.

[10] Ibid.

[11] Ibid.

[12] Ibid.

[13] Ibid.

[14] Ibid., October 1993

[15] Ibid.

Chapter 17

OPERATION EVACUATION

Behold, I tell you a mystery; we shall not all sleep,
but we shall all be changed.
—1 CORINTHIANS 15:51

For our citizenship is in heaven, from which also
we eagerly wait for a Savior, the Lord Jesus Christ;
who will transform the body of our humble state
into conformity with the body of His glory,
by the exertion of the power that He has even to
subject all things to Himself.
—PHILIPPIANS 3:20, 21

So far this book has been a taxing experience to read, I'm sure, as well as it was to write. Most of the subject matter until now has not been pleasant. I'm sure it has not been, what they call in publishing circles, "an easy read." Of course, it should not be, given the subject matter.

We've discussed the sad state of the human race, the rise of deceiving spirits, the move toward a one-world government, the coming great deception, environmental degradation, the spread of disease and plagues throughout the world, starvation on a mass scale, the eternal conflict in the Middle East and the international tumult that is leading the planet inevitably toward Armageddon.

Not exactly light reading. And it's very easy to be consumed by these life-threatening crises that now surround us—to be mired in the gloom and doom. Well, there's no way to soft-pedal it. This planet is on a death dive. We are rapidly approaching the end. But I want to keep all this in perspective for you—just the way Jesus did when He foretold the events we are witnessing today.

Approaching the End

For instance, in Luke 21:11, Jesus is predicting the conditions that precede His return. He said there would be great earthquakes, famines and terrors and great signs from heaven.

"And there will be signs in sun and moon and stars, and upon the earth dismay among nations, in perplexity at the roaring of the sea and the waves, men fainting from fear and the expectation of the things which are coming upon the world,"

Jesus tells us in verse 25. "For the powers of the heavens will be shaken."

I believe we're beginning to witness these things. But I don't want you to faint from fear. And I don't want you to become numb to these dramatic developments, either—even though these events are occurring in concert with all the other signs we are warned to expect in the last days.

Our Blessed Hope

Why? Because there's good news in all of this—in fact, the greatest news ever to be proclaimed on the face of the earth. It's what Titus 2:13 calls our "blessed hope."

And Jesus told the disciples a parable, the Bible tells us in Luke 21:29:

"Behold the fig tree, and all the trees; as soon as they put forth leaves, you see it and know for yourselves that the summer is now near. Even so you, too, when you see these things happening, recognize that the kingdom of God is near. Truly I say to you, this generation will not pass away until all things take place. Heaven and earth will pass away, but My words will not pass away. Be on guard, that your hearts may not be weighted down with dissipation and drunkenness and the worries of life, and that day come on you suddenly like a trap; for it will come upon all those who dwell on the face of all the earth. But keep on the alert at all times, praying in order that you may have strength to escape all these things that are about to take place, and to stand before the Son of Man."

The Need to Be Alert

You know, I believe the Christian church, for the most part, has become numb to the clarion call of the prophetic word. We are the generation this verse is about. We need to be alert. We need to be aware of what is happening right before our eyes. But in spite of all these things, be excited.

I know it's tough when you think about the suffering and the misery that will accompany this good news. We should pray for our fellow man. We should be on fire to evangelize in the short time we have left. But we also need to keep our eyes on Jesus and live in the light of His return any moment!

I, for one, am not waiting around to see the rain forests disappear. I'm not going to stick around to see famine envelope the earth. I don't have any interest in seeing a nuclear war. So, I'm getting out of here. And so are you if you know Jesus Christ.

Do Not Fear

So don't be afraid of what is written in this book. The only person who needs to be afraid today is the one sticking his head in the sand—the one saying: "Oh, nothing is going to happen. The world will just go on as always." These people have nothing else to believe in but this world. What else can they think?

Everyone recognizes the danger today. But only Christians have an answer. We're in a countdown that's going to end with the coming of Christ. He'll come for His own first—secretly. And that's what I want to address in this chapter—that mysterious event known as the Rapture.

It's Evacuation Time

In the last chapter we examined the persecution the church will experience in these endtimes. Satan is behind all hatred of God's people—whether it's the Jews or true Christians. And, as you've seen, Satan is going all out to destroy the true church right now. But God is going to wait only so long before He evacuates us. And, you know, when you remove your ambassadors from a hostile situation, it's tantamount to a declaration of war. When God's ambassadors are not only rejected, but are mostly under persecution, God will declare war on planet Earth.

That's why He's going to pull us out. Because we are ambassadors for Christ—or we should be. And God wants to get us out before the real shooting war begins. This is what we call *The Rapture*. In I Corinthians 15:50 we are told that Christians cannot inherit the Kingdom of God in their mortal bodies. But there will be certain people, the Bible tells us, who will do just that for a short period of time.

How Do You Become Eligible?

Who are those people? You and me—if we have received the gift of pardon that Christ purchased for us by dying under the penalty of our sins. Only those of us alive right now on planet Earth—the Christians of this generation—can possibly take part in the Rapture.

"Behold, I tell you a mystery," Paul relates in I Corinthians 15:51. *"We shall not all sleep, but we shall all be changed, in a moment, in the twinkling of an eye, at the last trumpet; for the trumpet will sound, and the dead will be raised imperishable, and we shall be changed."*

That's right. Before real judgment of the nations begins— before the seven-year horror we call the Tribulation—believers will be caught up to meet Jesus in the clouds. This is not yet the Second Advent. Jesus will return to Earth to save man from himself seven years later, with all of us—in glorified bodies— following behind.

Some Will Not Die

There's a vivid depiction of this event in I Thessalonians 4:13-18: *"But we do not want you to be uninformed, brethren, about those who are asleep, that you may not grieve, as do the rest who have no hope. For if we believe that Jesus died and rose again, even so God will bring with Him those who have fallen asleep in Jesus. For this we say to you by the word of the Lord, that we who are alive, and remain until the coming of the Lord, shall not precede those who have fallen asleep. For the Lord Himself will descend from heaven with a shout, with the voice of the archangel, and with the trumpet of God; and the dead in Christ shall rise first. Then we who are alive and remain shall be caught up together with them in the clouds to meet the*

Lord in the air, and thus we shall always be with the Lord. Therefore comfort one another with these words."

Here Paul gave the Thessalonians a detailed account of the Rapture. Apparently, there was concern among the Thessalonians that those alive at the time of the Rapture might not see their dead loved ones again. Paul assured them that the dead in Christ would actually precede those of us alive at that moment, and that we would all be caught up in the clouds together.

My First Encounter

I remember the first time I heard about the Rapture. I was listening to an on-fire young minister from Texas by the name of Jack Blackwell. I was so excited by what I heard that day I couldn't sleep for a week.

But before long, my excitement about the Rapture was challenged by some people who called it a "false doctrine." I was even confronted by a minister who was determined to straighten me out.

It was this debate, however, that caused me to begin a detailed study of scripture for myself. It was this conflict in particular that changed the entire course of my life. It was during those days that I realized I would never be happy apart from studying and teaching the Bible.

My Early Training

All other ambitions faded for me. There were times during my studies that I experienced the presence and leading of the Holy Spirit in such power that I literally became ecstatic. I would equate it with the feeling you get when you lie in the ocean and the waves wash over you—only this was a physical experience of God's love pouring over me.

It was during this period of intense systematic study that I became completely persuaded that the Lord Jesus Christ would come for the true Christians before the Tribulation. This conviction was based more on my own careful study of the scriptures than what my teachers shared with me.

Now, you and I both know that many sincere believers disagree about the timing of this event. Some say, for instance, that the Rapture will occur at the same time as the Second Coming. I have written extensively on this issue in other books and articles, and also have a video set called *The Rapture Factor*, so I don't want to devote too much time to this theological dispute here. But let me just throw out one or two verses to consider.

In Luke 12, Jesus tells believers to be ready for His return. He concludes in verse 40 with this: "You too, be ready; for the Son of Man is coming at an hour that you do not expect."

Don't You See It?

The Lord tells us that He will come for us—the believers—at an hour that we do not expect! Now, let me ask you this: If believers were around to see the emergence of the Antichrist, the invasion of Israel by Russia and the other signs of the end we expect to see during the Tribulation period, how could they possibly not be expecting Jesus to come? The Second Coming comes at the height of the most devastating global war in history. Any believer alive at that time would certainly be anticipating the imminent return of Jesus as predicted by the prophets. Yet Jesus also tells believers that He will come for us suddenly and without specific warning signs.

We are snatched away before we even know what hit us. We are then taken directly to His Father's House where he has already prepared a place for us (John 14:1-4).

In the Second Coming Jesus gathers all survivors to the valley just outside the Temple Mount, and there He separates believers from unbelievers. The believers remain on Earth as mortals and re-populate the millennial earth in His kingdom. The unbelievers are cast off the Earth directly into eternal judgment (Matthew 25:31-46).

Now, if the Rapture had just occurred, there would be no mortal believers left on Earth. There would be no need for a judgment of separation, because the Rapture would have already done that. And the biggest problem of all, there would be no mortal believers on earth to populate the Millennial Kingdom of the Messiah.

There is no way to reconcile the two descriptions of Jesus' coming apart from there being two stages of the Second Coming. The first is secretly for the Church before the Tribulation period begins. The second is public and with awesome displays of judgment as the Messiah Jesus comes to save mankind from totally destroying himself and all life on this planet.

It Could Happen Today

And the first stage—the Rapture—could literally occur at any moment. It could happen today!

"But, Hal, how could that be?" you might ask, "The Temple has not been rebuilt. All of the prophetic pieces are not yet in place." Not true, my friends. It could happen today. Everything else that needs to take place could easily occur either in the short interlude before the actual beginning of the last seven years, or within that period itself.

I believe we are on the very brink of it. No one knows exactly when it will happen. Don't believe anyone who tells you he knows. I don't know the day or the hour. But Jesus gave us a way of knowing the general time. Just read Luke 21:29-32. Study the parable of the fig tree in Matthew 24:32-34. The first leaf on the trees indicates that summer is near. We don't know exactly what day, just that it is near. We have already seen those first leaves in the profusion of predicted signs happening all around us.

This Is the Generation

And Jesus tells us that the generation that sees these things will see the fulfillment of all the prophecies leading to the Second Coming. Israel has been reborn. We are already experiencing the beginnings of persecution. False prophets are emerging. Deceiving spirits are leading many astray. The world is on the march to a new political, social and economic order. We're seeing the changing weather patterns, the plagues, the famines and the earthquakes. All the signs are there.

I tell you, it's time to be alert and going about sharing the Gospel with those you don't want leave behind. All who are truly born again and in God's forever family are soon going to stand before the Son of Man. Use the time we have left wisely. Solomon counseled, *"The fruit of the righteous is a tree of life, and he who is wise wins souls"* (Proverbs 11:30).

Be Prepared

Some believers regretfully will be raptured while out of fellowship with God. This may result in a loss of rewards for service, but not participation in the Rapture. We base this on the same foundation upon which we base our salvation. It is *"by grace through faith, and that not of ourselves, it is a gift of God."* There is no scriptural basis for a partial Rapture. The Rapture must be based on the same principles as salvation. Paul told the Corinthians, *"We all will be changed."* Now, since Paul assured all the carnal Corinthian believers that they were going to be changed, that ought to settle the issue.

One question that always comes up in any discussion of the Rapture is how such an event could be rationalized and explained by those who remain on planet Earth. If you asked me this question 25 years ago after I had written *The Late Great Planet Earth*, I don't think I would have had a clue. But events of the last two and half decades have given me some insights.

How Will It Be Explained?

Believe it or not, there are already people—cultists and New Age gurus—who are calculating just how Christians might be eliminated from the earth. In his book *Global Brain*, New Age theoretician Peter Russell explains his belief that each human being represents a brain cell in the mind of God. Some of the cells, he says are cancerous and cause division and malfunctions in the universe. The cancerous cells are the people who cling to the tired old theology of the past. Can you guess who they would be? Look in the mirror, Christian.[1]

Several New Age leaders, including Russell and John Randolph Price, author of *Practical Spirituality*, say their "spirit guides" revealed to them in the 1980s that these cancerous elements—you, me and other believers in the Word of God—will not be allowed to interfere with mankind's next quantum leap or evolutionary step.

What will happen to them (or us)? These people will be exported into the non-physical realm or "removed" from the Earth. Sound familiar? Does it sound like a grand explanation for the coming Rapture? Don't be surprised. Satan has long been preparing the world to accept and rationalize such a momentous and supernatural development.

They Can't Wait for Us to Leave

Look how closely many of the New Age teachings parallel (falsely, of course) the scriptural prophecies of the endtimes. Dr. Christopher Hyatt, for instance, predicts that true enlightenment for mankind will only come after a major global holocaust.[2] New Age guru Alice Bailey contends her Tibetan master, Djwhal Khul, channeled a message through her that one-third of mankind must die by the year 2000.[3] John Randolph Price claims he was told by his spirit guide that as many as 2.5 billion might be killed in the final holocaust.[4] And even the peace-loving Maharishi Mahesh Yogi says the "unfit and the ignorant won't survive" the transition into a New Age.[5]

In a New Age publication, Hyatt addressed the "Christian Fundamentalist Problem." How will this force be overcome? "I see that the Earth still requires some blood before it is ready to move into new and different areas," he said.[6]

Hyatt and other New Agers believe that their own millennium is being held back by the presence of Christian believers.

They must be destroyed before the dawning of their imaginary utopia.

"I foresee, on a mass scale, that the New Age is not going to come into being as so many people believe and wish to believe," Hyatt adds. "I see it as requiring a heck of a lot of blood, disruption, chaos and pain for a mass change to occur."[7]

OK, it sounds like the New Age movement is preparing to justify the persecution of Christian believers. But how, specifically, will the political and religious leaders of the day be able to explain the disappearance of every born-again Christian from the face of the Earth? How will they explain away the Rapture?

There are several possibilities. The New Age movement appears well on its way toward providing an explanation. An element within the movement claims there will be a sweeping away from the Earth of all non-believers and unprogressive beings before the New Age is ushered in. This, of course, would be a perfect explanation of the Rapture, as no Christians could ever participate in their new false world religion.

Exported to the Spirit State

"In the New Age view, the cleansing and healing of Mother Earth involves the removal of all those who have a negative consciousness," explains Christian occult expert Tal Brooke. "Unity of all religions—even Satanism and witchcraft—is positive, but to insist that Jesus is the only way to salvation is not only undesirable, it is dangerously negative. Christians are at a lower and inferior level of consciousness. They are an inferior spiritual race."[8]

Christians, the New Agers hold, send out negative thoughts and are thus responsible for the environmental degradation of the planet. Mother Earth can only be saved when these negative Christians are removed. Some in the movement are suggesting that the "Christian problem" might just solve itself.

"Millions will survive and millions won't," states best-selling New Age author Ruth Montgomery. "Those who won't will go into the spirit state."[9] The spirit state? Could this not be an *a priori* explanation of what happens to Christians in the Rapture?

Alice Bailey, too, suggests that the emerging New Age force is not only "destructive," but "ejective," too. In other words, not only will it wreak death, but somehow it will cause its counter-force (Christians) to be purged or spit out. Again, is this not a convenient rationalization for an event the Bible predicts will occur to save Christians from a judgment about to befall the entire planet? Of course, Christians won't really be ejected from the earth. They will be withdrawn from it by the power of God.

But Satan and his minions are clever. They know how to twist the truth just enough so that, while still believable, it fits their ends. How will they explain why every Christian on the planet suddenly disappeared? Well, they're already cooking up their plans.

References

[1] Peter Russell, *The Global Brain*, Tarcher Publications, Los Angeles, 1983

[2] Dr. Christopher Hyatt, *Magical Blend*, 1987, No. 16, page 22

[3] *Life Times*, Winter 1986-87, page 57

[4] John Randolph Price, *Practical Spirituality*, Quartus, Austin, Texas, 1985, page 19

[5] Maharishi Mahesh Yogi, *Inauguration of the Dawn of the Age of Enlightenment*, Maharishi International University Press, Fairfield, Iowa, 1975, page 47

[6] Dr. Christopher Hyatt, Ibid.

[7] Ibid.

[8] Tal Brooke, *Mystery Mark of the New Age*, Crossway Books, Westchester, Illinois, 1988, page 156.

[9] Ibid.

Chapter 18

THE REALLY GOOD NEWS

*He saved us, not on the basis of deeds which
we have done in righteousness, but according to
His mercy, by the washing of regeneration and
renewing by the Holy Spirit....*
—TITUS 3:5

*For by grace you have been saved through faith;
and that not of ourselves, it is the gift of God;
not as a result of works, that no one should boast.*
—EPHESIANS 2:8, 9

*For I would have you know, brethren, that
the gospel which was preached by me is
not according to man. For I neither received it
from man, nor was I taught it, but I received it
through a revelation of Jesus Christ.*
—GALATIANS 1:11,12

The heavy lifting is over. If you're stressed out over anything you have read in this book to this point, I want you to let go of that anxiety. It's time for the really good news.

Yes, it's true. The world is going to hell in a handbasket. There's no question about it. As we have seen, even the secular experts can't argue that one global crisis or another is certain to catch up with us. But now I want to take the time to show you how easy God makes it for us to join His eternal family.

That's what you need to do with the time you have left on this earth—make sure you are forgiven and have claimed a pardon that is reserved and fully paid for with your name on it. Many of you are already in God's eternal family. But I want you to know right now that if you have any doubt whatsoever that your sins are forgiven, you can be certain. You can really know God before you finish reading this book. If you are unsure about your own relationship with the Lord, then I want you to read this chapter with an open mind.

When Jesus came the first time, He came to take your place and mine. He came to take upon Himself the guilt and the consequences for every sin you'll ever commit in your life. And then He voluntarily died in your place. When He did, He paid for all of your sins and He purchased a pardon for you with your name on it. There is actually a pardon in heaven with your name on it. But it will only become effective when you receive it by a prayer of acceptance.

The Power of the Cross

How do you claim it? You can only receive it one way—as a gift. If you could do anything to earn it, it would not have been necessary for Jesus to die for you and me. You can't earn it. You can never deserve it. But if you're sitting there thinking you can never be good enough, you're thinking entirely the wrong way. None of us could ever earn it. It's a gift—pure and simple.

But you must be willing to accept that gift. If you're willing to receive the pardon that Christ died to give you, all you have to do is receive. He only wants you to be willing for Him to come into your life and change it. You can't do this, but He will by His power as He changes your heart and its desires to His desires. He gives you eternal life the instant you receive Him and His pardon.

If you want that gift—if you want that pardon—please pray this prayer with me right now, whereever you are. First, read these words over and make sure you are comfortable with them. If so, speak them—from your heart—directly to God:

The Prayer that Changes Your Eternal Destiny

"Father, I thank You that Jesus died for me. I confess I have broken Your laws. Forgive my sins. I receive the pardon right now. Lord Jesus, come into my life. Give me a new heart with new desires. And by Your Spirit, give me the power to live a life that is pleasing to You. Thank you for forgiving me as You promised. Thank You for the gift of eternal life."

If you prayed this prayer —prayed it with as much sincerity as you have right now—then you can be assured that the Lord has prepared a place for you in heaven. Congratulations and welcome to the family of God. No matter what you've done in your life, you've received a full pardon in God's eyes. That's how easy it is for you. But it wasn't free—it cost God the life of His beloved Son in your place. Just thank Him for such love to you.

Understanding Grace

It just doesn't seem possible, does it? It doesn't make sense. Why? Because the gospel of the grace of God is not something that we mortals would devise ourselves. It is contrary to our nature. Our human nature would never have come up with such a concept.

Grace goes opposite of human nature. Paul emphasizes this fact in his epistle to the Galatians. He didn't receive it from men but rather from a direct, supernatural revelation from Jesus Christ.

God couldn't have chosen a better person to explain this principle than Paul, because there had never been a man more opposite to grace in his personal life. Paul was the most zealous of all those who tried to live by the law of Moses. He brags about that in Philippians chapter 3, where he says, "as to the righteousness which is in the Law, found blameless. But whatever things were gain to me, those things I have counted as loss for the sake of Christ."

Listen to Paul

No one ever tried harder to gain God's acceptance through his own good deeds than did Paul. But Christ had to completely reverse him 180 degrees and overcome his nature.

What was this gospel of grace that Paul taught? Look at Galatians 2:14. He recounts an incident that happened while he was in the churches of Galatia.

> But when I saw that they were not straightforward about the truth of the gospel, I said to Cephas [the Apostle Peter's Hebrew name] in the presence of all, "If you, being a Jew, live like the Gentiles and not like the Jews, how is it that you compel the Gentiles to live like Jews?"

The Galatians, you see, had been fellowshipping in the grace of God until some representatives of Jerusalem came down and preached a different gospel of human merit and the law. Whenever you see somebody trying to get people to live by the principle of the Law, you will find that their message is based on fear, guilt and obligation. That's the motivation.

Contrary to Human Nature

Again, that teaching can be very convicting because deep within human nature is this willingness to believe that you don't get something for nothing—especially something so wonderful as everlasting life. But Paul explains to us in Galatians 2:15,16 that we are not justified by the works of Law principle. Law assumes that we have human merit—that if we try hard enough we can qualify to be accepted by God.

"Walk by the Spirit, and you will not carry out the desire of the flesh," Paul tells us in Galatians 5:16-21. "For the flesh sets its desire against the Spirit, and the Spirit against the flesh; for these are in opposition to one another, so that you may not do the things that you please. But if you are led by the Spirit, you are not under the Law. Now the deeds of the flesh are evident, which are: immorality, impurity, sensuality, idolatry, sorcery, enmities, strife, jealousy, outbursts of anger, disputes, dissensions, factions, envying, drunkenness, carousing, and things like these, of which I forewarn you just as I have forewarned you that those who practice such things shall not inherit the kingdom of God."

You see, without the indwelling of the Holy Spirit, we are all doomed to walk in the flesh, which is a word for our old sin natures. This sin nature will be with us as long as we are in these mortal bodies. But through Jesus' power within us, we are liberated daily from the flesh's power over us. We simply cannot walk in the flesh and the Spirit simultaneously. That's what Paul is saying. God has left one thing up to us—to choose to say "no" to the desires of the old nature and then to trust Him to put it down.

Understanding the Law

There has only been one system that God authorized if we want to try to work our way to Him—the Law of Moses. If you want to try it, good luck!

But Paul teaches us that no human being that ever lived will ever be made righteous in God's sight by works of Law. Once you're driven to despair by trying, God offers the miracle of grace. Then He shows us that the same grace that provided salvation—free and without merit—will also provide the inner motivation, direction and power to live the way God wants you to live. This is all possible because God's Spirit has taken up permanent residence in us. And He is there to guide, encourage, teach, strengthen and empower us over the temptations of sin as we trust Him to do so.

To be justified doesn't just mean to be without sin. It means God has declared you to be as righteous as Christ. The moment you believe He died in your place for your sins, you receive the pardon that He purchased. Immediately in the court of Heaven, God judicially declares you as righteous as He is. You are permanently made acceptable to Him. Your position from that moment on is one of being acceptable in His presence.

How to Live a Christian Life

We are to live the Christian life after that, but it is not to become more acceptable to Him. We are to live the Christian life because He wants us to attract others to faith in Christ and because He wants us to accumulate rewards which He is delighted to give us to enjoy for all eternity. That's the only purpose for which we are left here.

In my 38 years as a believer, I have seen leaders of the Southern Baptists, Methodists, Episcopalians, Catholics and others all acknowledge that they are not living under the Law of Moses, but then they substitute their own law. Then some teach what you must do to be saved or stay saved. Christian ministers of every denomination have tried to combine Law and grace. The Law must be kept with all of its demands and all of its impossible standards, or else it cannot fulfill the purpose for which it was given. The Law was given to drive us to despair of self effort as we try to keep it. It leads us to accept grace as the only means of pleasing God. On the other hand, grace must be kept free—you can't do anything to earn it or deserve it, or else grace is by definition no more grace. Law and grace are exactly opposite concepts.

The Bible puts it this way, "But if it is by grace, it's no longer on the basis of works, otherwise grace is no longer grace. (Romans 11:6)

What does the Law demand? Perfect obedience. God doesn't grade on the curve on our Law—keeping. In James 2:10 it says: "Whoever keeps the whole Law, yet stumbles in one point, he has become guilty of all." But, as Paul points out, Jesus' death was our death. And all the demands of the Law against you were taken out on Christ when He died for you. And when you believe in Him, you're joined with Him in a perfect union of life. When you're joined with Him, the Law has no more demand on you. That's what Paul is saying.

Obedience Under Grace

God doesn't demand perfect obedience. He knows we're incapable of offering it. His main message to us today can be summed up in this: "Walk moment by moment in dependence upon His Spirit." If we fail to trust Him, we will sin. Then we must confess our sin specifically to Him and claim His forgiveness. Then turn from it and trust Him again. He promises, "If we confess our sins, He is faithful and righteous to forgive us our sins and to cleanse us from all unrighteousness."(1 John 1:9)

Now, you might say, "I'm not strong enough to do that. I'm not sure I have the power to change." Well, God will give you that power if you make the first move. That's what the Holy Spirit is all about.

The power to live the Christian life comes from the Holy Spirit and from the confidence in the knowledge that Jesus died for our sins, was resurrected and sits in heaven at the right hand of the Father where He prays for us continually. But I hope that the message of this book gives you another motivation for living a life of righteousness. It is my prayer this book provides you with a foundation in biblical prophecy and the blessed hope that Jesus is coming back soon!

Living Like His Children

When you believe that His return is imminent, you are truly motivated to live like one of His children. Do you hear what I am saying? He is our Father. We are His children. Ours is a very personal, loving God.

Jesus died for us—personally. He promises to come live in our hearts—personally. He maintains relationship with us—personally. And the whole point of this book is to show you that He is coming very soon to redeem this planet and rule over it—personally.

Easy to Get Lost

You know, the Christian life should be one of great joy. After all, we live knowing that we have been forgiven by God for every sin. We live knowing that we will live forever in paradise. We live knowing that God will provide for us and not burden us with more than we can bear.

Yet, even the most godly of us sometimes gets lost. We get caught up in the things of the world and forget to keep our eyes on Jesus. It's easy to do. But, again, God knows we're just human beings. He created us. He understands us. He makes allowances for us. That's the beauty and the power of God's loving grace.

Why do those of us living in the Spirit sometimes stumble? Because living in the Spirit is difficult for human beings. We are still mere mortals—even those of us who have been saved and filled with the Holy Spirit. Walking with the Spirit requires a constant determination to trust Him and not ourselves.

Immerse Yourself in the Word

How do we prepare ourselves for it? We must immerse ourselves in the Word of God. Our study of the scriptures should have as its goal a greater knowledge about the Author and how to trust Him more. The Bible is not just a collection of stories, after all. It is God's manual for our lives. It is His way of allow-ing us to get to know Him—to understand His personality.

It is God's own goodness—not our own intelligence or sense of justice—that brings us to a change of heart. Think of where you've come from. All of us have committed terrible sins in our lives. We've all fallen far short of the mark. Yet, God still loves us. He loved us enough to send His only Son to die a horrible death so that we could be forgiven and received as His children.

Don't Wait

Sadly, most people may never acknowledge that simple, lifesaving, lifechanging fact. Even today as we see the world around us unmistakably preparing for the Lord's Second Coming, the vast majority of the world's people remain oblivious. Some even consciously turn away from the evidence—disregard it. I know people who say: "Yeah, Hal, what you say makes sense. But I'll wait a little longer before I receive Jesus and His pardon. I'll wait until I've lived a little more before I turn my life over to Him."

My friends, there's no way to put this nicely. That is a prescription for an eternity in hell. For one thing, you may literally never have the opportunity again. Life is preciously short and unpredictable. None of us knows for sure whether we will be here tomorrow. We don't know if the Lord will come today. This is a decision that cannot be put off.

Furthermore, if you are not willing to receive such a gift of pardon today, knowing that your eternal destiny is at stake, why wouldyou make the right decision later? It's highly unlikely.

Take the time right now, if you will, to open your heart to God in a way you never have before. Acknowledge the fact that Jesus Christ died on the cross for your sins. Humbly ask Him for forgiveness and eternal life. This is the only way to be sure of your fate for the future. If the Rapture comes tomorrow, make sure you're one of those who will never taste of death.

Afterword

WHAT TO LOOK FOR IN THE DAYS AHEAD

It may seem like it's a little early to be planning a party, but the world's elite are gearing up for the biggest New Year's Eve shindig in history. No, it's not this year, or even next year. I'm talking about the one set for the Great Pyramid of Cheops in Giza, Egypt, on December 31, 1999.

That's right. The pyramid—the seventh wonder of the world—has been specially reserved with the Egyptian government. About 3,000 people from all over the world will be invited to what is being billed as the World Millennium Charity Ball. More than half are to arrive on the ocean liner Queen Elizabeth II, which the group has also reserved.

The event will feature the top entertainment acts in the world, and distinguished citizens like former President Ronald Reagan and his wife, Nancy, who have already made reservations.

Gone by 2000?

Just for the record: I'm not planning to attend. In fact, looking at the state of the world today, I wouldn't make any long-term earthly plans.

We may be caught to meet Christ in the clouds between now and then—just as I described in an earlier chapter. Could I be wrong? Of course. The Rapture may not occur between now and the year 2000. But never before in the history of the planet have events and conditions so coincided as to set the stage for this history-stopping event.

Surely, this will be a show that surpasses any Great Pyramid millennium bash.

Ancient Curse

You know, there's an ancient Chinese curse that goes: "May you live in interesting times." If ever there was a generation more "cursed" than ours by interesting times, I can't think of which one it might have been—perhaps the one which witnessed the first coming of our Lord Jesus Christ nearly 2,000 years ago. Maybe now that you have read all this material, you've found it a bit overwhelming. Maybe you're a little confused. I believe the only way to understand the big picture is to look at the various categories of signs that the Bible predicted would come together just before the return of Christ.

In the opening pages of this book, I provided an overview of the prophetically significant events that have occurred since the publication of *The Late Great Planet Earth.* I want to spend the final pages of this book discussing what I expect to see happen in the hours and minutes we have left. As always, my predictions are made on the basis of my own study of the scriptures—not on any extra-sensory powers or personal gifts of prophecy.

A Look Back, a Look Ahead

The first chapter of this book deals with the sad state of the human race. While universally man seems more lost than ever before, the fact that people are rejecting God in the West, in the United States, in nations that have a strong Judeo-Christian heritage, is particularly alarming and distressing. America was the only nation in the world literally and consciously founded on

Christian principles. Most Americans have no sense of history. They think the American experiment is a permanent fixture in the world. Yet the nation has only existed for a little more than 200 years. And it was nearly torn apart irreparably just over 100 years ago. America, my friends, is not eternal.

Is America Facing Judgment?

Is America facing judgment? Sadly, I believe it is, especially if we don't dramatically and quickly turn away from our nihilistic, self-centered, humanistic ways. The Lord has blessed this nation so greatly, and because of those blessings, we have a profound responsibility. If we don't live up to it, God is going to withdraw His blessings. Is there any hope? Yes, as always, if we turn our hearts to God and recommit ourselves to the biblical vision of our nation's founders.

However, America does not appear to play an extraordinary role in the endtimes events. When you examine the scriptures dealing with the last days, there are some obtuse allusions to other nations, which play supporting roles before the final curtain falls. But I can find no direct references to a nation that is unmistakably America.

Sometimes when I read Isaiah 18:1-2 (KJV), I wonder if it might be referring to the United States: "Woe to the land shadowing with wings, which is beyond the rivers of Ethiopia: That sendeth ambassadors by the sea." That could have some reference to America, or it could be another nation. But the very fact that the United States is so hard to find in the last days prophecies indicates to me that America will be fading from power in the final hours before Jesus returns. It hurts me to say this. I find it incredibly sad. I am about as patriotic an American as there is. But I can think of no other explanation. Either the U.S. is going to somehow team up with the European Antichrist power or it may be militarily or economically destroyed.

Why would God allow this? Well, no other nation has been so blessed, yet, like the ancient Israelites, we have become proud and haughty. We don't thank God for our blessings. We take them for granted. That, my friends, is always a sure recipe for disaster with God. Even worse, we have removed God and the Bible from the public life of our country.

So, I hope I am wrong. But I am expecting America to slip into a secondary role as a world power in the coming days. Just think of the silly little social experiments this country is conducting with our military preparedness—gay troops, women in combat, radical defense cuts. Foolishly, the White House has even abandoned the Strategic Defense Initiative and the idea of a shield against incoming intercontinental ballistic missiles. This decision alone could prove to be our national undoing.

The Harlot Church

I expect to see more and more mergers between Christian denominations and more emphasis on ecumenicism. When Jesus returns the second time, He finds a planet operating under a one-world religious system. We can see the signs as we move toward that system today. But, soon, I expect to see even more dramatic breakthroughs for the harlot church.

The New Age and humanist movements are already laying the groundwork. When a man comes along working signs and wonders and the true believers are removed from the planet, things will move very quickly.

The New World Order

Yes, you can practically see the handwriting on the wall at the United Nations and the European Commission halls in Belgium. Now the United States has also agreed to its own version of regional unification with the North American Free Trade Agreement. The world is hurtling toward a global political system. How quickly can it happen? Think how quickly the Soviet Union fell apart. Think how quickly the Berlin Wall came tumbling down. We live in interesting times. The worldwide dependence on computers will increase. Look for an expansion of networking. Look for a worldwide supercomputer network to be established.

Signs in the Heavens

Yes, we've been witnessing the changing global weather patterns now for about 25 years. But we haven't seen anything yet. Soon the world will witness the greatest quakes ever known, new and old volcanoes erupting with incredible fury and spewing dust and ash into the atmosphere. Look for unprecedented environmental degradation—perhaps the result of nuclear fallout. But there's nothing we as a people can do about it. It's too late to reverse the adverse effects of industrialization. Look for rising concern about the greenhouse effect and ozone holes. And also look for even more inexplicable signs and wonders in the heavens. Might we soon experience a bonafide close encounter of the third kind? I fully expect it. But, as I discuss in some detail in this book, the aliens will not be visitors from another planet. They will be spirit-creatures—demons unleashed from Hell to deceive man about who he is and who His God is.

Plagues and Famines

Yes, I expect AIDS to wreak even more havoc on our planet. But there may be even worse plagues. Look for diseases thought extinct to make comebacks. Medical science will not be able to keep up with the epidemics, disease and famines the world will experience in the days ahead.

The Middle East

There will be no peace in the Middle East as long as the world entertains the Arabs' fanciful visions of dividing and conquering Jerusalem. Peace would only be possible if, by some miracle, the Arabs realized that their ambitions for military and economic hegemony over Israel were delusional. Don't hold your breath that such a conclusion will be reached without Divine intervention.

Israel is facing world pressure like never before. Because the Arab world has been successful at framing the debate over the Middle East as a struggle between downtrodden Palestinians and powerful, heavily armed Jews, Israel is dangerously close to compromising its own security needs. It may have done it already. More importantly, look for the Middle East—and Israel and Jerusalem in particular—to become the obsession that troubles the world.

The Temple Rebuilt

The preparations are being made. And those working on the plan in Israel to rebuild the Temple say it could be accomplished in less than a year! At the same time, the worldwide Islamic threat will only worsen. Terrorism will increase. There may be some limited wars in the Middle East. I wouldn't be at all surprised, for instance, to see Iraq once again test the United States militarily—perhaps even with another incursion into Kuwait. How would the world respond this time? Don't count on the United States coming to the rescue again.

The Role of Russia

Russia plays a critical role in the final chapter of history. We may see a change in leadership. We may see a return to authoritarianism. What I am certain we will see is a growing alliance between Moscow and the Islamic nations of the world. China, meanwhile, will grow in power and influence—perhaps even surpassing Japan as an economic power. But expect China to form a regional alliance with Tokyo and other Asian nations. The most dramatic geo-political trend we will witness is the rise of Europe. The stage is now set for rapid unification—political, economic and military. There is a vacuum of leadership at the moment. But that will change. Pray, however, you do not stick around to witness it.

The False Peace

Don't look for any major wars. But there will be no shortage of minor skirmishes. The world is moving toward a period of false peace. We may even see more dramatic agreements forged in the Middle East. Do not believe that these will be lasting treaties. Only the Lord Himself can resolve the deep-seated hatred and enmity brewing in the world just beneath the surface.

The Coming Persecution

Even though believers won't experience the worst of the tribulation period, we will undergo more persecution as we move closer to that time. More and more, we are going to see the press and government and the culture at large ignore anything positive from the conservative Christian movement, especially those who are interested in biblical prophecy.

And that's not all: crime will worsen, cheating will abound. There will be a near total breakdown in morality in the coming days, as families are further broken down. Man, we are being told, has evolved to the point where he can set his own moral standards. Each of us must be given the freedom to do what he pleases. The result: more pornography, sexual licentiousness, gambling, illiteracy, drunkenness and drug addiction. Next, the meaning of the family will be lost.

Government will be looked at as man's only savior. The right to own and control property will be routinely abrogated by a bigger and more bloated government bureaucracy—not only in the West but throughout the world.

But the big question, of course, is: When is Jesus going to return? When is the Rapture going to occur? It's funny, I get unsolicited manuscripts virtually every week. Usually they involve some elaborate scheme that details the exact day Christ is going to come. I believe very strongly that when Jesus said no one would know the day or the hour, He meant no one would know the specific time.

In the same context, he commanded us to know the general time. We are there, folks. We are living in that general time. We are the generation that will see "all these things." With that knowledge, aren't you glad you know Jesus? Isn't it nice to know that God is going to raise up a believing remnant of true Christians and give one last great offer of the free gift of forgiveness and acceptance in Jesus Christ before snatching us out of the world as it plunges toward judgment? Isn't it nice to be certain about your eternal fate?

As Christians, we should not be pessimistic and drop out of the world out of despair for its travails. We should be rejoicing in the knowledge that Jesus could return at any moment. This should and must spur us on to share the good news of salvation in Christ with as many as possible.

Even though He may come today or tomorrow, we should plan our lives as though we will be here on Earth for our full life expectancy. Don't drop out of the world. Don't stop working for righteousness on this planet. Make the most of the time we have.

Also, as the world becomes more chaotic and troubled, we as believers need to be steadfast, because we know where things are headed. We can rest assured that Christ will protect us until His purpose is finished, and then we will be taken up to be with Him in heaven.

It's late, but there's still time to bring many others to salvation. And that is our final mission.

Tally Ho! Maranatha!